WALLACE
LEGEND OF BRAVEHEART
BOOK 7

WARLORD

SEORAS WALLACE

Ist Edition

Published in 2021 by Wolf and Wildcat Publishing

Copyright © Seoras Wallace 2021

Seoras Wallace has asserted his right to be identified as the author of this Work in accordance with the Copyright, Designs and Patents Act 1988

ISBN Paperback: 978-1-8383470-4-8
Ebook: 978-1-8383470-5-5

All rights reserved. No part of this publication may be reproduced, stored in a retrieval system, or transmitted in any form or by any means, electronic, mechanical, photocopying, recording or otherwise, without the prior permission of the copyright owner.

All characters and events in this publication, other than those clearly in the public domain, are fictitious and any resemblance to real persons, living or dead, is purely coincidental.

A CIP catalogue copy of this book can be found in the British Library.

Published with the help of Indie Authors World
www.indieauthorsworld.com

www.facebook.com/InDiScotland

Wolf & Wildcat publishing
Associate: Jade Macfarlane
+44(0)7766 584 360
www.wolfandwildcat.com
www.facebook.com/Wallace.Legend
Clan Wallace PO Box 1305 Glasgow G51 4UB Scotland

Dedicate to the memory of a great clansman…
RIP
Roy Ramsay
- A Wallace -

Acknowledgements

Big thank you for the writing support from
my hard working family and friends

About the Author: Seoras Wallace

After a career in the film industry spanning over thirty years, in such films as Highlander, Gladiator, Rob Roy, Braveheart, Saving Private Ryan and many more. In 1997 following a serious horse riding accident, Seoras turned his valuable experience to becoming an author, and parallel to his professional life. Seoras has also served as acting chief executive of the Wallace Clan Trust for Scotland.

"An experience like no other," said Seoras, "One of the constants in my vocation has been the revelation of private or secretive documents and accounts from many unusual sources that gave me a wholly different perspective of William Wallace, that shaped him as a man who became a nations Iconic patriot and world hero in the eyes and hearts of many. At first I used to think that the information I witnessed was too incredible to be true, but when certain parts of that narrative repeated from different sources, another story from the academic norm began to emerge. Growing up in a remote west coast village, that was extremely patriotic and nationalist, I was taught from the clan elders at an early age the family legend of Wallace, but that too did not match the publicly available narrative. On my many travels around the world, especially after the release and success of the film Braveheart, people would often say upon hearing my account, "You should write a book about the Wallace." "I have always replied that no one would ever believe it, but following my accident, I decided to leave the family legacy as a fact based fictional narrative for my family and future generations, almost as a historical bloodline diary. The epic account I have written about the Life and Legend of William Wallace has been an inspiration and brought to me a newfound love for the man, the people and the country he fought for. Many who have been test reading the epic series as it developed, have a constant response that stands out more than any other comment, "Seoras, I've researched what you've written, and it's true…" My reply has always been… "Naw… it's just fiction!"

The Bruin Hoose

Wrapping their heavy brats and winter mantles around them, Sir Hugh Braidfuite and his son Brian both try to keep warm and dry as they leave their Lanark townhouse. They hastily make their way down towards the Bruin hoose, while traversing through a cold early morning mizzle now falling upon Lanark town. Thick sticky mud from the churned-up market streets cling to their boots, weighting them down as they deftly rush through the well-trodden narrow walkways that lay between the many clusters of trader's stalls and little obhainn's, all of which are enveloped in a thick blue hazy smoke, emitting from the many morning vittal fires. Though unsaid, both of them are acutely aware that the atmosphere has noticeably changed from the previous day's merriment of the extended Lanemar fair. As they approach the Bruin hoose, Brian enquires, "So Dá, why does Marion keep doing this?" Sir Hugh looks at his son curiously, "Why does she keep doing what?" Brian replies, "The Bruin hoose, ah mean, now that Marion is wed and she's settled down with big Wallace, and wie them now with a second wain on the way, you'd think she would be passing on her duties o' the Bruin to Brannah, or to one o' the other townie maids." Sir Hugh smiles and sighs, "Ach son, it's just the making o' her. She remembers how her own family suffered in times o' famine. Yie well know that it's in her character to be making sure that the poor and unfortunates of this shire gain food and warmth, for she's the Aicé o' the Bruin after all." Brian quips, "I could run the Bruin hoose Dá, now that Marion is making family life with Wallace. And what do yie think about this, maybe we could get them all to come and live with us down at Lammington? Ah like big Wallace, he makes me laugh, and no-one gives me trouble now wie' them knowing he's my brother-in-law." Smiling, Sir Hugh climbs up the few steps then he pulls at the long-bolts to open the main doors of the Bruin hoose. He pauses a moment then speaks to his son, "Brian, I could wish for nothing better than for them all to be staying with us down in Lammington. But ahm afraid that as long as young Wallace is always between the law and peace, then it's best that we maintain things the way they stand for now, as we don't want to be having any trouble from the English." Brian says, "Aye, ah know that Dá, but these English lords offer us neither comfort nor any kinda certainty for the future, no' with their brutal martial laws and barbaric punishments for the smallest o' transgressions."

"Ah cannae be faultin' your observations there son."

Brian continues, "It would appear that all of us in the whole of Scotland's realm, are behavin' like a load o' wee timirin' mice attending a hungry tam-cat feast."

Sir Hugh frowns at the thought; then he says, "Aye son, I've never known the likes afore, it would appear to most that we're living in the time of a realm dying in its entirety." Brian grins knowingly, "Not all o' the realm Dá. Many of ma friends are tellin' me the Galloway Gallóbhet and the outlawed forest hunters are refusing to bow down to the English, they spit upon hearing the very name o' that English King called Longshanks, far less would they ever be bendin' their knee to him neither. Everyone about this shire is talking about how the Gallóbhet are trying to rally all the freeborn Scots to rise and fight like men against this English oppression, but ah think that it's no' se' much use really, not when most of our noble's sit-up, sup and dine with those English lords. Some o' ma friends are even saying that if their families suffer any more injustices from the English, they'll run away and be joining the renegade brigands, especially the brigand Chief they call Mac Álainn mòr." Sir Hugh gazes at his son standing before him. He sees in him an expression of the wide-eyed innocence of youth, with much hope and great expectation abundant in his eyes.

The youthful, almost feminine appearance of Brian; momentarily reminds Sir Hugh of his dear late wife Cornelia, who died not long after Brian's birth. Sir Hugh feels a spirited resonance in his son's words, then a sudden realisation occurs to him, "Now then Brian, you wouldn't be thinking of running away, would you?" Brian walks up the steps of the Bruin hoose, removes his sodden brat and shakes off the rainwater while considering his fathers question, he enquires, "Answer me this first then Dá, what will you do when the English come to take me away to fight for them in their foreign wars, and come for me they surely will?" Sir Hugh has considered the possibility often, but he hasn't come to any conclusions yet, other than he would do all that is within his power to keep his son safe with him at home and by his side. He has considered sending him to shelter with Wallace, but that must be a last resort to send his son to live with a wanted outlaw. He replies, "It won't come to that son."

"But what if it does come to that Dá?"

Sighing, Sir Hugh is slightly annoyed and frustrated that he doesn't have an answer, he blusters a reply of sorts, "Then we'll deal with it in good time." Brian looks at his father curiously, then he states with great gusto and pride, "Then ah will tell yie this truth with certainty Dá, when the English do come for me, I'll run away for sure and join with the brigands or Gallóbhet, there I'll learn how to fight, for I'll never leave you and my sisters unprotected and at the mercy o' these evil English soldiers. I've seen what they do to the poor unfortunates Dá. I've also heard lots o' stories from ma friends and they've been tellin' me o' many ancient noble families like the MacDuff's, Comyn's, Mackie's, Graeme's, even much more powerfull clans than ours that have already been slaughtered or put to the sword, almost extinguishing their race. We're the last of our blood now Dá, we cannae let that happen to us."

Putting his arm affectionately round Brian's shoulders, Sir Hugh walks him into the darkened front storeroom of the Bruin Hoose, there Brian enquires, "What do you think is going to happen with Hazelrigg's son Arthur, now that he's lookin' to betroth our Marion, especially when he finds out Marion and Wallace are already wed?" Sir Hugh thinks a little while upon an answer, for he himself has got many grave concerns about the outrageous demand the son of the new Sherriff of Lanark should be wed to Marion, simply for the purpose of politic… and 'for good breeding' as he was told by sheriff Hazelrigg in no uncertain terms. Sir Hugh replies, "Yie are askin' me far too many questions Brian. Now go, git… I need yie to get to the back granary store and see what vittals we may prepare for the poor folks arrival." Brian walks toward the store doors, but he has another question. "Dá, what do yie think o' this? I'd heard Arthur Hazelrigg made the claim, when he first saw Marion walking from the chapel of saint Kentigerns, he instantly fell in love with her, but surely that can't be right Dá, can it, looking at someone then falling in love with them, naw, no' just like that?" A mixture of mirth and the seriousness of the situation crosses Sir Hugh's mind, as Brian continues relentlessly with his questions, "I read once the original law of English chivalry stated, if you loved another man's wife and you killed that same man, the law of chivalry under god's protection, is you could take the dead man's wife as your own to sire noble blood by her at your will, is that right Dá?"

"Aye it is son," laughs Sir Hugh, "the chivalric laws for them there bold English knights, aye, they are so very different from our own laws in so many respects."

"What laws do we have then Dá?" enquires Brian, he continues, "There seems to be no' any law that can protect any Scot against English ill-will and their cruelty upon us, that's for sure." Brian pauses thoughtfully for a moment, then he says, "Wallace won't let anything happen to us or to Marion and Brannah Dá, will he, for he's the man? Anyways, I don't like Hazelrigg's son, he stinks and his feckn breath smells so bad." Sir Hugh laughs out loud, he says, "Now you be listening to me son, there's so many questions coming from yie, too many in fact, now ah need you to get away and be doin' all yer chores, or there will be none fed from the Bruin hoose this day." Brian reluctantly agrees and walks towards the granary doors; he stops again for a moment, still pondering… "Dá?" enquires Brian. Sir Hugh snaps, "What is it boy?"

"Do you really think it was our Wallace that did it Dá?"

Sir Hugh, now getting exasperated by all the endless questions, enquires brusquely, "Do I really think it was Wallace that did what?"

"In Ayr town," replies Brian, "yie know, the story we heard about the riots there, when many English soldiers were supposedly killed by Brigands from the Wolf and wildcats. Ah had also heard some sayin' that the brigands were led by the notorious outlaw and Brigand Chief called William

Wallace, is that our Wallace they're talkin' about Dá?" Sir Hugh shakes his head while struggling to lift a heavy sack of grain, he replies, "Look here Brian, that's all just rumours and scandalous bothy blethers that's all it is. It's more than likely it was just an inn fight or an argument at one of the ale stalls that simply got out of hand." Brian continues, "Then tell me this then Dá, why is it that Hazelrigg has ordered more of his soldiers to go quickly out o' here to follow de Percy's train to Ayr town? And why has he sent for more English troops to garrison Lanark? Everyone is talking about it, they're saying that during the Ayr riots, Wallace was joined by the Brigand chief Mac Álainn mòr and that most feared o' chiefs o' the Dregern Gallóbhet, Sean mòr. Everybody is sayin' that the Scots all fought like warriors of the fabled Tuatha de Cruinnè Cè of olde Scotland."

"For feck's sake Brian," exclaims Sir Hugh, "are yie never goin' tae shut up?" He points angrily at the back granary store doors, "Move it boy, for I have more than enough to be thinking about than inn gossip and idle rumours. Now move yourself ah say, if we don't have the place ready by the time Cornelia gets here…" The expression suddenly changes on Brian's face. "Cornelia… Dá, you just said Cornelia… ah think that yie really meant to say Marion, didn't yie?" Brian pauses when seeing the expression of sadness descend upon his father's eyes. He continues, "Cornelia, that was my mothers name, wasn't it?" Sir Hugh nods his head mournfully. "Aye son, it was, when we first brought Marion and Brannah here as foundlings, we gave Marion your mother's name, for the bonnie lass has the same spark of loving kindness in her heart as your dear Maw." Brian smiles, "Marion Cornelia Braidfuite Wallace… that's some mouthful, isn't it Dá?"

"You're going to get a mouthful yer no' expecting if yie don't get tae work," growls Sir Hugh. Brian laughs, "What do you think will happen here if the English Sherriff finds out about Marion and Wallace, do yie reckon there will be big trouble? If there is, I'll pull out ma sword and smite the English dead, or ah'll send them back to England, especially that big prick Arthur. Dá, you can't let that fool Sudron anywhere near our Marion..." Sir Hugh is about to reply, when he thinks he hears what sounds like slow hand clapping, coming from the storeroom doors directly behind Brian. He looks curiously at the doors then back at Brian. He sees the puzzled look on his son's face too. "What was that noise Dá?" enquires Brian. Sir Hugh replies, "I don't know, I thought ah heard something or somebody doin' somethin' behind the store doors?" Brian looks at the doors and mutters. "That was strange?" Sir Hugh says, "Open the doors then, it's probably some old hungry worthy who's come in through the back wynd for a scrub feed." Brian leans forward and opens both the doors, he jumps back startled...

Standing in the doorway is Arthur de Hazelrigg, with a leery self-important look on his face, still slow handclapping. Beside him are four large and surly looking men-at-arms, all with their swords drawn menacingly at the ready.

"Haze, Hazelrigg..." stammers Brian.

"Hazelrigg?" exclaims Sir Hugh, "what are you doing here?" Arthur de Hazelrigg replies, "I came through your granary store quarters to requisition your stocks my lord Braidfuite. And it's a good thing that I did, for I believe your words of sedition would never have been so freely spoken in front of my father and I otherwise." Before Sir Hugh can reply, the front doors burst wide open and more English soldiers come rushing in, with their swords drawn and bills at the ready. Sir Hugh and Brian are immediately manhandled up against the granary wall. "Hold fast there you filthy traitors..." commands a swarthy looking English soldier.

For a few moments, the terror felt by Sir Hugh is extreme amidst all the confusion. He has no idea why the English are suddenly treating him this way. Three English soldiers point their swords towards his heart and another two soldiers point bills menacingly towards Brian. Sir Hugh can't yet find the words to demand an answer, nor has he the fortitude to enflame the manic looking soldiers who have treated them so.

A voice barks out a command from the main door, "Stay your weapons…"

Immediately Sir Hugh and Brian look to the entrance and are relieved to see Sherriff D'Levingstun in the company of Sherriff Hazelrigg. D'Levingstun commands the English soldiers once more. "Alay your weapons I say." Sherriff Hazelrigg smirks, then he nods at the leading soldier, who looks coldly into the eyes of Sir Hugh, then spits in his face. Brian immediately lashes out at the soldier, who quickly pins the hapless youth against the wall by the throat. Sherriff Hazelrigg speaks as he approaches Sir Hugh, "You must forgive my men their vigour Braidfuite, but they are perturbed by news that so many of their friends have been waylaid and murdered in Ayr town but yesterday. Apparently, as I am reliably informed, by someone that you harbor amongst our midst. This is treason Braidfuite, and I myself have just witnessed the sedition of your son, when he attacked one of our King's soldiers but a moment ago."

D'Levingstun is enraged.

"Hazelrigg… I will have no disrespect shown to the family of Lord Braidfuite in my presence, particularly when you base this outrageous supposition upon trivial hearsay and the obvious provocation of the boy by your men." Hazelrigg glares at D'Levingstun, "I shall tell you this D'Levingstun, if it had been any other Scot who had spoken to me thus, or had tried to defend a felon who attacked the body of a common English soldier before my very eyes, I would have had his hands cut from his body by now and he would already be swinging on a rope outside these doors, with my hunting dogs feasting upon his balls."

"Aye Hazelrigg," replies D'Levingstun, "sure yie would, but as yie know, I'm no' any ordinary Scot who bows and scrapes to a fair-weather Englishman such as you. Should you wish the house of D'Levingstun to seek redress from our lord King Edward because of a lowborn rascal such as yourself, then so long as I'm the acting Sherriff of this shire, you will heed my words with a caution befitting of your station." Hazelrigg replies, "That may be so, but not for much longer I'll wager." Hazelrigg turns and glares ominously at Sir Hugh, while trying to hide his own embarrassment upon being chastised by his senior, de Levingston, especially in front of his own men. He says, "Well then my dear Braidfuite, I'm sure you're not too disturbed by my soldier's excesses, are you? If it is so, then I shall have them punished appropriately for the disrespect shown to your rank, if you think it so well deserved."

"M'lord Lord Braidfuite," says D'Levingstun, "I do humbly apologise to you for such base and uncouth behaviour enacted in my presence, in particular from those supposedly representing the crown of England." But Sir Hugh's mind is in too much turmoil to really be hearing de Levinstun's apology. It is not the disturbing episode that concerns him; it is that Arthur de Hazelrigg has probably heard most, if not all the conversation between himself and his son Brian, from behind the closed doors of the granary, but Arthur shows no sign that he has overheard the whole conversation, only maybe part of it. Sir Hugh watches keenly as Arthur raises a hand to cover his mouth; then he speaks quietly into the ear of his father. Sir Hugh speaks, "This misunderstanding is quite regrettable D'Levingstun, especially upon hearing this terrible news of their brother soldiers being attacked. But I beseech you Hazelrigg, do not punish your men, we shall just put this unfortunate incident behind us."

Hazelrigg says nothing by way of a reply, but simply turns to his son Arthur.

For a few moments, Hazelrigg speaks quietly to his son, then Sir Hugh watches as Arthur grins, turns and rushes out the door as though on an important mission; he is quickly followed by his bodyguard and henchmen. Sherriff Hazelrigg says, "Now then Sir Hugh, I must inform you that my men shall be clearing out your warehouses and barns immediately, all the foodstuffs and any other vital necessities that are required for the needs and sustenance of my men and servants up at the castle. And I may add, because of recent attacks placed upon the Kings authority by felonious Scotch outlaws and the likes, including the heinous murder of King's officers. My Lord de Percy has issued orders that punitive taxation shall be applied immediately in this Sherrifdom, in order to pay for more soldiers to guard all roads and wagon trains. If these new taxes are not paid upon demand, then it is by martial order that all chattel, stock and goods of worth are to be seized and forfeited to the crown, and the aforesaid miscreant who refuses to pay these taxes or pay suitable compensation in kind, is to be punished immediately and most severely."

"But you cannot do this my lord Hazelrigg," exclaims Sir Hugh, "the traders of this…" Hazelrigg interrupts, "Stay your tongue Braidfuite, I can, and I most certainly will apply the orders of my lord Percy. Though of course, this measure doesn't apply to your good self, well, not personally, but all of the foodstuffs, dried meats, fish and grain that you have stored here in these barns that you call the Bru, Bruin or whatever, they are all to be seized by our King's orders, for it is merely hand-outs for the old or idle vermin of this shire anyhoo; and most certainly sustaining other worthless indolent's hereabouts that are also of no productive use to our King, therefore they are obviously of no use to me." Sir Hugh replies, "But this is vital food necessary for the old and needy of Lanark parish and all o' the surrounding shire my lord, you cannot be taking away their only source of sustenance and warmth, for they will surely starve or die of cold and hunger."

Sir Hugh looks to D'Levingstun for support, but D'Levingstun is unable to help and simply shakes his head in futile dismay. He says, "I'm truly sorry for this Sir Hugh, but a series of incidents from the border marches of Galloway to the precincts of Ayr town, has enflamed both lord de Percy and King Edward himself, and as Hazelrigg is soon to be taking command here in this shire, these reprisals and requisitions are direct orders that he executes on behalf of King Edward of England, which I cannot countermand."

"My oh my..." says Hazelrigg, "you two Scotchies appear to be rather peeved. Look you both on the brighter side my good fellow's. These wretches that you feed and dispense succor from this place are naught but a burden on this community, therefore it would appear to me, they are beyond any usefulness when they cannot feed nor clothe themselves. So why should we bank food for these depraved cretins, when we have many fine English yeomen who are here to protect you that require that same sustenance? These wretches that you feed will soon be crow or rat food anyhoo, and with your young men to be drafted into King Edward's army; and your young noblewomen betrothed to be breeding with a much more superior race of men, you and your fellow countrymen should be demonstrably grateful that we only seek to ration all these valuable resources. You shouldn't baulk at such a magnanimous elevation of this realm's status Braidfuite. We English are all men of honour and of stout loins, who simply strive to bring true civilisation here to you Scotch."

"Hazelrigg..." growls D'Levingstun, "I swear, you do push me to my limits..."

Raising his hand, Hazelrigg laughs, "I jest... I merely jest with you my dear Levingstun. I only thought to add some levity to the moment and brighten up such solemn faces. Where is this wit and humour that I've heard you Scotchmen are supposed to possess?"

Hazelrigg looks to the soldiers guarding the entrance to the Bruin hoose, he snaps his fingers, instantly more English soldiers come in and begin ransacking the granary and all the food stores of the Bruin hoose; then they load everything onto large wagons at the rear of the building to take it all to the castle. Sir Hugh pleads again with Hazelrigg, "Please my good sheriff, the needy of this town will surely starve now that you have taken all their food and sustenance..." Hazelrigg laughs, "So be it my dear fellow, then starve they must, for as I say, if they cannot toil for their sustenance, then they are no longer of any use to me or good king Edward. Anyway Braidfuite, all that fare will be better appreciated in the stomachs of my men than in some Scotch savage of no account. D'Levingstun, what say you?"

Exasperated, D'Levingstun replies, "I have important duties that I must attend to Hazelrigg. I'll meet with you later this eve in the castle, where we shall discuss this sordid affair. Sir Hugh, with your permission, I shall call on you later at your townhouse." Hazelrigg says, "I wonder about you Levingstun. I have been well informed regarding your ability to master this shire, but by your pallor, I fear that you really know nothing of the discipline or the wit that is required to be lording even over English chicken shit." D'Levingstun retaliates, "Do you mean the chicken shit that spawned the likes of you Hazelrigg, a parasite fathered by a louse from a sow's arse..." As Hazelrigg and Levingstun continue to spat insults at each other with barbed words, Sir Hugh glances at Brian, urging him to leave.

Brian takes heed and begins to make his way tentatively towards the back doors. At that moment, D'Levingstun turns away from Hazelrigg in a rage and walks directly out through the swaying rear doors of the Bruin Hoose. Hazelrigg, watching de Levingston leave, notices Brian...

"And where do you think you are going young Braidfuite, I didn't give you permission to leave?" Brian hesitates, "I... I'm going outside for a piss Sir." Hazelrigg laughs then walks menacingly toward Brian; he then puts his arm aggressively around Brian's shoulders and pulls him close, all the while looking ominously into the eyes of Sir Hugh. "This young lad of yours wishes to piss Braidfuite, now then, what should we do about this? You see Brian; those filthy brigands that do dwell in those evil woodlands surrounding this God-forsaken place, well, they might attack you and take you away. Nay lad, you stay here with me. I want you to piss in the corner over there while I discuss some more serious and contentious matters with your father." Brian scowls at Hazelrigg, who says, "Go on boy... do as I say, or you will feel the weight of my sword belt off your bare back, have no doubts about that."

Hazelrigg smiles, then, in a swift movement, he smashes the back of his hand across Brian's mouth, knocking him to the ground. Immediately Brian pulls out his dirk, but Sir Hugh steps forward and easily kicks it out of his hand. Hazelrigg's men move forward to strike Brian down again, but he scurries away and cowers against a wall. "A wise decision young Braidfuite." says Hazelrigg with a grin, "You are aware are you not, that any form of sedition is to be met with immediate execution if it so favours the slighted, and you did this mischief before the witness of my men, therefore you have surely slighted me boy." Sir Hugh moves forward, but he is held fast by two yeomen, he says, "Hazelrigg, I beseech you, please… do not harm my son."

"We shall see about that," says Hazelrigg. "This insolence cannot go unpunished."

Many hours pass, with Sherriff Hazelrigg meticulously interrogating Sir Hugh and Brian, regarding the whereabouts of Wallace and his camp, but to little or no effect. The questioning is interrupted when the front doors of the Bruin hoose are barged open and Arthur de Hazelrigg walks back inside, he glances knowingly at his father, grinning while mock wiping his mouth and brushing down his loose tabard. A signal that is noticed by Sir Hugh, but the meaning he couldn't possible yet fathom. Sherriff Hazelrigg kicks Brian hard up the backside. "Be off with you boy, you are dismissed, now get out and piss elsewhere if you must, for we have no need of your sullen impudence here." Hazelrigg sighs, then he says, "I had heard that you Scotchies were fearless and very brave, but it would appear so that you are all little more than a gathering of timid simples, who piss themselves in fear upon hearing some fine English humour. Go Braidfuite, get out of here before I change my mind."

Hazelrigg suddenly slaps Brian across the face, bursting his lips, he says, "Now let this be a lesson to you boy, never raise your hand to your betters again. Think yourself lucky that I am in a charitable mood." Brian wipes the blood from the corner of his mouth; then nervously, he walks towards the doors of the Bruin hoose while the English soldiery laugh out loud at his timidity. An English soldier leans close behind Brian's ear, cups his hand then he shouts aloud, "BOO..." Brian immediately jumps away, startled, wide-eyed and flailing his hands ridiculously about in the air, causing even more hilarity and amusement for the Hazelriggs and their English soldiery. Brian glances shamefaced at his father, who furtively nods for him to leave now and get back to the safety of their townhouse.

"GO NOW..." commands Hazelrigg. Brian drops his head in great shame and anger. Feelings of utter futility and rage are building up rampant inside of him as he walks towards the main doors of the Bruin hoose, he looks back and scowls. Arthur de Hazelrigg laughs and waves his hand frivolously, he says, "Away with you my little Scotch mouse."

Shamefaced, Brian closes the Bruin hoose doors behind him, then leans against the old oak doorframe, infuriated. He hears laughter coming from the English soldiers, he wants to rush back in and confront them, but he can't find the courage. Wiping away tears of anger, he rampages through the market streets, completely oblivious to English soldiers assaulting and beating people with staves then ransacking their goods. Finally, Brian reaches the townhouse, he kicks the door open, storms in then slams the door shut behind him as all his emotions are released. As the tears begin to flow, he hides away his face in his léine sleeves; then he squats behind the door, crying tears of shame. For a long time, Brian is lost in his own little world, deep in his own morose thoughts, then he realises that a female voice keeps calling out his name.

"Brian..." says the frail voice. He looks up and sees Brìghde, he is startled, for she is standing before him, completely naked and holding little Mharaidh close to her bosom, crying in her arms. Brian composes himself as he stands up to try and understand why Brìghde is naked and crying. He rushes over and embraces her with a care. Amidst his confusion, he sees that she is obviously in a deep state of shock.

"Brìghde what is it, why are yie crying so, what's happened to yie, why are yie...?"

Suddenly an ominous feeling sweeps over him, he looks up the stairs toward the door of Marion and Brannah's sleeping chamber. Brìghde sobs and points up the stairs towards his sister's chamber door, instantly he understands that something malevolent is very wrong in the household. He hastily bounds up the stairs and bursts into the bed chamber, there, much to his horror, he see's a bloodied battered Marion and Brannah, both naked and huddled together in the corner of the chamber. Immediately he grabs at some hemp sheets from their crib and runs over to cover his sister's nakedness. "Marion..." he cries, "what's happened here, who has done this evil to you?"

Marion looks up and then she immediately clings tightly to Brian, she sobs, "Oh Brother..."

Brian looks down at Brannah, who is cowering away desperately, her eyes puffed and swelling from an obvious beating as blood still trickles from her nose and mouth, and noticeably from between her legs. To his dismay, he notices that blood is smeared all over her inner thighs. Marion cries out, "Brian... please, please listen to me, you must never tell William of what you have seen here this day, nor our father, I beg of you, do not tell anyone, do you hear me, you mustn't..." Marion falls silent as tears fall freely down her cheeks. Brian pulls back from Marion, it's then that he sees that she too is bleeding heavily between her legs, but unlike Brannah, her blood is extremely blackish in colour. Feeling himself falling into a state of utter confusion, Brian stammers, "Marion, I must tell Wallace and father, I cannot let this..." At that moment, Brìghde wanders into the room; apparently she is still in a daze and deep sate of shock. Marion rushes over to her and quickly takes little Mharaidh into her own arms. Brian glances at the distraught Brannah and rushes to be by her side to comfort her, but she screams murderously and claws violently at his face, causing him to immediately pull away from her.

"Brannah, it's me…" he exclaims "it's Brian…"

Brìghde wanders over and huddles down beside the terrified Brannah, in a pathetic attempt to protect her from any man, even from her own brother.

"Their wits are gone." Says Marion, who appears completely oblivious to her own brutalized condition and her nakedness. She approaches Brian, "Listen to me little brother, Wallace, Moray and Stephen, they must never hear of this… do you hear me, do you promise me. They nor anyone else must never be told of what has happened here this day. Now give me your word?" She grabs Brian firmly and looks into his eyes, "Give me your word on oath little brother? For if any of them find out, they will surely try and avenge this great wrong, and we shall lose them all to the gallows or axeman of the English." Brian stammers, "I… I can't Marion… I must tell them of this…"

Marion's eyes glisten ice-cold as she commands, "NEVER are you to speak of what has happened here to anyone Brian, for our very lives now depend upon your silence." Brian looks at Marion, but instead of acquiescence and resignation, he demands, "You must tell me who has did this to you and the girls Marion, for I'll surely seek out revenge myself for what they have done to you all?" But Marion ignores Brian's demand and turns away to offer solace to Brannah and Brìghde instead. She says, "Come here to me Brìghde, we must make this house fair once more, we'll make it as though nothing has ever happened."

"I will go and get father," exclaims Brian, "he'll know what to do…" but Marion and the girls now appear to be in another hellish trance-like world, ignoring his plea. Brian runs to the door and looks back at the three despoiled young women.

"I will bring father…" Again, there is no response from any of the young women. Brian races down the stairs and smashes his fist into the door, in his heart he knows Arthur de Hazelrigg is responsible. He barges into the main hall of the townhouse, desperately looks around, then he sees and grabs his father's sword. He secures the sword then rushes outside and into the market square. Without wasting a moment, he barges and pushes his way thoughtlessly through fleeing crowds, knocking people over or into others, such is his enraged emotions that he neither sees nor cares for anything else but his sister's outrage.

Eventually Brian reaches the front doors of the Bruin hoose, without thought, he smashes his way through the doors and rushes inside, instantly the scene before him dumbfounds and appalls him. Sherriff Hazelrigg turns then smiles upon seeing Brian enter. "Ah, young Braidfuite, at last, we've been expecting you to return…" Suddenly the doors slam shut behind Brian and he is struck viciously on the back of the head and knocked down to the floor. A few moments later, somewhere in his haze and pain, Brian feels the weight of strong men pinning him down to the floor, compressing the air out of his lungs and binding his arms firmly behind his back, while others tightly bind his ankles together.

Throughout his pain and giddiness, he stares at his father in complete bewilderment and confusion. He sees that his father has been stripped naked, bound and severely beaten. His arms have been forced behind his back and his wrists tied to a long rope hanging from a butcher's hook, affixed high in a roof beam. Sir Hugh desperately tries to use his eyes to signal Brian to get away and escape from the situation. Sherriff Hazelrigg studies Brian, leers; then looks once more at Sir Hugh. Something is about to happen and Brian can sense it, suddenly he calls out, "Nooo…"

"You are much too late now my little Scotch seditioner." Sneers Hazelrigg. He then turns and nods affirmatively towards a couple of burly soldiers holding on to the far end of the rope bound behind Sir Hugh's back, they immediately pull on the rope, very slowly and deliberately, causing Sir Hugh to be forcefully hauled up onto the balls of his feet with his arms outstretched behind him, the soldiers suddenly jerk the rope, causing a gut-wrenching scream to exhale from Sir Hugh as his shoulder-blades rotate awkwardly, stretching muscles and tendons to their limit in his back.

"Now…" Commands Hazelrigg.

The soldiers, relishing the blood-curdling screams of pain coming from Sir Hugh, begin to haul Sir Hugh slowly and methodically high up into the air, untill the lord of Lammington is hanging just below the ceiling hook with his arms outstretched behind him, now ripping and tearing his shoulder and back muscles asunder. Sir Hugh screams out in excruciating pain as he slowly swings below the beam like a human pendulum, his own body weight progressively tearing and ripping up his shoulder muscles and back tendons. Hazelrigg nods and the soldiers loose the rope, suddenly Sir Hugh drops towards the floor at speed, but the soldiers suddenly grip the rope firmly, violently jerking Sir Hugh's body before his feet could touch the ground. The full weight of his body, supported only by his backward extended arms, completely rotate the shoulder blades, dislocating and forcing his arm bones mercilessly out from their rotator cups. Sir Hugh screams and howls in great agony. Sherriff Hazelrigg laughs aloud, "Ah, the sweet sound of the Scotch songbird." The Sherriff viciously grabs Sir Hugh by the jaw, "So tell me my Lord Braidfuite, where does this Wallace Brigand make his filthy nest? Tell me now, or it will be much the worse for young Brian here, and of course, let us not forget about your pretty maids." Sir Hugh cannot reply; such is his pain, but Brian cries out, "Please my lord, I do beg of you, we know not where Wallace hides away, other than it is somewhere deep in the heart of the Wolf and wildcats…"

Sir Hugh sobs, jerking the rope and causing him more extreme unbelievable pain with each little movement. His mind begins to swim and he becomes nauseous. Suddenly he project vomits into the face of the Sherriff. Hazelrigg throws his head back in disgust; then he smashes his fist hard into Sir Hugh's face. "ARTHUR, come here boy," commands Hazelrigg. He glances at Brian then issues a command to his son, "Arthur, you try and find out the truth of it all from Braidfuite's runt here." Arthur de Hazelrigg grins; immediately he grabs Brian by the hair and yanks him to his knees, he sneers as he enquires, "What is wrong with you little Brian? Is it the stench of both your sister's cunnie's upon my fingers and peg that leaves you so silent, is this what you meant earlier when you said I do stink?"

The enormity of the situation paralyses Brian with fear and rage, but before he can muster any words of reply, he is hauled roughly to his feet and dragged over to stand face to face with his father. Sir Hugh pleads through the mist of excruciating pain, "Please my lord Hazelrigg, please, please… do not harm my only son. We know not where Wallace is, if I surely did, I would seek him out and kill Wallace myself with my own bare hands, if you would only…" Sherriff Hazelrigg nods to his men, who then place a snare-rope around Brian's neck, then the other end of the rope is thrown over the same butchers hook that his father is hanging from, they then unbind the rope around his legs that he may stand freely. Hazelrigg moves closer, till he is almost nose-to-nose with Sir Hugh. "Now, do tell me Braidfuite, where does this Wallace brigand have his camp, where does he shelter?" Sir Hugh drops his head as tears roll down his face, "I don't know my lord, please oh please God help me I don't know, this is the truth…"

Impatient, Hazelrigg nods to his rope men once more.

Suddenly Brian panics when he feels the thin wiry rope begin to tighten around his neck. Bewildered, he looks at his father as the sudden rush of burning and choking pains of slow strangulation are instantaneous, then he is hauled up into the air to hang mere inches from his father's face, with his feet barely touching the ground.

"Braidfuite…" enquires Hazelrigg, "would you see that your son be hung, rather than divulge this Brigand Chief's location?" Sir Hugh wails, "I don't know, please God, oh God I do not know…" Hazelrigg replies, "Alas then my friend, surely you have just murdered your own son." Brian begins kicking out wildly, desperately trying to get his feet to reach the ground, but it is to no avail while he hangs by the neck on the rope slowly strangling him, his body violently convulses as it tries to purchase air to breathe.

"Drop him." Commands Hazelrigg. Sir Hugh cries out as Brian falls helplessly to the floor, gasping in precious air at the feet of his father. "Thank you my lord, I…" gasps Sir Hugh, "I, I thank you, thank you." Hazelrigg gains close to the face of Sir Hugh then enquires, "You have one more opportunity to end this distasteful calamity for your son Braidfuite, just tell me where Wallace's camp is, it is that simple, that's all you have to do to end this, what do you know of the whereabouts regarding this common brigand and murderer William Wallace?" Stupefied, Sir Hugh gazes at Hazelrigg while trying desperately to remain conscious throughout the mist of searing pain, he replies, "I... I cannot tell you what I do not know my lord, please, I'm begging you, just spare..." Hazelrigg, in a flurry of a rage, looks to his men and commands, "Again..." Instantly, a bewildered Brian is hauled high up into the air once more, the thin rope biting deep into his neck. Once again he is eye to eye with his father. The horror and helplessness shared by father and son is incomprehensible. Brian's body begins to involuntary convulse and shudder. He kicks out, causing the rope around his neck to tighten. His eyes begin to bulge out and his tongue protrudes grotesquely while guffaws of laughter erupt from the English soldiers watching Brian's contortions, due to the pressure of strangulation; this heinous display also amuses the Hazelrigg's. Two of Hazelrigg's men step forward with daggers drawn then begin to slowly slash Brian's armpits, then they draw their blades over the skin to reveal his ribs, causing him immense agony.

"Look see father," smirks Arthur de Hazelrigg, "The little mouse pisses himself as he does this amusing Scotch jig before us. See how he now pokes his tongue out at us. That is so amusing." The more he chokes, the more Brian kicks and jerks as the rope bites and cuts deeper into his neck, much to the continuing amusement of the English soldiers. "Higher." Commands Arthur. The soldiers immediately haul Brian upwards, to the point where he continues to flail and kick wildly, but with each kick, he strikes Sir Hugh in the face, making his own physical pain greater and his mental anguish and terror indescribable. Sir Hugh cries out for mercy as Brian tries in vain to gulp in precious air during his horrific fight for life, but Sir Hugh's cries are ignored. An eternity passes for Sir Hugh as Brian's desperate fight to breathe begins to slowly ebb and falter. The horrendous scene continues for many moments longer before Brian's tortured body eventually hangs limp, other than the occasional involuntary muscle spasm and minor convulsion. Sherriff Hazelrigg nods and the English soldiers slowly release the rope with amusing little body-jerks, till Brian's face eventually rests mere inches from that of his father. Sir Hugh weeps as he looks into his son's dead eyes, the whites of his eyes now red, due to blood vessels expanding and bursting with the pressure, eyes that are now bulging grotesquely from his head; his purple tongue now swollen, protrudes and drips a viscose syrupy saliva from his mouth. The stench of Brian's bowels now releasing uncontrollably, fills the room. Hazelrigg commands his men to open all the doors of the Bruin hoose as Arthur covers his nose; then he says, "Who stinks now my disgusting little dead Scotch bastard."

Sherriff Hazelrigg looks at the pitiful condition of Sir Hugh, "Twas' of your own making Braidfuite. All of this unpleasantness could so easily have been avoided, if only you would have told us where the brigand chief Wallace is hiding, that was all." Arthur enquires, "Can I cut the old goats throat now father?" Hazelrigg replies, "No, not yet, drop him down too, for it's obvious that he knows nothing of Wallace."

"But why not kill him now father," enquires Arthur, "he's a rebellious seditioner after all?" Hazelrigg replies, "We will still need him to sanctify your marriage to the maid, for I am determined that this wedding shall go ahead as planned."

"What?" exclaims Arthur, ... "but father? I pegged her like the lying whore she is, then my men played much rapine upon her too, and that of her damned sister and their maid... was it all for naught?" Sherriff Hazelrigg slaps Arthur hard across the face. "You will marry this Scotch bitch Arthur, or believe you this of me, you will soon be joining young Braidfuite there if you do not, for I don't have the same squeamish qualms as that of his father..." Hazelrigg pauses a moment, then he enquires, "So none of those women of the Braidfuite house knew anything regarding the whereabouts of Wallace?" Arthur replies, "I'm sorry father, but, eh... I didn't really enquire, as I hadn't heard everything clearly that was said through the doors when the pissing mouse and his old cretin father spoke earlier?" Hazelrigg grabs his son violently then he slaps him hard about the head and beats him to the ground, "You fool, now you tell me you may have been mistaken as to what you say you heard from behind that door... Lord tell me this isn't true, tell to me now that every word you heard was sacrosanct?" Hazelrigg hastily waves his finger at two soldiers, whereupon they immediately release their grip of the rope binding Sir Hugh, dropping him to the ground like a sack of pulverised meat.

Sir Hugh struggles to sit up, he raises his head, just enough to kiss the lifeless foot of his son. Sherriff Hazelrigg glares at Arthur, now lying prostrate on the floor at his feet. He shouts at him, "Get up on your feet you fool, I require you to tend to Sir Hugh's well-being, you shall now be responsible for making him whole and good once more, for if we have struck down an innocent lord who could have elevated our family name to greatness... My God, If Lord de Percy hears of this bloody foolishness and it is truly a miscarriage enacted here this day, we are done for you fool, done for I tell you..."

Arthur quickly gets to his feet; then he enquires. "What shall we say about Braidfuite's son Father, what shall we report to Lord de Percy, that he was a traitor, planning sedition?" Hazelrigg replies, "Yes, that's good, we shall say that we hung him for sedition, and also for raising his arms against me, not just once, but thrice, despite the many warnings and by me graciously applying leniency the first two times. We have enough witnesses here to his treacherous misdeeds if required." Arthur exclaims, "Father, do you really wish me to actually wed that Scotch whore, especially now that she has been despoiled so?" Hazelrigg strikes his son hard and fast with an ironclad fist, sending him sprawling back to the ground, he is enraged at the thought that his son may have been mistaken about Sir Hugh's sedition, he growls, "Mark my words Bastard, you shall wed Braidfuite's whore daughter. then you shall breed her, for we need this shire and all of the titles that come with it. Dear God, you ignorant imbecile, if we have thwarted Lord Percy's plans for you to wed the maid, we may all end our days soon enough by hanging from a gibbet."

"I'm sorry father, I didn't realise ..." says a repentant Arthur as he wipes the blood from his mouth, he continues, "but I'm fairly certain about what I heard..." Hazelrigg grabs his son by the collar of his chainmail coif and pulls him close, raging in an absolute fury, he bellows at his son...

"You're sorry, you say you're fucking sorry? Then mark me this too boy, by the words that I say to you now, you will be more than sorry if lord Braidfuite dies because of your bloody incompetence. What I don't need to hear is any more empty and fatuous words from your bleating mouth. Now hear me well boy, you will now escort Lord Braidfuite with a care up to the Sisters at the Kentigerns infirmary, then you shall do nothing else but make purposeful plans to be wedded to that Scotch whore as soon as it is possible, and that boy, is the end of the matter... or I swear to you by the Holy Scriptures, I have other sons who will be ready to wed her in your place, then I will make sure that you will most certainly be joining young Braidfuite up there on a gibbet. Now look you, get moving and apply your miniscule brain to securing Sir Hugh's welfare, then get back here and clean this mess up."

Sherriff Hazelrigg wipes the vomit from his tabard and storms out of the Bruin hoose to witness with a grim satisfaction, the devastation his soldiers are now wreaking upon the inhabitants and traders of Lanark town.

Warlord

Bishop Wishart sits patiently on his steed as Lord Stewart rides up beside him, a few words are spoken in private between them, then they both turn to watch their small troop and entourage hastily assemble as they prepare to leave Lanark town. A slight disturbance behind Wishart causes him to look around. Amidst the thronging crowds now gathering to leave the town after the Lanemar fair, he sees two of his trusted men come rushing towards him. Wishart leans over and the two men speak to him quietly in his ear. After a few brief moments, Wishart sits up and nods for all his men to quickly mount their horses. Lord Stewart sees the colour draining from Wishart's stern face. Curious at this sudden change in Wisharts pallor and demeanor, he enquires, "What's the news that appears to ail yie so Wishart?" but Wishart sits expressionless on his horse, his usual ruddy cheeks now turning a deathly grey, his hazel eyes deeply focussed. "Wishart?" enquires Stewart curiously. "What did those two men say to you?"

Upon hearing Stewart's voice, Wishart appears to snap out of his deep thoughts; he turns to look at Stewart then he mumbles, "A change of plans."

"What do you mean, a change of plans?" enquires Stewart, "I thought we were heading for Glasgow?" Wishart replies, "When we're clear of the port gates, we'll stop near the Cartlan

Bridge, there I'll tell you all. Just remember this Stewart, when we reach those gates, no matter what is said to us or what I may say by reply, do not show any unfamiliar reaction, or all may be lost." Stewart gazes curiously at Wishart, he knows him well enough to be aware that his mind is working ahead in some political game, and he is satisfied for the moment that he will find out the answers to his questions soon enough. Wishart nudges and walks his horse forward, while Stewart signals for the small troop and entourage to follow on.

It isn't long before they arrive at the north port barbican gate of Lanark town, now manned by veteran English soldiers, who appear to be stopping everyone, stripping them of all their goods and chattel, then turning the unfortunate people back into the confinements of the town. Any who show resistance are severely beaten, while others are bound in ropes and chains then led away to the castle dungeons. Stewart looks at Wishart in trepidation. "What goes on here Wishart? This appears to be something extremely serious, those English soldiers do not shirk away from committing severe brutality… look see, they're refusing exit to everyone, what's happening here, what's really going on, why are the English stopping everyone and leading others bound in chains to the castle?" Wishart says nothing as they slowly approach the North port.

On arrival at the gates, English soldiers point their keen edged halberds directly at Wishart, Stewart and their entourage. Archers standing on the parapets above on the fortified town wall, keep arrows nocked-taught and pointing straight at them. A guard captain gruffly enquires, "Where do you think you're going Scotchie? No one has given you permission to leave, have they? None of you Scotch are permitted to travel abroad under the martial law orders of the Sherriff." Wishart appears to be non-fussed, "I am bishop Wishart of Glasgow, a good friend and confidante to Sir Henry de Percy, baron of Alnwick, Northumberland, Governor of Ayr, Galloway and Cumberland. I return to my diocese to arrange for his lordships forthcoming visit to the greater Glasgow guilds council in a few days." The captain replies, "You are going nowhere Scotchman, now dismount I say while we search your baggage…"

"CAPTAIN…" calls out Sherriff de Hazelrigg as he comes strutting over.

Waving the captain aside, Hazelrigg enquires, "You're leaving us so soon my good Bishop?" Wishart replies, "Aye Hazelrigg, that I am, for my work here is done. But I can see quite clearly that your work here just begins." Hazelrigg laughs out loud; then he says, "It's Gods work that I do too my dear Bishop, God's work. I am sure you will appreciate and must surely agree, we must be ridding this realm of shit and heathens if we English are to even begin to try and civilise your Scotch beasts of the field."

"Aye Hazelrigg," replies Wishart with a smile, "it's God's work that you're doing right enough. I've already heard of master Braidfuite's gallows jig for sedition, and also that of the rapine of the Braidfuite sisters and their household servants. So, tell me this Hazelrigg, what is the purpose of this cruelty that you have set upon Lord Braidfuite in particular, is this also supposedly God's work?" Hazelrigg grins nervously, then he replies, "Surely it's a truth you do have many ears abroad Wishart, but don't you know, that I and all Englishmen here in these our new territories, have been prior absolved of all the necessary deeds that may be done by my hand, by my sword and also by my soldiers, all in order that is necessary to bring the word of God and true Christianity to this wretched land? You see my godly Wishart, you and I, we are both servants of the true faith, therefore we can do no wrong in the eyes of the Lord, particularly if we obey our anointed king's commands. For it does say oft in the Holy Scriptures, as well you know, that all philistines and heathens who turn their face against Christian Kings, the emissaries of the Almighty, are therefore the true enemies of God, and so, they do forfeit their wives and daughters as bonded slaves, in that, we may do with them as we please." Wishart looks firmly into the eyes of Hazelrigg, he says, "Then God will surely bless you in particular good sir."

Disregarding the pleasantries, Hazelrigg says, "I don't trust you Wishart, I never have, but then, you have only ever offered me praise, pleasantries and assistance since we first met. But I shall still keep a hawk's eye on you my good Bishop, even though I unfortunately require your blessing for the wedding of Arthur to the maid."

"Clear my way at once Hazelrigg," says Wishart, "for I return to Glasgow to prepare for lord de Percy who intends to hold a Guild council and court there in a few days time. You wouldn't wish it so that he thought you to be the cause of any delay would you, notwithstanding his urgency in establishing peace and taxation within his jurisdictions? Must I remind you that I have his favour, and his ear. I ask only this of you, not to be testing Lord de Percy's humours, for if you delay me now, I believe you would have lord Percy most certainly thinking of you to be obstructive to his cause... and to his needs." Hazelrigg scratches his chin, "Hmm, perhaps that may be so my lord Bishop, so go, you now have my permission to leave." Wishart glares at Hazelrigg, "No sir, I am leaving as I please, not by your mistaken sense of authority over me, which only our lord God has." Hazelrigg grips the reigns of Wishart's horse firmly, "Take heed my good Bishop, for I shall be watching you." Wishart ignores the taunt, pulls his reigns from the hands of Hazelrigg and walks his horse forward. "May God keep you safe my lord Sherriff." Hazelrigg hears the bishop's words, which does not sit well by his own interpretation. Wishart does not look back as Hazelrigg nods to the captain of the guard to raise the blockade, allowing Wishart's entourage to leave Lanark unhindered. Upon clearing the towns north port gates, Stewart enquires, "Forgive me Wishart, but what the fuck just happened back there at the gates with Hazelrigg? Is this about the information your men brought to you earlier that caused your pallor to change, young Braidfuite hung for sedition and the maid, her sister and their maid servants have been raped, and what was this that I heard you say about a cruelty placed upon Sir Hugh?" Wishart replies, "Aye, yie heard it right."

"My God…" exclaims Stewart, "this is an outrage." Wishart says, "God does his work in mysterious ways Stewart, but at least Sir Hugh and his daughters are still alive." Stewart shakes his head and mutters, "I can't believe that this has happened. If I were young Wallace, I wouldn't rest till I had my revenge upon them all…"

Soon they are a good distance away from Lanark Town and crossing the Cartlan Bridge. Wishart turns his horse and leads the entourage away from the North road, down the wooded hill and into the olde Moose mill orchard beside the river Clyde.

"Why have we stopped here?" enquires Stewart. Wishart replies, "Stewart, bring me forward your two best horsemen and fleetest horses, I urgently require them to take a message for Robyn of Loch Sloy, I need him to come to me as soon as possible." Stewart sits back in his saddle then waves for his best outriders to come forward. He enquires of Wishart, "You desire the presence here of Robyn o' Loch Sloy, Robyn

Hodde MacGilchrist…? But he's a hundred miles away in the west highlands Wishart, what do you require of Rob that is so urgent?" Wishart replies, "No Stewart, MacGilchrist will be waiting for us at the Loudoun hill, with many men from Bothwell, Avoch and Petty." Stewart enquires, "But, he's young Andrew Moray's man… why would he be waiting there for us?"

Before Wishart could reply, the two riders approach. Wishart speaks with them briefly, then they turn and gallop off at a fast pace north towards the Loudoun hill.

"We must move quickly Stewart." Says Wishart, "I've sent your outriders to find MacGilchrist and his men, they're to meet up with us at Comunnach castle or en route. When we do meet with him, we will all move directly into the Wolf and wildcats through the glen Afton pass." Stewart enquires, "And why would we be doing that?" Wishart replies, "We urgently need to seek out the Wallace's camp in that woodland wilderness." Stewart exclaims. "Have you gone completely mad Wishart? You would dare to take a troop of horse and an imminent Bishop into the Wolf and wildcat lair? That's a death sentence in the making my good bishop, for all of us. I will tell you this, there are far worse things in there I fear than just Wallace's contemptible Gallóbhet, there are many evil spirits and demons lurking in those woodlands too, who do feast gleefully upon wandering fools… and likely enough they feast well on well-fed Bishop's too." Wishart replies, "We must go in there and find Wallace's camp regardless of your fears Stewart. If it is too much grit required for you to muster, then you may retire to the Loudon hill or any other place of safety and wait there for my return."

Stewart angrily moves his horse forward and pulls across the front of Wishart, blocking his path. "Answer me this then Wishart, what are MacGilchrist and Moray's men doing at the Loudoun hill? Will you tell me what the fuck is really going on inside your head?" Wishart tries to pull his horse around Stewart, but he is met and parried with every twist and turn. Wishart's anger flares, "Do not waste our time here Stewart, we need every breath we can muster to find young Wallace, and quickly. Any vantage we may gain in advance of Wallace finding out about what's happened to Braidfuite and his kinfolk this morning, in particular, what's happened to the maid, it will be the better for all of us."

Reluctantly, Stewart turns his horse away and walks alongside Wishart then says, "This is another bloody tragedy." Wishart replies, "Or perhaps Stewart, it's the opportunity I really needed." Stewart pulls his horse to an abrupt halt. "Opportunity you needed?" He exclaims, "Surely not Wishart, tell me that my ears just heard a falsehood. Surely you would not use the demise of young Braidfuite and rapine of the maids to your own advantage?" Wishart shakes his head, "Oh, spare me the chivalrous disquisition Stewart, you're not that naïve. There is naught that you, I nor anyone else can do to change what's already happened, or would you have it that I stand idly by and watch while both Wallace and Moray throw their lives away needlessly, in some bloody futile gesture of exacting revenge or in saving face by chasing misguided honour, or would you have me nurture their need for justice, the kind of justice that would be useful not only to us, but perhaps saving their lives and that of many others too, who would surely suffer if their hot-bloodied sense of retribution went unchecked?" Stewart nudges his horse slowly forward. "I don't know Wishart, it's hard to accept that you're so cold as to use the pain of those two young men for your own gain, maybe you're not the man I thought you were."

"It matters not a damn what you think of me Stewart," says Wishart, "what is vitally important is what's about to happen."

Wishart then looks directly into Stewart's eyes, "You must listen to me, for our people, our realm and our very future is a stake right now like never before in our history, and if nothing is done and done soon, it's more likely than not, even your own illustrious bloodline will soon follow that of others in this realm and ended soon enough by this English king. We must use this terrible tragedy, not just to our own vantage but to the vantage of Wallace and Moray themselves, and most importantly, all of Scotland. It may seem to most, that the killing of young Braidfuite in Lanark is just another murder among the many perpetrated by the English tyrants, but I truly believe that it may be the spark that will light the fires to eventually unite all the people of our realm, or would you have it that things stay as they are, where-after we all gather around just wringing our hands and talk of how terrible it all is, then we sit and do absolutely nothing?"

"I don't know what we should do?" ponders Stewart, "I hear what you say, and it does make a sense, of sorts… but look you to what happened after the heinous massacre of thousands of innocents in our great port of Berwick by the English, or the bloody slaughter of our footsoldiers after the battle of Dunbar, absolutely nothing was done, except that most of the nobles, magnates and clergy of this land all rushed to swoon themselves and lick the feet of Longshanks. If at any time there was to be a rising of the people of this realm, it should have been on those two occasions not after the killing of just one young lad. I wish so much that something could be done to end this usurper's cruel heel grinding down on our necks, but I fear now you're too late, with so many of our best leaders and warriors dead or imprisoned in an English dungeon." Wishart enquires, "What would you have me do then? Would you have it that young Braidfuite back there and the thousands of others throughout this realm to have perished so cruel and needlessly, have all died for nothing? Will young Braidfuite simply just be another poignant tragedy soon to be forgotten, or would you rise with others to bring this usurpers rule to an end, before it brings an end to all of us?" Stewart begins to understand the logic being used by Wishart.

"Perhaps you're right there Wishart," says Stewart, "perhaps there is some merit in what you're saying, I can begin to see that now, but why young Wallace, and why young Moray? It would seem to me a bloody foolish venture to be risking all upon two lovelorn youths to foster a rising. Why not use the merits and warlike prowess of the MacDuffs, Douglas' Graemes and Comyns or any of the other great families who have suffered so greatly too, why do you dwell upon those two in particular?" Wishart replies, "I wish I could answer that fully for you Stewart. All I have ever known is that many would fight for love of country, love of their brother soldier, even love of their faith, but I ask this of you, who is better to lead the fight for our very survival, than those who put love of family first. Other than that, I'm not really sure and cannot explain as to why it is those two youths appear to have been chosen by God himself, but there is one thing that I and many others are most assured and have no doubts about whatsoever, it will be those two hotspurs and those who follow them that will lead our realm forward into a bloody war that is sure going to come."

"Aye your right Wishart, I do know that when Wallace and Moray find out about this tragic affair in Lanark, there will be nothing and nobody to stop them seeking their blood tax." Wishart says, "This is why we must get Wallace out of Scotland now Stewart, at least gone long enough till I and others that I'm in league with, can bring everyone of importance in this realm together, as they did once before for our late king Alexander, God rest his soul. From the highest of lords and magnates, to the lowest of field tillers, we must bring all together who are prepared to rise and fight. We need this combined unity from all the souls of our realm to drive this foreign army away from our borders forever." Stewart says, "Aye, you certainly talk a good fight there Wishart, and it may be so that you're right in your ploy, but…"

"I am right," replies Wishart curtly, "think of it man, in all of our long history, whenever the people of this land rise as one to fight a common enemy, we've never been defeated, not by the imperial Romans, not by the Jutes or the Angles, not ever by anyone. Even in our own lifetime Stewart, the ill-fated attempts made by the feared Norsemen to lord over us ended in their own ignominious failure, those warriors who had defeated almost all of Europe, including the English, they may all have invaded us, but none has ever subdued us. Trust me Stewart, this small backwater as Longshanks' lickspittle men would call us, and this almost insignificant incident in Lanark, is just the beginning of something much bigger than you or I may yet comprehend, but believe me this, we cannot yet have Wallace and his Gallóbhet seeking retribution by blood tax for what has happened, or all our plans will be undone. If we fail in this duty, then I fear we will never get a second opportunity to rise, this is why we desperately need time, enough time to be fully prepared and get all of Scotland united, this is the reason we must get Wallace away from here as quickly as possible before he finds out, or all may be ruined before it has begun."

"I know what I would do if I were Wallace," says Stewart. "If I found out that… My God Wishart, this 'insignificant incident' you speak about, for the maid and her sister to suffer such rapine and bereavement… I myself cannot yet accept so easily what's been done to those poor women and their father, and then to the young fella Brian too." Wishart says, "It was a terrible deed done to the Braidfuites." Stewart replies, "Aye, amidst the thousands of other evil deeds done upon us all." They both continue talking in great depth as they wander forward awhile on their horses along a secretive drove road towards Comunnach Castle, with everyone else in somber mood and deep in thought about what has taken place in Lanark.

"So then tell me Wishart?" enquires Stewart, "What actually happened with young Braidfuite to be the cause of his execution?" Wishart replies, "I was told the young idiot drew his blade on Hazelrigg in front of the sheriff's own men, not just the once, but a few times. Apparently the first time he was told to go home, the final time he returned he made to assault the Sherriff. Hazelrigg then had the poor young fool hung for sedition." Stewart looks away into the distance towards the misty covered peaks of the Wolf and wildcats. "Dear God Wishart, I have to agree with you, it is certain that when Wallace hears of this calamity, there sure will be blood awash in the streets of Lanark town, I know him well enough that your plans will be naught but a forlorn afterthought when both he and his followers find this out. And if we are to be the messengers, then I don't hold out hope for us seeing another morn in this lifetime." Pausing a moment, Stewart thinks long and hard on what he has to do; he says, "I don't know if I can face young Wallace and keep my peace for long Wishart. I like him, he's a good spirit, but my face must surely give away my hidden secret."

Moving his horse close to Stewart, Wishart speaks to him quietly, "You must listen to me now Stewart, I and a few others have spent a long time laying out meticulous plans to regain our sovereignty and independence, but now, now those plans must change, not the structure of what we must do, only the timing, and that's mainly due to Longshanks leaving to start a war in France, but also it's because of what's happened in Lanark too. It's true that young Wallace will hear of this tragedy soon enough, but it is too soon for him to yet know. Believe me this Stewart, no-one has any doubt that both Wallace and Moray are the principle keys to unlock what will happen next, so it's for this reason that I am personally going into the Wolf and wildcats to seek him out and gain time for Scotland." Stewart is puzzled, "I still don't fully understand, why we do not simply tell Wallace when we meet him."

"Listen to me Stewart," says Wishart, "already you and I both know of this wretched business in Lanark, as do all the men of our troop. It will be short in time before young Wallace's spies travel with this news, once they escape the precincts of Lanark, if they have not done so already." Stewart enquires, "How then will we find Wallace in the Wolf and wildcats? Even the English armies fear the very name of that god-forsaken place and will not enter. And no disrespect is intended towards you personally Wishart, but it's widely known that the Gallóbhet murder or kill anyone simply for amusement that enters that damned forest un-invited, and with you being of the Holy cloth, an enemy of their ancient faith as they see it, that's something they would relish..." Wishart interrupts, "I must risk all to reach Wallace before his spies or by any other means the news reaches him first. I must make sure he is out of the country before he hears of this." Stewart is bewildered, "His wife and her sister repeatedly raped, their father tortured and Wallace's brother-in-law dead, and you want him out of the country?" Wishart replies, "Aye, we only need a few days to set other plans firmly in motion, then we can let Wallace and Moray loose to do what they will. It was initially planned for him to leave in a few days time, but now it must be immediately." Stewart enquires, "How do you propose to find Wallace in that vast woodland, and even if we're successful in finding him, how are you going to convince him to leave the country? And then Moray, for he is imprisoned in England."

"Have no doubts," replies Wishart, "when we enter the Wolf and wildcats, Wallace or his men will find us soon enough. And to answer your second question, I sent word to him before this tragedy, to go to Invergarvane and meet Morrison mòr in a few days time. There he is to board a ship that will take him to England, I'm reliably informed he is already preparing to leave." Stewart is completely baffled, "Now you lose me Wishart, what's going on in that head of yours, why is Wallace going to England?" Wishart replies, "I have many good friends in England at the Benedictine priory of Birkenhead in the shire of Chester, near to where young Andrew Moray is being held captive by the Justiciar of Chester castle, Sir Hugh de Lacey."

"So, what has Wallace got to do with this affair?" enquires Stewart. Wishart replies, "I've brokered a deal for young Moray's ransom with de Lacey, now I'm sending down Robyn MacGilchrist as Moray's Bondsman with the ransom siller to set him free, he's then to bring Moray back to Scotland with much haste. Wallace is going too, for it's well known that he's a close friend of Moray. I initially thought to send Wallace with MacGilchrist, under the pretext of welcoming Moray with a friendly face, thereby removing him from the realm, at least long enough for me to prepare for my next move. But now, with the murder of Braidfuite's son and poor Marion and Brannah suffering grievously at the hands of the English, imponderable actions have already overtaken my original plans, this is why we must make certain that Wallace leaves the country before he hears of this, at least for a few days."

Pondering, Stewart says, "You sound certain about Wallace leaving Scotland so easily." Wishart replies, "I know young Wallace will attend Moray willingly, according to my spies, he and the Moray are bond-close brothers and soon to be kinsmen." Stewart replies, "I really hope you're right about all o' this Wishart, for ah reckon that you're playin' your hand awfy close to your chest, go canny ma' good Bishop, for sometimes that play can also be a fool's hand. You'd better be prayin' hard that your plan succeeds, for if Wallace does remain in the country, and it's only a matter of time before he does find out what's happened… also, if he finds out that you have been playing a willing part in all of these evil doings, you may well be a recipient of his vengeance." Stewart further enquires. "How much are you paying for the Moray ransom?"

"One thousand silver Merks," replies Wishart.

"WHAT…?" exclaims Stewart, "I've never heard of such a ransom prize outwith a kingship?" Wishart explains, "Sir Hugh de Lacey is heavily indebted to Longshanks for this amount or thereabouts, that's the main reason he took six Scots nobles prisoner at the battle of Dunbar, for ransom purposes simply to be paying off his debt to the English Royal treasury. Apart from young Moray, there's also Alan le Marschal, Thomas Moncrieff, Patrick de Montalt, Hugh Lochore and Matthew de Eyton's ransoms still to be paid. We'll try and bring them all home soon enough, but it's mainly Young Andrew that we require to be returned more than the others, for his stepmother is Euphemia Comyn, she's the sister of the red Comyn, and their mother is Eleanor Balliol, the sister of our King, therefore, if we bring young Moray's house to our table, he will surely bring on all the might of the Comyns and Baliols too."

"Yie reckon so?" says Stewart. He enquires, "Yie think that the fire now set in our noble youngblood, is goin' to be the answer to securing an army for pushin' the English out o' Scotland do yie? If you're thinking of bringing all o' those young nobles back home, with Longshanks' taxmen bleeding us dry, that will be a mighty sum well beyond anythin' that our realm can afford. Tell me then Wishart, where did you raise such a sum for young Andrew's ransom?" Wishart replies, "From Moray's own kinfolks, but mainly from his uncle, David le Riche, he's the wealthy prior of Bothwell. More came from his elder brother William, and a fine contribution was also raised from the church diocese' of Glasgow and Saint Andrews. I have also gained finance from other good friends of the cause to bring them all home."

Stewart says, "I see your play now Wishart, though I fear young Andrew's father Lord Moray, may be lost to us soon, for I hear he lays sickly to death in an English dungeon. But by bringing young Moray back, aye, you will most certainly secure your planned banditry adventures from him and his followers up in the northeast. With you also having Wallace stirring up trouble down here in the southwest, and both o' them being kindred spirits with the Braidfuite sisters… my God Wishart, setting them up against the English with their hot blood for revenge with all the men that will follow their banners, this will be enough for your plans to ignite a proper resistance."

"Aye," replies Wishart, "those two young hotspurs will be the spark we need to light a grand fire under the English and illuminate Scotland's road back to freedom."

"Freedom?" repeats Stewart. He smiles knowingly then says, "With risings in the North-east and southwest, two places full of savage and barbarous warriors where the English fear to tread, I can see now that by stirring the bile of Wallace and Moray, you could have the English easily trapped betwixt the two. But what of the men of the border marches and the western highlands?" Wishart replies, "Nial Campbell of Lochawe is committed and will rise all of his warriors in the west. MacDuff will raise all his men and the remnants of the Guardian army in the mid-east of Fife. And you my friend, you will command the men of your household and kinfolks, with additional support of the lower west coast Islanders and border marches bowyers. The houses of Comyn will rise to the southeast with Sir James Douglas and de Graeme the younger to the mid-west."

"Grand," grins Stewart, "You'll soon have these English usurpers trapped in a deadly rat-box, with no escaping the wrath of Moray and Wallace as your pretext, and no blame or inference of collusion regarding our noble or clerical classes attached. Now I truly understand why our late king Alexander had placed so much faith upon your shoulders. What you're setting in motion with Moray and Wallace being seen as warlords, and with the English being so busy chasing the heads o' Wallace and Moray in the opposite corners o' Scotland, you'll tie up a substantial amount of their men looking for brigands and bandits. And by what you're sayin', you will be bringing back into play the old army of the King... and the English won't see that coming. A master play if you and your associates can pull this off Wishart, this will surely give everyone hope and time for all of our great houses to assemble and raise their banners as one."

Stewart pauses a moment, then he enquires, "But Wishart, we both know that war is never enough, no matter how sweet any victory may be in the field, we both also know that astute politic, money and powerfull friends abroad are necessary to put Scotland firmly back in contention as a free trading sovereign realm. So, tell me this ma' wily bishop, who else is part of this cabal, if I may be so free?" Wishart replies, "I cannot reveal all at this moment in time. For more do come to our banners each and every day, but I can tell you that I shall be meeting with Duns Scottis, William Lamberton, Fraser of Saint Andrews, Bernard of Kilwinning, and Archibald of Brechin very soon. We're preparing to draft a radical document of royal reformation on behalf of the people of Scotland for the Holy See, a document that will most certainly free us politically from this English usurper's tyranny. All we require right now is enough time to gain favour with His Holiness and obtain his blessing and a Papal Bull, then we will sign and resume our allegiances with the Hanseatic trading federation, Philip of France and Eric of Norway, then finally my friend, we will be rid of this barbaric English despotism for all time."

"Alexander de Ergadia," says Stewart, "I noticed that his name is missing from your prominent list of theologians?" Wishart frowns then he replies, "He most certainly is associated, but I regret to inform you that he's been imprisoned by Longshanks in the tower of London, along with many other formidable nobles from the north-west Islands, Argyle and Ross. But I shall tell you this information Stewart, his MacDougal sons, along with the Mac ua' Ruaidhri clan and Morrison mòr's men, they are all labouring furiously and building a large fleet of Birlinns to ensure Longshanks' navy will never blockade our ports again, for they will inflict a high cost upon any English admiral who would dare to try." Stewart enquires, "Then you must tell me this then Wishart, how so is it will you contain Longshanks ardent supporters and fleets from the Clans of Ranald and Alistair óg McDonald." Wishart replies tersely, "Their angst to be licking the arse of the English king will soon be quashed by the Birlinn fleets alliance' under the leadership of Lachlan MacDougal, Morrison Mòr and Ruaidhri Mac Ruaidhri. I've also been well informed that Alasdair Comyn, John's brother, is also preparing to ally his substantial west-coast fleet to the Birlinn alliance, between them my friend, they believe that they can muster enough men to fill a one-hundred oar Birlinn every davoch, from the Rhinns and Machars up to the mighty Éilean Siar, a formidable and powerfull alliance to lay the usurper's allies low."

"Very impressive indeed Wishart, and speaking of the Comyns, what about freeing the red Comyn too, he's another young spur who will be able to muster a great house to the cause, and we will surely need the Comyn house to ride with us from the outset to succeed, but I hear that he's locked away in the tower of London for ransom? And what about young Brus of Annandale and the Brus claim to the throne of Scotland?"

"I'll answer you," replies Wishart, "The red Comyn sails for Flanders as we speak, he's under a bonded oath to Longshanks, but both his bond and his oath were given under duress, therefore worthless in the eyes of true men of honour, he'll soon escape or find a way to return, and if King John Baliol does not return, it looks as though it would be most likely Edward Baliol, the Kings brother, who succeeds to the throne, but he lies in an English dungeon too. If not him, then it would be the red Comyn whom the Guardians and magnates will crown as the next true King of Scots, not the house of Brus, for they have previously shown that they have too many divided loyalties, both the father and the son. Robert, the young earl of Carrick, well, he's already sworn the name of Brus solemnly upon the Holy Gospels and sword of Thomas a' Becket, committing their fealty and loyalty to the King of England alone. The Brus family have too many great estate properties in England and France to lose, should they seek the crown of Scotland solely for themselves." Stewart says, "Aye, that may be the truth of it, but there is such bad blood between the houses of the Comyn and the Brus, this could yet spark another civil war?"

Pondering a moment, Wishart replies, "I know of this bitter animus Stewart, but not withstanding your own house of Stewarts, the houses of Comyn, Campbell, Moray, Graeme, Douglas, Baliol, and MacDuff's with all their collective kinfolks, could bring an enormous army to the field in support of the cause of Scotlands freedom, an army Stewart, such as we've never seen before in this realm, an army that would easily match the size of both Scotland's old Guardian armies. Also, if Wallace truly is the warlord of those savages of Galloway, and young Moray draws his forces from the North… and if we cannot bring all together in a single alliance with all of Scotland's nobles, then I agree with your initial concerns, where any other support for the Brus to take the throne would thrust Scotland back into a civil war. The Brus claim must be sacrificed for the sake of the greater alliance, which in turn would mean that too great and overwhelming a force would be ranged against them. No Stewart, I have no doubt that the house of Brus would soon stand down after much consideration. I believe they would shrewdly cut their losses and remain fairly contented to be living a comfortable life on their estates in England."

"You think?" laughs Stewart. "I fear that you greatly underestimate the hunger the Brus faction has for the throne of Scotland." Wishart replies, "I did once before Stewart, but never again. There has to be a loser in all of this, and I must support whomever the church, Guardians and the council of magnates deem to be best suited to free Scotland from the grip of Longshanks… And to keep it free, therefore, it falls that it must be for us all to support Comyns claim after Baliol, for it is the superior claim to that of Brus through the criterion of primogeniture, and by all of us abiding by the propriety of the recognised and established Laws of kingship, this will surely gain us unqualified approval and support from the Holy Father in Rome."

"Fair points you make again Wishart," says Stewart, "but I must ask you this, why do you not rest easy with the English yourself? You could be well contented sitting in front of your little fish loch up at the Bishops Palace near Glasgow for the rest of your life. What drives you so Wishart? What restless spirit beats in that heart of yours that you would risk all for Scotlands freedom?" Wishart replies, "Bishop Bek has been antagonising our church for such a long time, in order I believe, to stir a seditious reaction from us. I also believe his actions are there to justify the taking over of all our religious orders to bring the wealth of our church into English hands. I'm sorry to say that I didn't see this happening earlier, but Bek's cohorts and many others, even within our own church, have been appointing English scribes, priests and Bishops to all our major and minor benefices, there they've been busy altering our historical accounts. I don't know the full reason for why yet, but I tell you this Stewart, I do not, nor will I ever accept English siller to keep my mouth shut, simply to make myself an easy life… all I know is this, I must do all in my power to protect Scotland and her people."

Stewart says, "I understand what you say Wishart, I feel the same way… I have also heard of these interfering scribblers at work upon our antiquities. It's been said to me oft' that when Longshanks removed our original records of antiquity, he dumped them all into the sea just east of Newcastle, supposedly lost in a storm on their way to London." Wishart scowls, "Longshanks, may he rot in hell… That sacrilegious usurper King has also stolen the Black Rood of saint Margaret, Scotland's holiest relic, a piece of the true Cross of Christ. He has also removed an Lia Fàil away from Scone and had it placed under his own throne down in England." Wishart remonstrates, "Did you know that when Longshanks took away the sacred stone to Westminster Abbey, he paid one hundred shillings to a common carpenter for a base throne to house an Lia Fàil, then he costructed a majestic headboard to hold the royal and ancient crown of the dynastic Llewellans? He now calls it all, St Edward's Chair, or even more fanciful would you believe, he's named it the throne of King Arthur."

"What's the reason for all of that foolishness?" enquires Stewart curiously.

"The reason?" replies Wishart, "The reason that he does this fancy, is to convince everyone to believe he is the fabled King Arthur reincarnate, summoned by all that is holy to return to save and rule over all 'Britons' as he would call us. Also, these heinous actions of his on our account are deliberate, in that, we Scots may never anoint nor raise again to bless our own sovereign Lord upon our sacred relics. That I believe, with all the other machinations and cruelties that he employs upon our people, is to ensure that future generations of our countrymen may never again feel pride as a free people. He and his cohorts want to make certain the people of our land believe they are forever dependant upon England's charity for the very sanctity of life itself. That's the reason Stewart, not only do the English need our wealth and vast resources, the English, they appear to need our history too..." Wishart pauses as though he has had a revelation. "I see it now Stewart, we both know that Longshanks is a ruthless but also a very pragmatic King, and his claim to the throne of Scotland is extremely tenuous at best and mostly based on a series of great falsehoods. Apparently he needs an inviolable historical credibility with the Pope, to make his claim upon our realm utterly justified in the eyes of His Holiness, therefore, hence God. Add to that, Bishop Bek's attempted Anglicisation of the Church in Scotland into accepting English rule, I see now that there is a much greater purpose behind these actions that makes Scotland's submission to Longshanks but a small piece to a greater puzzle. I fear that we are nothing more than a small account to be paid to service a much greater purpose for this conniving English king." Stewart laughs, "Is this Wishart the Breitheamh Rígh, or is it the politician, maybe even the elder o' the Cruinne-Cè talkin'? Or perhaps it's all three that does this conferring with me now?"

Wishart smiles wryly as they ride on with great haste towards Comunnach Castle.

After a while riding along the old drove roads in silence, Stewart says, "I was just thinking there Wishart, do yie remember when my brother James was forced into a marriage with that English lord of Ulster's sister, Erdigia, as part o' the deal to keep his freedom when he had to submit to Longshanks after the battle of Dunbar?"

"Aye, I do remember, she's the sister of Richard Óg de Burgh, the red Earl of Ulster, I remember when he sailed from Ireland with many hundreds of his Irish levies to support Robert le Brix, when the old fox of Annandale made his first play for the crown of Scotland during the Pact uprising." Stewart says, "Aye, that's the man I'm talking about. Well, as luck would have it, my brother and the red Earls sister, they actually found love for each other." Wishart enquires, "I had been informed that the marriage you speak about was a calamitous arrangement and a bad affair for your family?" Stewart replies, "In many ways aye, it was, but as yie know, the marriage kept my brother away from being taken as a prisoner in chains to the tower of London, to be ransomed or die at the hands of an English axeman. But I will tell yie this, even though we lost many things to this imposition of English governance, so much more than just the Sherrifdom of Kintyre and keepership of Dunbarton castle, thankfully my brother now lives, but as a man who is bonded under a martial oath to Longshanks." Wishart says, "I fear we all lost something precious during that fight for our independence, but at least your brother is free and not rotting away in an English prison somewhere, like so many others we know and love, who now wait to be ransomed." Stewart says, "But Wishart, there's something else we gained from that marriage." Wishart enquires, "Aye, and what would that be?" Stewart replies, "We gained a unique and extremely valuable inside information source regarding de Burgh and his plans with Longshanks." Wishart is curious, "Explain yourself fully Stewart, what's the detail of this valuable source, and to whom do you refer?"

"Erdigia herself," replies Stewart, "she's never spoken in any great detail, but it's apparent to us that her life and body was sorely defiled in the English court, she's made it plain she has no love for Longshanks. There's something Erdigia told us recently that I never thought o' much importance, but perhaps now, this information may be useful to you and help our cause, maybe it'll help turn Brus in favour of your plans." Wishart is curious, "Be careful there Stewart, for you're beginning to sound a wee bit like a religious cleric with your political maneuvering." Both of them laugh at the comment; then Wishart enquires, "So what's your point?" Stewart replies, "It would seem that after the recent death up at Cardross of Roberts wife, Isabella of Mar, it's a well-known open secret between the two families, that the red Earls daughter Elizabeth and Robert Brus of Annandale, they're both se' sic' in love from their childhood trysts, that one day soon they will be joined as man and wife."

"And what use could that information be to me..." says Wishart. Suddenly Wishart looks across at Stewart, almost in amazement. "Stewart, this snippet might be the final little key to unlocking the family of Brus from the chains of Longshanks grip. This news may also bring to us the house of Brus into the fold of nobles that we need, it may also gain us the time we require to bring both the guardian's military might together alongside Moray and Wallace, then Stewart, then we may raise all their followers into one single great army of the people..."

"What?" exclaims Stewart, "what are yie thinking Wishart?"

"Don't you see?" says Wishart, "If we can bring the house of Brus on board without stirring up another civil war, then we would have all the major houses of Scotland finally on our side, and with all those houses, the Guardian army, Moray and Wallace's commoners..." Wishart is almost ecstatic. "All we are needing is just a little more time Stewart, just enough time to unite all of Scotland under one banner." Stewart is intrigued, "But what if Robert Brus makes a play to fulfill his grandfather's ambitions, to take the throne of Scotland by force, how then would we stop him without fighting both the Brus factions and Longshanks too?" Wishart replies, "You and I Stewart, we would act as legal arbiters on his behalf, but we would make certain that his claim would eventually fail, through reasoning, not a bloody war." Stewart enquires, "How do we organise that, it's a well-known fact that you cannot walk ten paces for a piss without bumping into one of Longshanks spies or paymen?"

"Time itself will surely favour us Stewart," replies Wishart. "especially if we bring Brus on board very soon. Your reference to Longshanks with his spies and paymen, well, we will let them know surreptitiously through little facts escaping and by rumours, that the nobles of Scotland are planning to hold an armed conference of objection to his English administration... perhaps we should hold it at the Irvine sands." Stewart enquires, "Why Irvine?" Wishart replies, "Because Irvine is the martial stronghold of the Guardian army, it also holds Scotland's main royal armoury, this will give the English cause to pay us attention. We will make it so as not to arouse suspicion from the English that it's an act of war, this is in order for them not to send a full army against us, but just enough of a smaller force, in that, we could drag out the negotiations as much as possible and make it appear that after much deliberation and parleying with them, we would finally acquiesce then capitulate."

"This play makes no sense to me," retorts Stewart, "why risk all, then capitulate?"

Before Wishart can reply, an outrider suddenly comes galloping at speed towards them. The rider pulls his horse to a halt beside Wishart and Stewart. "My Lord, good Bishop," he gasps, "There's a Clachan up ahead, there are many English soldiers, and they, they..." Stewart exclaims, "That's Pádraic Mackie's place. I know him well, for I have traded many horses with him in the past. What's with your angst soldier?" The rider appears pale, out of breath and there is a look of terror deeply etched in his face. His shaken demeanor is not lost to Wishart and the others of the troop too. Wishart demands, "Speak up man, what ails you?" The scout regains his breath, "The English, they've slaughtered everyone down there in the Clachan ma lord, every man woman and child..." Before Wishart or Stewart could ask any more questions, a squadron of English soldiers ride fast towards them, their lances menacingly at the tilt. Within moments they have Wishart, Stewart and their entourage troop completely surrounded. The lead knight of the English squadron circles Wishart without saying a word. Wishart enquires, "What's your business here?" The young-looking lead knight casually replies, "Nay, it is you who must answer my questions. So tell me Scotchman, what is your business hereabouts?" Wishart replies, "I journey to Comunnach castle to meet with Lord Cospatrick of Dunbar." The knight replies, "But he no longer dwells there. Tell me then my lord... Bishop is it? Would you like to try again? What is your business on these goat roads so far from my king's highway?" Stewart grips his sword, "Have a care with your tongue Englishman. I am the Mormaer of Lennox, Sir John Stewart of Bonkyll, son of the High Stewart of Scotland. This holy man that you now address is the venerable Bishop of Glasgow, Robert Wishart."

Wishart notices the tabards and boots of the English riders are spattered and sodden in blood. Wishart speaks, "I was unaware lord Cospatrick is no longer in his residence, I had thought to rest and break food and wine with him, before I journey onwards to meet with lord Sir Henry de Percy in Glasgow in a few days time." The young knight's demeanor swiftly changes. He laughs and looks round at his men, then glancing back at the Scots troop, he looks directly into the eyes of Wishart. "Lord Percy my dear Wishart, is my father. So, you must tell me why then that I have never heard him speak your name before... do you have any port passes to travel? For you must know I'm sure, that no Scotch, be he a high or low born, may be between towns or abroad in this realm, unless it is in chains or to some hilltop gibbet? And you are aware are you not, that any who does defy or does break this law, is to be put to death immediately, by orders of my King... regardless of their station?"

"I have heard it so." replies Wishart, "Then you will also recognize the seal of lord de Percy on my port passes." The young knight leans forward and swiftly grabs the port passes away from Wishart's hand. After scrutinising them, he hands them back. "My name is Marmaduke de Percy dear Wishart. Please do convey my best regards to my father when next you greet him." Wishart puts away the port passes as De Percy continues, "Your grace, it is not safe to be so far from the Kings highway, there are many brigands who lurk hereabouts, waiting to ply their evil trade upon the unwary. I am sure you appreciate my zeal when first we met?" Wishart replies, "I've never knowingly been mistaken as a brigand sir knight, but I do thank you for your concern for my safety." De Percy laughs, "There is a hamlet ahead of you my good Bishop, perhaps you should avert your eyes as you pass by, for what you may witness is not for the stomach of such an imminent man of God as you appear to be." De Percy laughs again; then he spurs his horse on to a canter. His squadron raise their lances away from Wishart's entourage; then they too canter off in the direction of Lanark.

"Smug bastard," curses Stewart, "did you notice the blood all over their horse's hooves and boots?" Wishart replies, "I did..." Stewart watches the departing English squadron, growling to himself, "Bastards..." Wishart walks his horse forward in the direction of the little Clachan. It isn't long before the bishop's entourage comes to the first of the smoldering ruins, where the bodies of men, women, children and even dogs, lay scattered asunder in bloody grotesque forms. Each and every living being they see has been mutilated, trampled or decapitated, their skulls being placed in little pyramids around the Clachan ruins. The stench of death and scent of warm blood from opened guts fills the air, causing everyone to pull out rags to cover their mouth and nose. As they ride slowly through the carnage and detritus, they halt in the centre of the Clachan; for the sight before them causes many of Wishart's entourage to wretch involuntarily. Stewart exclaims, "God as my witness."

A light rain begins to fall as Wishart dismounts and walks over to a cow-skinning gibbet, where the more desirable young girls and women of the Clachan, have obviously been defiled then mutilated in a most barbaric fashion. Fires had been lit below their feet and objects forced between their legs. Most of the females that can be seen, from the smallest of girls to the eldest grandmothers, have had their breasts, lips, ears, nose and eyelids cut from their bodies. Only Stewart has ever witnessed such vicious barbarity before. Wishart's entourage and Stewart's troop, all men of piety or simply ordinary town guard soldiers, are in total shock or being violently sick. Wishart immediately falls to his knees, clasps his hands and prays fervently. Stewart dismounts close to the ghastly scenes and looks at the tortured faces, then he hears a faint groan coming from what appears to be a young girl. He looks closer into a once pretty face, he jumps back startled as the wide bloodied gawking eyes move and look at him through a black-burned encrusted face, the poor creature bares her teeth, so white against her seared black flesh, then she emits another groan.

"Some of them are still alive…" cries Stewart. "Look out for any more survivors…"

Men from the troop quickly put aside their revulsion and rush to where Stewart is now gently untying a mutilated young girl from a wagon wheel spar. He calls out, "Look about everyone, some of the others may yet show signs of life." With the help of some of the men, Stewart carries the young girl across the blood-soaked ground and lays her down carefully upon a pile of dry clothing. Audible screams begin to come from the girl as her body begins to shake violently. Stewart hastily takes off his mantle and covers the girl as Wishart comes rushing over, he exclaims, "Is she still alive?" Stewart says nothing as he wipes the drizzle from his face, then he leaves to search for any other survivors. Wishart kneels beside the girl, all the while uttering the Trinitarian formula as he quickly makes the sign of the Holy Cross.

After a long and fruitless search, everyone gathers around Wishart and the young girl. Stewart returns and says, "I found the body of auld MacKie Wishart, he's been flayed, emasculated, then left to slow roast over the smithy forge, I had to…" Wishart notices Stewart struggling to continue with what he has seen, and obviously what he had to do. Wishart enquires, "No other survivors then?" Stewart replies, "None." Standing up, Wishart looks at Stewart, then he speaks quietly… "I shall say prayer for all of the unfortunates from this Clachan, then we must leave this place and make with much haste to find the Wallace camp, regardless of meeting with MacGilchrist and the men of Moray. Every sand-grain drop of time we tarry here, our opportunity to end this wicked madness diminishes." Stewart glares at Wishart, "What the fuck are you talking about lord fuckin' Bishop… what fuckin' opportunity?" Stewart takes off his helm and throws it to the ground then he stands nose to nose with Wishart.

In a rage, Stewart says, "I'll go no further Wishart, for this girl will not die here all alone. I will tell you this too, ever since we left Lanark and you told me of your plans, I had my doubts about facing Wallace knowing what I know… but now, now I am thinking to bring him my banners then standing by his side. This is not the first time I have witnessed such barbarities, but it will surely be the last, for I will go back to my shire and raise my men…" Wishart interrupts, "Hold your wits together man, don't you see, for all of this wickedness that lays before us, this will be a scene that shall be repeated a thousand-fold or more, if we do not stop the English rampaging through our country with impunity, and we have none other as yet to stop them, other than his

Holiness." Stewart replies, "I care for naught at this moment in time for anything other than the peace of this young girl Wishart. I tell yie this too, if I was to meet with Wallace now, at this very moment, and he still be ignorant of the rapine and murder in Lanark, I would tell him so and be done with it… you mark my fuckin' words Wishart, I will tell him what has happened and I'll bring all of my bannermen, kith and kin to the field to faithfully stand by his side in his endeavors."

Grimacing, Wishart says, "Stewart, this is why I must make absolutely certain that Wallace is out of the country to bring Moray back. Should we recklessly condone the raising of arms throughout the realm now, in an unplanned armed attack on the English host, it is a folly as it is most certain that we will fail, then I fear, Longshanks will surely abandon Flanders and France to strike back at us with such a fearsome retribution, that this day will mean nothing, all these deaths will mean nothing… and this cannot be. My friend, I need you to yet hold your grit firm, for I have a foreboding it will be so calamitous if you don't, such actions as we have witnessed here this day, will only be the beginning of the apocalypse of our realm."

A soldier cries out, "Many riders are fast approaching us, I think it is your outriders my lord." Stewart's outriders gallop wildly into the Clachan, followed by a large troop of mounted Gallóglaigh. Wishart whispers to himself, "MacGilchrist…"

The Gallóglaigh ride into the Clachan where MacGilchrist dismounts then he walks at a fast pace towards Wishart, apparently oblivious to the human carnage strewn all around. MacGilchrist's loud voice booms out across the silent Clachan. "Wishart, what are your plans?" He continues as he closes in on Wishart and Stewart, "I should be riding into Invergarvane right now, preparing to sail with Morrison mòr's fleet bound for Birkenhead, what demands do yie make upon ma attention that are more important than that o' ma Moray kinsman?" MacGilchrist looks around the scene then speaks with no obvious care, "There is naught we can do here for these souls now Wishart. Hayde here is going to take us directly to Wallace's camp in the Wolf and wildcats, but we must be leavin' now, there's no time to be wastin' with the dead when it's the living that's needin' our help." Wishart replies, "I urgently need to ensure that Wallace goes with you to Birkenhead, now, this very day. I have orders and vital information for both him and the Moray." MacGilchrist queries Wishart, "Wallace is to come with me?"

"Aye, that is so," replies Wishart, "but we must leave now, I will explain all to you as we travel towards his camp." Wishart looks at Stewart, who says, "I'll be waiting here with my men Wishart. When the soul of this young girl is gone from this world, we'll build funeral pyres for her and her clan. Then I'll await your return at the castle of Cospatrick." Wishart nods positive then turns to MacGilchrist... "I'll say prayers for the fallen of this Clachan MacGilchrist; then we shall leave this place." MacGilchrist moves to protest, but he sees that all men of both the Avoch and Bishops entourage are kneeling as one in the light rain. Wishart begins to pray. Hayde and the Wolf and wildcat Gallóglaigh stay silent while remaining in their saddles.

The prayers conclude then everyone mounts their horses.

Wishart puts his hand upon his friend's shoulder and says, "I'll leave my entourage here with you Stewart. There's no need to be risking their lives on this mission; it will also eliminate any tongue from revealing what has happened in Lanark at the Wallace camp, I believe that this part of the journey is best done myself. I must get MacGilchrist to tell Wallace all that he needs to hear and nothing more, in order that he fulfills my mission. I'll send word to Morrison mòr at Invergarvane to ensure he leaves from Scotland with Wallace immediately after both he and MacGilchrist arrive at the landings. And later, when Wallace finds out that he was tricked and seeks retribution, it is on my head alone, no-one else's." Wishart sees much anger and conflict in Stewart's eyes. "May God protect you Stewart. It may be that some day you will understand my methods, as I fear you think them perfidious to you now." Stewart replies, "May your God protect you too good Bishop." Wishart looks curiously at Stewart, as though an insult had been intended, but he also feels an ancient pull of faith between them, a faith much older than Christianity that is the true bonding between them both in this cruel place of slaughter. MacGilchrist calls out, "Come Wishart." Stewart watches as Wishart rides off with MacGilchrist, Hayde. Moray's men and the Wolf and wildcat Gallóglaigh, he waits patiently till they all disappear into the thick grey mist cloaking the great woodland wilderness. He knows that Wishart is determined absolute on his precarious mission to get Wallace out of the country and to bring young Andrew Moray home to Scotland.

On route to the Wolf and wildcat enclave, Wishart tells all to MacGilchrist of his plans for the raising of the royal war banners in both the North and the South of Scotland. He also discusses with him the opportunity for a gathering upon the Irvine sands. After a while, Wishart relays in detail what has happened in Lanark. Big Rob MacGilchrist appears surprisingly devastated at the news regarding the fate of the Braidfuite's. Wishart says, "Yie must be heeding me well MacGilchrist, if Wallace finds out what's happened over in Lanark before you sail, and he makes a break for land… you must attend to him as needs be. For Wallace may yet undo in moments what many of us have planned for years, because of his need for revenge…" MacGilchrist enquires brusquely,

"And what o' young Moray. What do I do if he too finds out about the rapine o' his sweetheart when we land back in Scotland by return?" Wishart looks at MacGilchrist and says, "In the name of God, I absolve you of all actions that you may deem necessary, even if it's to sacrifice the few to save the many, then you must… for the sake of all of Scotland, Moray must be returned to the North before he too finds out."

MacGilchrist says nothing more as they ride on towards the camp of Wallace, for despite his love and duty to his kinsman Andrew Moray; he knows the bishop is right. He enquires, "Of all these plans that you and your brokers are plying Wishart, who will be the King of our realm once we rid ourselves of this bloody scourge, we both know that Baliol, though he himself be a good man, has lost the faith of both the people and the nobles?" Wishart replies, "We must keep our faith in John Baliol returning to claim the throne, but if not, most likely it will be his brother, or John Comyn." MacGilchrist exclaims, "The Red Comyn? Why not Moray, a fine young noble fella that yie place so much faith upon?" Wishart replies, "No MacGilchrist, though I feel that young Andrew has everything that Scotland needs to be our king, it must only be John Comyn as is set down by our ancient laws of Kingship and primogeniture." MacGilchrist enquires, "Then what is to become of Moray when all of this dirty business is settled?" Wishart replies, "We shall endeavor to have Andrew elevated to the position of his father as the imminent Justiciar of Scotia."

Nodding agreeably, MacGilchrist enquires, "What of young Wallace too should he survive, for he is naught but a lowly commoner?" MacGilchrist smiles then continues, "Just like me." Wishart too smiles, he says, "He will be a warlord that inspires the common people, and should he survive that, I believe a simple knighthood and some landed estates to heal his wounds will be reward enough." MacGilchrist says, "Aye, that's about right in thinkin' o' Wallace, a Warlord in the making. Ah do like the young fella greatly Wishart, ah truly do, but I doubt that he has much time left to be breathin' in the air o' this world, he's always getting into trouble with the English, and he's reckless. Each time he encounters conflict; it's greater in its intensity, or success as we would call it, than the last. But you and I both know that the nobles will never take orders from someone as lowly as he is, he could never hold a position of power above any nobility." Wishart replies, "I have no intention of Wallace being in any position to give orders to nobles. My plan for Wallace is to use his growing popularity with the common folks, not just in Galloway, but also in the shires and marches of Stirling, Aberdeen and Dundee. His function will be to serve both the red Comyn and Moray as their second in command, he can be raised no further than that." MacGilchrist says, "I reckon yie are right there Wishart. Young Wallace is clever and a very smart hunter of both beast and men, and he's also a good leader of men at times too, and those that do follow him, which are many and still growing in their numbers every day, they sure are all dedicated men and women, all with a fearsome reputation for a good fight, especially those Gallóbhet and their Irish counterparts, who all claim him as their leader. But ahm afraid that he has his limits. A good thing is, I know he is as close to Andrew Moray as any brother could be. Aye, your thinkin' is sound by me Wishart, Wallace will make a fine warlord and he'll serve Moray and the red Comyn loyally. Aye, William Wallace, Warlord o' the Wolf and Wildcats… that does it for me."

Warlord

WARLORD

Witness or Victim

n the Welsh English border of the Wirral peninsula, an early bright and warm morning sun causes a thick mist, almost mystical in its appearance, to rise eerily from the still calm surface water of the ambling Afon Dyfrdwy, River Dee. Nearby on the riverbank, a young sheepherder sits idly by without a care, chewing on a sweet grass stalk while he watches his flock being herded and corralled by his loyal dogs, then something un-settling stirs his senses. He looks up and scans across the river estuary, but there's nothing apparent, nothing untoward. He keeps a focus on the centre of the mist, and waits, for he knows that something is out there, but he is not sure what it is. Then he hears the faint sounds of light water turbulence, a regular but feint splashing sound, but still he sees nothing. He whistles for his dogs to bring the sheep closer to him; then he gets up and forges himself partway into a nearby willow coppice where he takes shelter. Suddenly, he is startled when two swans appear, flying gracefully out of the mist, he watches, almost mesmerised as the mist majestically spirals behind the beating wings of the swans. But something causes him to keep observing. The young sheepherder waits and watches, then he sees something very strange… '*A monster*' he thinks. Then eerily, a large dragonhead bow slowly emerges from the mist; then another dragonhead bow also begins to appear, then another. Petrified, the young herder pushes himself deeper into the willow coppice for perceived safety, as three large and fantastical dragonheads totally emerge from the mist. Beginning to shake with fear, the young herder thinks to himself, *'Vikings…'* He waits a little longer and is amazed to see three large Longship Birlinns fully appear, moving almost silently now, with the minimum amount of wind billowing into the great Blue Angel sails. The three Birlinns glide silently past the sheltered herder on route towards the landing docks on a nearby riverbank. Almost three days have passed since Morison mòr's Blue Angel Birlinn's had left the shores of Invergarvane for the Wirral peninsular priory pier near Chester Castle, on the northwest coast of England. Morrison mòr says, "Ah don't like this Wallace, ah'v told MacDougal and Ruaidhri to hold their Birlinn's off a'way from the landing pier so as tae cover us."

As the Blue sails are hoisted high, the Birlinns glide slowly to a halt, then the scene becomes deathly still, with everyone aboard the three ships remaining silent, while keenly watching all routes leading to the riverside boardwalk. Patiently they wait…

Morrison mòr groans, "Ahm still no' likin' all o' this feckn quietness Wallace." William replies, "It should be fine enough Morrison mòr, the English will be lookin' out for us. At least they'll no' be huntin' us, and that'll make a fine change."

Suddenly a watchman calls out from the high-mast nest, then points landward, "there they are now, look, they're all coming out from just below that tree-line over there…" Looking to see exactly whereabouts the watchman is pointing, William sees a large troop of English knights riding out from the priory forest and making their way down the main drag towards the pier, with many foot-soldiers bearing polearms running alongside them. Morrison mòr says, "Are yiez sure this is no' just another trap for yie Wallace? Ahm fuckin' tellin' yie, yiez had all better be keepin' a sharp eye out on those bastards, ah don't feckn trust them, they might want tae just capture you lot for tae ransom yiez too." William replies with a wry smile, "We're no' worth anything by way o' a ransom Morrison mòr, that's likely why Wishart sent us. Anyways, Stephen of Ireland has got our best Gallóbhet bowyers and slingers ready if this gets all fucked up…" Morrison mòr replies tersely, "It's no' the fuckin' English ahm worried about Wallace." William enquires, "So what's eatin' away at yer angst then?"

"It's big Sean mòr over there," replies Morrison mòr, "do yie really think that he's the best man to help hand over the ransom siller for young Moray?" William smiles again at the thought, then he replies, "Aye, yie could be right there, we all know that he'll likely be in a cold sweat by now, but his word o' honour I reckon is just that wee bitty greater than his urge to keep the ransom siller… ah hope."

William and Morrison mòr turn their attention back to the English troop and soldiers now nearing the landing pier. "There he is now…" exclaims William, "there's Andra Moray, he's riding alongside that heavy lookin' big knight." Morrison mòr says, "Are yie sure that yer ready for this Wallace?" William replies, "Ahm as ready now as ah'll ever be ah reckon." he turns and looks at Sean mòr, who nods back at William with a fierce look of grim determination. William mutters to himself quietly and with much hope… *'Don't you do it Sean mòr, we cannae risk it for the life o' Moray.'*

As the English delegation reach just a short distance away from the pier boardwalk, Sean mòr suddenly calls out to William, "Lets get the job done and get out o' here Wallace, for ah'v a real bad feelin' about this, the sooner we set sail back to Scotland, the better it'll be." Rob MacGilchrist walks up from the stern of the Birlinn and leans on the gunnel beside William, he waves across to the other Birlinns, where MacDougal and Ruaidhri have already prepared thirty Wolf and wildcat Gallóbhet to land with them. Each is an experienced archer or crossbowyer and weighted with two full quivers of arrows and bolts, all are armed with their notorious ring spears. The Gallóbhet have travelled in tandem with Morrison mòr's Birlinn. Their specific mission in the event of an attack by English patrol ships, is to defend Moray's Birlinn at all costs, even to sacrifice themselves if necessary, so that the Birlinn of Morrison mòr could run with the wind and deliver its precious cargo back to Scotland.

"That's young Andra Moray right enough," Rob says, "Sean mòr, you get yer men to carry those ransom chests ashore now, move, let's get goin.'"

The Birlinn of Morrison mòr eases portside onto a birth at the landings, where Rob and Sean mòr step over the gunnel onto the pier boardwalk. They lead a small band of tough Gallóbhet off the Birlinn and walk towards the approaching English deputation. The contrast between the appearance of the English knights and their guards, dressed in their fine armour and brightly coloured tabards, is dramatic by comparison to the Scots and Irish Gallóbhet, who are all dressed in heavy skins and leather plate armour. As the two groups gain closer to each other, William can see that Moray has his wrists manacled in chains, but otherwise, he looks to be in relatively good health. Stopping yards from each other, the English knight makes an introduction, "My name is Sir Hugh de Lacey, Palatine lord of Chester Castle…"

"Robyn of Loch Sloy, I'm…" De Lacey interrupts, "I do not have a care for who you are Scotchman, to the point, I believe that you have brought the ransom silver for Moray… just let me see it?" Rob glances at Sean mòr, who nods to a group of his Gallóbhet struggling to hold up five heavy looking sea chests. The Gallóbhet move forward and place the sea chests at the feet of de Lacey, then they back off. The tension is fraught between the two groups, as everyone waits to conclude the ransom handover. William winks at Moray, who grins at seeing his old friend. Rob calls out, "Are yie all right there Moray, did they treat yie fair and well?"

"It could o' been better Rob." replies Moray.

Two of de Lacey's men, who are weighing the thousand pounds in silver, soon complete their task, they glance at de Lacey, nodding towards him in the positive.

De Lacey looks behind him and indicates for two guards to bring Moray forward. "You are free to go now Moray, though I do hope that we see you again, as your reckless adventures do make great profits for me." Moray replies, "I cannae say it was a pleasure de Lacey, for it wasn't, but if yie ever show yer face anywhere near Scotland, you can be real certain that I sure will return the compliment…" Suddenly a scream is heard as one of de Lacey's men holding a sea chest, falls to his knees with a Gallóglaigh spartaxe blade buried deep in his face, then a second Englishman falls down beside him, with two arrows buried deep into his chest…

For a mere second, everyone is stunned and confused, then more arrows strike down guards on either side of de Lacey. A blood curdling yell is heard as Sean mòr launches forward and cuts the arm clean off the guard nearest de Lacey with his spartaxe. Big Rob shouts out to Moray, "Run for the Birlinns Andra…" William reaches forward and grabs Moray, then he pulls him to the relative safety of the Scots delegation as vicious fighting breaks out in front of them between the two groups near the pier-boardwalk. Heavily armoured knights immediately surround de Lacey to give him protection, then they beat a hasty retreat while de' Lacey's foot soldiers advance on the Scots. Rob shouts out to William, "Move it Wallace… you make sure to get Moray on board that nearest Birlinn damn quick, we'll hold off the English as long as we can." William and Moray run along the pier, as volleys of deadly arrows and crossbow bolts fly past them in both directions. "What the fuck…" exclaims Moray. As they reach the head of the pier, they both run fast and jump over the war shields fixed on the side of the Birlinn for protection and land into the safety of Morrison mòrs Birlinn. Andrew enquires, "What the fuck's goin' on Wallace, what just happened there?" William replies, "I haven't got a clue, everything was fine and then…. ah just don't know what happened?" Amidst the frantic chaos, they both chance to look over the side of the Birlinn, only to see Sean mòr and his men struggling to run at speed towards them. Meanwhile, the rest of the Scots delegation led valiantly by big Rob, desperately fight their way back as a rearguard.

"Fuck," exclaims William, "ah don't believe this…" Moray enquires. "Yie don't believe what Wallace?" William replies, "Its big Sean mòr, the mad bastard, would yie believe it Moray, that's all o' your ransom money in those big sea chests, he's gone and stolen all yer siller back…"

"What?" exclaims Moray, "But he cannae do that… can he?" But William doesn't hear Moray as he deftly picks up his longbow and joins in with the broadside fusillade of deadly archery loosing and vital crossbow cover for big Rob. The remaining rearguard of the Scot's, soon begin to pile unceremoniously into the sheltered deck of the landed Birlinn. The power and accuracy of the Gallóbhet bowyers on the other Birlinn's, proves to be too much for the English to follow big Rob and rearguard along the solitary pier boardwalk. Morrison mòr calls out at the top of his voice, "Cast away now, git the fuckin' oars out and drop the fuckin' sails…"

Sharp axes quickly cut through the landing ropes. As the great blue sails of Morrison mòr's Birlinns drop fast and immediately catch the wind; the Birlinn slowly begins to pull away from the pier. Everyone huddles behind or under the gunnel shields as an arrow storm from the enraged English archers, smothers the three Birlinn decks in a flurry of arrows and crossbow bolts. It's not long before the Birlinns are well out of range of the English archers and sailing north once more on the Irish Sea, it's then that everyone begins to appear from below or behind whatever cover they are sheltering.

Still hiding underneath two large shields now bristling with arrows, William and Moray look at each other, wide-eyed and incredulous; then they both burst out laughing. Moray exclaims, "What the fuck just happened there?" William replies, "Moray, I don't fuckin' know?" They hear a loud exchange of angry words nearby that attracts their attention. As they throw their shields aside, they see standing near the masthead, Sean mòr and big Rob violently confronting each other. "This doesn't sound se' good to me Wallace," exclaims Moray, "those two big bastards are lookin' as if they're set to go square at each other, and so do their men…"

"Quick Moray," replies William, "we'd better get up there and find out what's goin' on? If those two madmen are set to be fightin' then the whole deck will get caught up in whatever trouble is brewin' between them." Stephen of Ireland approaches, "Here you fellas, what the feck is goin' on up there?" William exclaims, "Stephen, what are yie doing here, I thought yie were over with MacDougal or Ruaidhri on another Birlinn?" Stephen grins, "Well sure now me foin big friend, as yee well know, or yie feckn well should, I'm no' fit to be runnin' a mean mile yet, so ah thought, *'Stephen me boy, you just jump ships and go ahead and help those fine fellas.'* So I did, and as Morrison's Birlinn was a lot closer to the fightin' here I am." William and Moray look at each other, grinning upon hearing Stephen's logical explanation. He continues, "Tell me fella's, what bleedin' happened, none of us were really expecting there to be any sort o' a fightin' back there?" William replies, "Ah dunno, but we had better get up to the masthead quick, before big Rob and Sean mòr set to kill each other."

The little group of friends close in on the fracas at the masthead, when they hear Sean mòr declare, "Fuck off MacGilchrist, it's fuckin' mine now…"

Big Rob appears perplexed as Sean mòr continues, "Yie got the Moray siller back didn't yie, minus ma share? So, what's yer fuckin' problem?" Rob replies, "But it was a ransom, yer supposed to hand the siller over in exchange for the prisoner." Sean mòr replies, "Ah know, and ah did, and once ah handed it over, it was theirs, so that means it was no longer yours, so what's it tae you big man?" Rob is animated, "Yie cannae do that at a ransom parley for fucks sake. Yie've likely caused the death o' the other prisoners de Lacey's holdin' tae ransom." Sean mòr is indignant, "We didn't lose any men, did we? We got Moray and all o' the siller back, now we are headin' home to Scotland, job done as ah see it. And don't think the sons o' our nobles still in de Lacey's dungeons will be slaughtered, when that fat English bastard calms down, he'll realise that siller is still the better part o' valour."

An exasperated Rob replies, "Fuck me Sean mòr, do yie no' get it in that thick fuckin' skull o' yours yet, when yer son three Fingers or whatever the fuck yie call him, stuck a fuckin' axe in the face o' one o' their men, then yer archers struck down the parley men, and as if that was no' bad enough, yiez took the ransom siller back, it will likely cause the execution o' more o' Scotlands sons… and all because o' your fuckin' greed for siller, Jaezuz, the English will never trust us again.

It was their ransom siller, not ours to take back." Sean mòr replies, "Exactly. Yie just proved ma point, it was theirs and so it was no longer yours, and then ah was well within ma rights tae rob the bastards to make it mine, and that's just what ah did..." Rob exclaims, "But why? The English as ah'v said to yie, they'll never trust us again doin' a ransom," Sean mòr laughs, "Och aye MacGilchrist, sure, it's no' like ma fuckin' life and awe ma happiness from now on in is dependant on whether the fuckin' English trust me or not? Besides, it's my siller now..." Still exasperated, Rob exclaims, "What do yie mean, it's your fuckin' siller now?"

As the heated debate over the ransom money continues, William says to Moray, "Ah think ah'v heard this story before..." Moray enquires, "What dyie mean?" William replies, "Ach, ahl tell yie about Sean mòr and his great love affair with Siller another time, ah reckon it's likely best to let them two sort it out between themselves; for everyone looks more amused by them than threatened, and ah reckon too that none will be taking sides on this." Moray smiles, then he says, "Get me one of the ships smiths over here and we'll get these chains off ma wrists."

On the seaward journey home, William and Moray hang out from the bow of the leading fleet Birlinn and celebrate like teenagers, whooping, cheering and talking of good times past, in particular, chatting about the love of their lives, Marion and Brannah. Stephen and Gormlaidh approach them, Gormlaidh says, "When we were runnin' for the Birlinns, ah noticed a few o' these wee barrels o' somethin' waiting to get loaded onto a wee boat..." William enquires, "What is it?" Stephen dips his finger into the bung hole of a barrel and then licks the golden coloured liquid, he replies, "I reckon it's a thing the English call Meade... it tastes no' much better than salty pig pish, but it does have a certain twang to it." Moray grins, "Then fill us up and we'll try it?" Stephen laughs as Gormlaidh hands out some horn cups and pours everyone a drink, then a long day and a fair wind, speeds the Birlinns Northwards.

As dusk begins to fall, there's a cheer from all the Birlinn crew's when the most southwesterly headland of Galloway is sighted on the horizon. William leans on the ships gunnels thinking of his beloved Marion. He smiles when he thinks of the bright eyes of little Mharaidh Morríaghan, when a familiar voice calling out behind him interrupts his thoughts. Approaching William, but appearing unusually solemn, Stephen says, "You need to be hearing this Wallace."

William turns to see a small gathering of his friends and two crewmen standing nearby. Curiously, he senses their apprehension. Stephen says, "These men have some interesting information for us."

"What's it all about?" queries William. Stephen replies, "They were in attendance when yer Wolf and wildcats fought the English and their isle-men on the Duibh hill at Invergarvane." William exclaims, "What?" he aims his next question aggressively at the nervous crewmen, "You two were there?" The crewmen recoil at the sight of Wallace's extremely animated expression. The moment seems frozen in time, then the crewmen seek protection by cautiously stepping behind Torrance and Gormlaidh. Stephen puts his hand up, "Whoa there Wallace, they were no' fighting against you. I'm tellin' yie that they saw what happened, and they're willing to tell us about everything they witnessed that day."

Stephen steps in front of the crewmen, just in case William hasn't properly heard what has been said. Faolán, Fiónlaidh and Eochaidh Gunn come forward upon hearing the comments. "Wallace," says Faolán, "I need to hear what happened to Lihd at Invergarvane." Eochaidh speaks, "Listen to them Wallace, I know the big skinny one there, he's kin to me. His blood is good and a Gunn, I know he would never betray one of his own."

Glaring at the two crewmen, William's mind flashes back to the fight on the Duibh hill at Invergarvane, a place where he had lost many of his closest and dearest friends. His expression relents, he says, "I'm sorry about that a moment ago fellas, so tell me, what's your names?" The first crewman replies. "Me, ahm Thu'barr Gunn from the sons of the Cruathnie chief Catha Guinnich." The second crewman replies, "Ma name is Parlán, a son of Malduin the warlord o' Arrochar." They all sit down with the two crewmen, for they have a need to hear an eyewitness account of the bloody skirmish above Invergarvane. Parlán speaks first. "We were fishing the mouth o' Garvane as yie do in our curraghs, and lifting the early mornin' catch, that's when we saw some northern marked Longships beachin' near to us on the longshore beachhead. We could tell by their banners it was the ships o' the clan Donald chief Angus óg and his isle-men on board the first two ships. The other two ships were Irish flagged, they were carryin' de Burgh's Irish levies from Ulster, there was another ship sailin' under the top-mast banner o' a big ugly fella called Aslikkør Ranald o' the isles." Gunn shakes his head, "He's De Burgh's man, a fuckin' treacherous big bastard. His men call that big Ranald fella Aslikkør, because he has no fuckin' honour and he's lower than a snake's belly, a dirty big bastard that one."

"Aye." nods Parlán in agreement.

"Anyways," continues Gunn, "We watched as the crews landed on the foreshore in the mouth o' the Garvane then they set up camp, a wee while later, we watched as a large squadron o' mounted English soldiers came over the drove road from the back o' Duibh hill, the eve before you lot arrived. It appears as though they were supposed to be meetin' the men o' the Longships." Parlán says, "They were commandeered by an English knight called Sir Henry de Percy." Gunn agrees, "Aye, we found out later from some of the crew, they were all meeting up at Invergarvane to go down south into Galloway to fight with de Brix's Pact against Baliol and the Comyn's forces." Parlán glances at Gunn, "What about the wee greasy rat-faced bastard that rode with de Percy, what's his name?" Gunn sighs, "Fuckin' Marmaduke de Percy, I won't forget him in a long time." William and Stephen glance at each other, but they remain calm in order to get the most information out of these two seamen. William enquires, "What's so special about this Marmaduke de Percy?"

For a moment, the crewmen look warily at each other, then Gunn says, "You tell him." Parlán pauses as though he didn't want to recall, for fear of William's reaction.

"Tell me fuckin' what?" growls William. Parlán exclaims, "Ach fuck, well, all o' this evilness regardin' what that wee bastard did, this was after your fight and you went down Wallace…" William commands aggressively, "Go on…" Parlán continues, "I'll tell yie straight Wallace, after the main fight, see that wee English bastard, he took great pleasure when he ordered the torture o' your surviving men and women, aye most severe it was, man he was so feckn cruel to them. We could only watch as the bastard took his time…" Parlan falters, then he continues, "It was their screams man, ah can only tell yiez this, it was a hellish scene to behold. We covered our eyes and ears for there was nuthin' we could do, fuck, there was nuthin' anyone could do to stop him… it was an awful bloody spectacle." Parlán pauses to think of what both he and Gunn had witnessed that day; then he sees that William is glaring at him. "Yie have to understand us Wallace," exclaims Parlan, "there was not a thing that we nor anyone else could do to stop him, or we would have suffered the same fate…" Gunn says. "He's right Wallace. When de Percy was finished his torturin' and cruelty with your folks, the dirty wee bastard commanded his men to hack the heads off yer folks and then he had them stacked in a big pile, he then ordered pitch to be poured on the severed heads to set them alight, but Angus óg stopped him…"

Parlán speaks, "Aye, we heard later on, that disgrace was a wee thing de Percy calls his calling mark." Groaning, William covers his head with his hands.

"Jaezuz, what did I do?" He looks over the gunnels of the Birlinn and sees the coast of Scotland, thinking to himself how many more times must he see this sight from a Birlinn, to many others it is just another beautiful panoramic landscape, but to him… He doesn't want to look, but he does, for there on the mainland is the place of his landing, Invergarvane. Though still in the distance, he could clearly see the river mouth and where the sweeping sands of the longshore rise up the bleak Duibh hill where this tragedy occurred. He knows it is where he will disembark this day; the nearest sea landing that will take him at speed to his home in the Wolf and wildcats… and his Marion. "Wallace," says Faolán who is standing beside him, "We need to hear all o' this." Parlan says, "Ahm so sorry Wallace, but yie asked, and we had to tell yie."

A demoralised looking William replies, "Its fine." He sits back down on a rower's bench to hear the rest of the tragic tale. "Wallace," says Gunn, "Ah tell yie, we've never seen such braw fighting as you fellas laid out to them that mornin', and yiez almost had them too, but what yiez did do is yie broke the back o' a strong fighting force that was intent on invading Galloway from the western seaboard." Parlán agrees, "Aye Wallace, we saw more Longships were on their way, when they landed they all gathered and had a big meetin' on the foreshore. It wasn't long before they must have concluded that you were a small forward hunter group, scouting for a larger force coming from the mainland, and because of what yiez did, you and your folks caused their forward force such injury and death, they turned their entire fleet back." William enquires, "How so?" Gunn replies, "They decided they couldn't risk getting caught in a trap, for many o' them still rankle over their defeat at the battle o' Largs. It appeared that they thought the better part of valour would be to get away as fast as they could, and not to be attacking Galloway as they originally intended."

"Another thing," says Parlán, "many o' Angus óg's crews had no stomach for to be fighting against the Scots anyway, and they'll have no truck with that dirty big bastard Aslikkør Ranald and his back-stabbin' ploys. We know many o' the crews, and their hearts are to be fightin' against the English, no' to be lickin' their feckn boots."

Lifting his head up, William looks at the two men... he says, "Detail to me all of what really happened that day, for I have little memory of that mornin's doin's."

Gunn and Parlán begin to recall how Angus óg, the English soldiers of de Percy, with de Burgh's Irish mercenaries and Aslikkørs men, camped on the sandbank shores of Invergarvane that morning. Gunn says, "We heard the English soldiers of de Percy boast to Angus óg's men how they had already carried out many massacres, rapines and murders in Galloway. They gave great detail about the foul deeds they committed. We thought they were just trying to impress the isle-men with their heroic stories, it was then that one of their guards reported seeing a spy watching them from a little way up the Duibh hill, they thought it was one of Baliol's scouts."

"Fuck..." exclaims William, he shakes his head while

running his fingers through his hair. He says almost despairingly, "That must have been Coinach right enough, ah had fuckin' told him not to go down there." Gunn continues, "De Percy thought there must have been more of yiez thereabouts after someone thought they noticed movement up at the old fort. Everyone was ordered to act and behave normally in the camp, while De Percy, Angus óg and Aslikkør waited on the spy retreating, they needed to let him think it was clear and free to return to where he had come from. They waited till they were certain the spy thought he'd escaped unnoticed, De Percy, Angus óg and Aslikkør split their forces into three, with one to follow the spy and the other two flanking the back o' the fort to surround yiez from three sides…" Gunn says, "We followed behind them at a distance, for we didn't know what was going to happen. We watched as the isle-men and de Percy's horsemen gain behind the fort, then we saw Henry de Percy lead the rest o' his men through the shore-mist straight up the hill, then fuck, all hell broke loose."

Speaking with excitement, Parlán says, "Wallace, it looked as if you ambushed them instead of the other way round, yiez sure caught them all by surprise." Gunn says, "Just as the front soldiers of de Percy got near the foot of the old fort, your men appeared on the ridge parapet, then the arrow storm yiez let loose, fuck me man, I have never seen anything like it in ma life before, or since."

"Aye," sighs Gunn, "we thought there were about a hundred o' yiez up there, for the arrow storm yicz sent down was pure relentless." Parlán says, "We saw when yiez hit someone with one flight, it wasn't just one arrow that hit them, it was two or three at a time, and with such a fuckin' ferocity." Gunn says, "Aye, so many of your arrows were ripping right out through the bodies of the mounted knights and soldiers, they stuck into men following behind. Some of your arrows even flew past us, we had to shelter behind a big boulder or yie would have stuck us too. Yiez near wiped out de Percy's force coming at yiez in moments, then we saw Henry de Percy's horse getting struck wie arrows in the neck and fall, throwing the rider and rolling over that wee bastard Marmaduke. Some men grabbed Sir Henry and dragged him away and they didn't stop runnin' till they were at Turnberry castle, near twelve miles away."

Everyone smiles at the remark, then Gunn says, "Suddenly yiez all charged down the hill into the remaining Englishmen, it was then we saw there was only about a couple of dozen of you fella's, ah will tell yiez this, even when the mounted unit and the Irish levies hit yiez from the flanks, yiez just kept attacking and chopping them down, it was incredible to behold. Then we saw you Wallace, we saw you getting hit in the back with a crossbow bolt and watched you fall over; a big warrior beside yie fell too, struck on the head by another bolt. We thought both o' yiez must be dead, but you and this other big fella just got back up on your feet, and I've never seen fighting like that before, you didn't just slash and stab at them, yiez cut ther' limbs and heads off as though they were stalks o' corn lopped off by a big feckn knife. We saw you pickin' up a spear or a lance, then you and that other big fella were near unstoppable." William sighs, "That would've been Bailey Wallace, ma big Cymran cousin you're talking about."

Glancing across at the Duibh hill, William is distracted, aware this is the second time aboard a Birlinn that the memories of his good friends and kinfolk come flooding back, then he hears Gunn as he continues...

"We reckon yiez might have won the day there Wallace, if yiez had all stuck together, but yiez got all fucked up when yiez split away into two wee groups, there was a bunch went directly at Marmaduke de Percy and they fought like demons possessed, they were bein' led by a wee wiry looking dark fella, he looked like an Egyptian with his dark looks. But they never really stood a chance Wallace, they took on far too many o' them to fight on their own." William says, "That would likely be Coinach ua Bruan, his complexion was dark, he was from one o' the Ceàrdannan clans o' Galloway, a dark-skinned race. His family were all butchered and it's likely it was that bastard Marmaduke de Percy who was responsible."

"A close friend?" enquires Gunn.

"Aye," replies William "Coinach was a great wee fella and a fine friend to me, but after the massacre of his family, he was a man with only vengeance in his heart, ah reckon that's who you saw going at de Percy with such a fury, and likely that was who you thought was the spy." Gunn replies, "Aye, that sounds like him right enough, b'Jaezuz, that wee fella could fight some." Parlán says, "See when you fell the second time Wallace, what was your kinsman's name, the big fella... Bailey was it?" William replies, "Aye." Parlán continues, "Well, the big fella Bailey, he shouted a war-cry over the noise o' the fightin' *'A WALLACE...'* He called out your name a few more times for the life o' him, then every single one of your Gallóbhet who could do, ran to where you lay wounded, all o' them fighting like demons to protect you, everyone except the wee Coinach fella and his young ones, when he fell badly wounded, about the same time that you went down, they stayed by his side and fought around his body tryin' to protect him." William enquires anxiously, "So tell me, how did I fall? I can remember mostly that me and Bailey were fighting for all we were worth; then it's all a blank after that, ah remember nuthin' else till I woke up in my uncles Keep about thirty miles north of Invergarvane." Gunn replies, "Wallace, if it had been a fair fight, well, it was ten to one in their favour, and that looked fair enough to us because o' the way you fellas were all fightin', it wasn't till some o' that big fucker Aslikkør Ranald's isle-men came in at your back…"

"Aye, typical fuckin' Aslikkør." exclaims Torrance.

Gunn is animated, "There was a big Ranald bastard standing no' far from the fighting, he was yelling and a' roarin' like a big mouthy fuckin' hero…" Parlán sneers, "Aye, far enough away from the fightin' though, we watched him skulking about in the background, yie know, one of those big fuckin' glory hunters, all Norse legend and no fuckin' hair on his balls. When he saw you were sorely wounded and disarmed, the big fuckin hero charged at your back and felled you with a mighty war mallet. When yie went down, he felled yie a couple more times, we both reckoned that no one could o' survived those kinda strikes." Gunn says, "It was yer man Bailey that swung on the big man, he froze at the sight of Bailey coming at him, then would yie believe it, there was a wee lass who was lying wounded on the ground, she sat up wie her short-bow then notched and loosed an arrow right up into the big fella's jaw."

"That would have been Lihd," says Faolán.

Gunn continues, "Ah tell yiez, that wee lass, she fought like a cornered wildcat that one, we saw her destroying many with her flights, then at close quarters she fair sliced them up wie two wee skinning knives before they got to her, but even at that, she stayed close to protect yie Wallace. Man, that wee lass, she was fearless beyond belief." William glances at Faolán, Fiónlaidh and Eochaidh, acknowledging the debt he owes to Lihd for probably saving his life.

"So, what happened next?" enquires William. Parlan replies, "See the big fella Bailey, well, he swung his sword in a mighty arc towards the big bastard, we thought he'd missed, but it was just plain amazing to see what happened next. The big bastard grabbed desperately at his throat, the surprise etched on his face was priceless, big wide eyes in pure disbelief, he looked as if he was twisting his head a wee bit to the side and about to cough, but then the big fella's head seemed to spring high up into the air and spin away from his shoulders. We couldn't believe what we had just seen, we watched as the big isle-man's head fell right beside yie, then his body dropped on top o' yie, that's when that Bailey fella shouted out your name. That's also when we pretty much knew who you were by then, and that's when what was left o' your men came running to be by your side to protect and stand over you."

"So how did it all end?" enquires William anxiously, "Why, ah mean, how did I get to live, when all o' ma friends didn't, how is it that I survived… tell me?"

Parlán replies, "Bailey and your men, they wouldn't leave what we thought was your dead body, by that time and after such a bloody encounter, the pile o' dead and wounded on top of you from both sides was gatherin' and so many, it wasn't till the last of your own men were too badly wounded and completely surrounded, that the fighting ceased." Gunn says, "That was when that slimy wee bastard Marmaduke de Percy appeared again…" Parlan agrees then spits over the side of the Birlinn. With great disdain he says, "That's when all the real butchery began."

For a moment there is silence, as everyone reflects on the account. Parlán says, "That big Aslikkør Ranald fucker, he'd hid himself well away all throughout the fight, apart from shoutin' the odds, but we could see that he was just waiting till it was well and truly safe before he and his bodyguard came skulkin' back to the scene. He joined up wie' De Percy then they both took their sweet time capturing all o' Coinach's wounded youngblood that survived the fight, then they had them beaten severely and tortured so bad, while

Bailey and the others were left to watch from their standoff position, still armed, but too badly wounded to maintain a running fight. But they wouldn't surrender yie up Wallace, proud men all." Gunn says, "Angus óg tried to stop de Percy and Aslikkør Ranald from torturing your young men, but he couldn't because he was outranked by that wee bastard and his Aslikkør lackie. All we could do was witness de Percy's evil." Parlán falters again… "Wallace," says Gunn, "De Percy had all o' their throats cut wie auld rusty guttin' blades, then he had them butchered up wie blunt axes."

"Fuck…" exclaims William, He stands up and looks up at the blue skies, shaking his head while trying to fight back the tears of pain and a rage that threatens to overwhelm him. Everyone goes quiet till William regains his senses and sits back down, he utters, "The hell of my kin's fate never had to be." He looks back at Gunn and Parlan, "Go on, I need to know everything." Gunn says, "Angus óg's men had your fellas surrounded. But Bailey and the survivors showed them no fear, they were still armed and defiant, it was plain to see they would kill many more before they would give up your body, and only then, after they had given up their own lives."

"So, what finally happened?" enquires William. Gunn continues, "De Percy offered your men quarter, but Bailey spat at him and told him to fuck off, we all knew de Percy had lied, but none would dare say it. Then, without warning, Angus óg ordered his bowyers to finish the day rather than lose any more men. Wallace, I must tell yie this, I believe that Angus óg chose a mercy on your Gallóbhet, for he was truly enraged at de Percy and Aslikkørs intent. I honestly believe his actions that day, saved your men from a terrible fate at the hands of that dirty wee English prick de Percy and that walkin' bilge-rat Aslikkør Ranald, a disgrace to his very name." Parlán says with a tone of pride and admiration in his voice… "Ah will tell yie this too, Wallace, it was a sight to behold, from where we were we could see that Bailey was severely wounded about the legs and chest, but he remained defiant. There was another three o' your men that I recognised from the fishing over at the isle of Arran, Andra frae Drum, Tam óg and big Seamus the quiet man. Though they were all badly wounded, they sensed what was about to happen, and would yie believe it, they all hauled together and charged straight at that wee fucker de Percy, and they almost made it too."

Gunn says, "Big Seamus was cut down by the long axes, Tam óg took about eight arrows before he fell. And bonnie Andra, even though full o' arrows, managed to get within striking distance of de Percy and struck him on the head with the flat o' his blade before he was overwhelmed. I say this with a sadness Wallace, but thankfully they died quickly, for what de Percy and Aslikkør had planned for them, was likely unspeakable. Wallace, your folks fought like mountain lions, all of them did."

Gunn sighs in awe of what he had seen.

"Last to fall that day was Bailey and the wee lass, he stood proud atop your fallen kinfolks Wallace, then he pulled the wee Gallóbhan up to her feet. We could all see she that was mortally wounded when he held her close in embrace, yie could tell that they both knew what was comin' but they stood defiant. As the fletchers of Angus óg loosed their flights, Bailey flung his sword right at them and shouted, 'A WALLACE…' before he and the wee lass finally succumbed. They died as real hero's o' Invergarvane Wallace, both o' us had never seen the likes before or will ever see their likes again, may the Aicé bless them." The little group of Gallóbhet sit silent awhile, all taken by grief and sadness, but they are also finding a sense of peace, knowing what had really happened on the Dubh hill of Invergarvane, but they also are aware that this would not be the end of the blood to be spilled, far from it. William enquires, "So tell me, how is it that I survived…?"

"It was Angus óg." replies Gunn, "That wee cunt de Percy was in a pure rage, he wanted to have all your heads cut off, piled high and burned with pitch, in order to be leavin' his brave wee calling mark for everyone to see, but Angus óg would have none of it. The impasse ended between them when the second fleet arrived and they had their meetin'. Angus óg ordered them all to leave Invergarvane immediately and sail up the coast to the Brus' castle at Turnberry, to join Sir Henry de Percy with his own badly wounded, and no' to be wasting no more time about it. It was then word came in that a large force of Scots horse were coming in fast from the north and east."

"Angus óg offered us a bag o' siller," says Parlán, "he said for us to push all the bodies into a wee gulley and torch them, but we told him to keep his siller, we reckoned he understood why. He also told us to leave the headless body of the big shite-bag o' Ranald who'd attacked yie from the back, he said it was to be feedin' the rats to keep them away from the men of honour's bodies, it seems even the big bastard's own kinfolk despised him." Looking down, Gunn says, "Angus óg, man he looked shamed at the evil deeds done that day in his very presence, for it was only after the battle that we saw that most of your men were just mere boys comin' o' age." Gunn says, "Aye, when we told Angus óg it would be an honour to lay to rest the heroes of Invergarvane without payment, he thanked us and smiled, for he showed the same respect to you and your Gallóbhet too Wallace. Some of the isle men stayed behind to help us, at great risk to themselves. They said nothing about betraying you when you were found alive.

Aye, it seems to us that Angus óg may even have saved your life." Astonished to hear this, William exclaims, "How, I mean, who was it that found me?" Gunn replies, "When Angus óg was lifting his own wounded, he signalled over to us where you lay, then he and his men simply moved away. We saw too from a little distance across the hill, that it looked as though he lifted one or two of Coinach's boys, he saw us watching, there was just something in his look and a feeling of knowing that passed between us… We can't be sure if it was Wildcat survivors or not, for every one o' the dead and wounded was a bloody unrecognisable mess, there was just no way of really telling who was who after such a bloody business."

"Who did they lift…?" demands William, "Are yiez sure about Angus óg finding one or two o' my men?" He suddenly grabs Parlán tightly by the throat, then he eases his grip upon seeing the look of fear in Parlán's face. Though shaken, Parlán grips William defiantly by the wrists; suddenly William let's go apologetically.

"Naw Wallace," replies Gunn, "we cannae be sure if it was any o' your men that he lifted or not, but there was something about a couple o' his wounded men that Angus óg made sure to keep well away from de Percy and that big shite Aslikkør Ranald, but we'll find out in the passing, for many of those Norse have big mouths, yie know how they like to boast. If we do find out anything Wallace, we'll let you know as soon as we can." Parlán speaks, "All of the bodies and bits o' bodies, disemboweled, headless, fuck, it was simply a butcher's carnage on both sides, it was impossible to know who was who, exceptin' for the wee lass and the big fella Bailey."

"It was a sickening detail," says Gunn, "but it was the least we could do. It took us a long while, but we kept going into the late o' light, for your men deserved a warrior's pyre. We had all but collected the remains of everyone, the last being the big headless isle-man who lay on top of you, when we pulled him off your body, that's when we found out that you were still alive at the bottom o' the pile of your kinsmen and yer enemies. Though a sight that struck us hard, was when we saw that the wee lass was laying there by yer side, she was holding both yours and the big Fella Bailey's hands, that's sure something that ah'll be takin' to ma own grave as a mother's comfort."

"Aye," says Parlán, "that's right enough, then some of the older good-wives and bahn-bhuidseach' from the fishin' bothies down at Invergarvane, they came up the hill to help us, and fair play to them, they spoke oaths and said some fine auld blessings of the Magda mòr and Cruinnè cè for all o' your men and the wee lass too. They blessed them all for their bravery, then the bahn-bhuidseach' released the mortal souls o' the dead up and away for the wild geese to take them on their final journey to Tír na Óg s' na-ill." The Gallóbhet, though satisfied in knowing, all appear slightly shaken after hearing this gruesome tale. William in particular, now knowing what had happened up on the Dubh hill, helps to partly heal the deep emotional wounds he has been carrying since that day… also, in him knowing that the bahn-bhuidseach' had said words of the Cruinnè cè faith for his kinfolk, comforts him. William looks to the west across the sea, then turns to Parlán and Gunn…

"So ma friends, what exactly did happen after yiez found me?" Parlán replies, "Well Wallace, we still didn't know for sure exactly who you were yet. We thought you were likely some noble's son, it wasn't untill one of the good-wives saw your clan colours and the dragon on your jack, that we all realised you were Céile Aicé, as are the both of us. Then we remembered hearing Bailey shouting out aloud, *'A Wallace…'* We knew for sure who you were then. The older good-wives tended to your wounds and it was Gunn here who pulled the crossbow bolt out o' the front of yer shoulder." Gunn says, "You were lucky that the bolt head had came right through your chainmail, for it was barbed, had it stayed in, it's dead you would be right now." Parlán says, "Aye, even then you looked as if you might not make it through the night, the old women and the bahn-bhuidseach' tended yie well. It was no' se' long after that a large troop of riders came fast towards us, they were led by Sir John De Graeme and Crauford the Sherriff of Ayr, with about two hundred of their men and some odd-looking fella called True Tam, he took over your welfare as soon as they arrived." Gunn says, "That's it Wallace, that's all that we saw that day."

Shaking the hands of the two crewmen, William says, "I can't be thanking yiez enough, ah reckon yie both saved ma life for sure." Parlán replies, "Naw Wallace, the heroism of your folks that day are legend and an inspiration to us all." Gunn says, "Ahm sorry for the loss of your kinfolks Wallace, but to witness such bravery was a privilege and will surely be passed down our families for generations to come, and it's more than likely you and your men saved the lives of hundreds in Galloway by destroying that force o' bastards." William turns and sees Faolán, Fiónlaidh and Eochaidh sitting with melancholy expressions. He also notices that Sean mòr is sitting quietly nearby too. A quick glance of unspoken acknowledgment gleaned from the dark piercing eyes of Sean mòr, unexpectedly soothes William's heart.

For a long time, the Gallóbhet all sit awhile in sombre silence, considering the account of the bloody skirmish at Invergarvane. Eventually, Eochaidh speaks, "I'm thankful we found out what really happened to Lihd and the rest o' the Wolf and wildcats." William glances back at Faolán. He remembers when he first met her in Galloway during the

Pact confrontation between Brix and Baliol, and they had remained close friends ever since. "Ah see yie watching that bonnie Gallóbhan Wallace," says Andrew, "Do yie know her well?" William replies, "Aye, ah met her years ago when she was leading a war-band during the Pact uprising, she's a natural leader o' both women and men and she fair knows her stuff Moray. I lost contact with her for a while, but fate would have it when I was in exile in Ireland, she was over there training young Irish bahn-Ceitherne in the arts of war, that's when we met up again. I'll tell yie Moray, I learnt much from her while fighting with the Irish clan chiefs and warlords against the English settlers." Moray enquires, "Whereabouts were yie in auld Erin?" William replies, "I was with the Irish Gallóglaigh fightin' all the way down Erin's lower east coast and about Corcaigh, then back up to Tír Eoghain and Aontroim."

William Glances at Faolán, who simply acknowledges William's expression of shared sadness and grief. She stands up then she says, "We're going up to the galley for some scran Wallace, Eochaidh Fiónlaidh and I have got much to be talkin' about, then we may settle this news with Lihd's family when we gain shore and return to Dun Reicheit in Galloway." Faolán, Fiónlaidh and Eochaidh make their way to the galley, while William turns his attention back to Gunn and Parlán. "I'll be thanking yie both for the information that yiez brought. I never was aware o' the whole story because o' what happened to me, but now that I do, I'm grateful. I need to know though about Angus óg and any survivors, if yiez find out anything, I'll make it worth your while." A solemn looking Gunn offers out his hand to William, as they clasp and shake hands, he says, "We wish no reward Wallace, for we feel kin to you and your people, if we do find out anything we'll get that information to you damn fast." Parlán says, "We'd better get back to our chores." William shakes Parlán by the hand, "I'm truly indebted to yie both." Gunn replies, "We're glad to have been o' service to yie Wallace, we just wish it had been news of good fortune instead of what we saw."

Parlán and Gunn leave William to make their way toward the bow of the Birlinn. Suddenly William spins round and calls out, "WAIT…"

Gunn and Parlán immediately turn around in response to William's command. He enquires, "Were there any of the Brus clan present that day or in the company of de Percy?" The two crewmen look at each other and shrug their shoulders. Parlán replies, "None that we're aware o'" William waves and replies, "Tá mo chairde."

Sitting back down on the rower's benches, Moray hands William a full horn cup of craitur, then he says, "That sounded sure like some bad shit that yie went through at Invergarvane Wallace." William replies, "Aye, it sure was, ah lost many good kinfolks and friends there Moray, it was all my own fault, and it sorely burns ma heart, even now." Moray says, "Well, at least yie know now how you got out o' that situation." William still appears to be deeply troubled by his thoughts. "Ah reckon it was ma own inexperience and indecision that was to blame for their deaths." Moray replies, "Wallace, it can happen to any o' us, and guilt is a hell o' a thing when you're a lone survivor… you take it from me, I've been there, but yie will learn to deal with it."

"Ah don't know Moray, those memories cut deep into ma thoughts, badly."

"Wallace…" says a deep voice behind him. William is suddenly jolted as a large cumbersome body slams down on the rower's bench beside him. "Sean mòr?" exclaims William. Sean says, "That was a bloody business that broke yie in at Invergarvane wie those mercenaries o' the Pact."

William enquires, "What do yie mean?" Sean replies, "Ah'v heard all o' the inn tales, both good and bad about the wee skirmish yie had up there, but it was rare to be hearin' it from folks who actually saw it happen. And with that bein' yer first real encounter with an enemy, you take from what yie saw and experienced as a bitter but a real lesson in life Wallace, really learn from it, or the death o' yer kinfolk will mean nuthin'." William replies, "That may be so Sean mòr, but it doesn't make me feel any better about what happened to ma kinfolks because o' my decisions." Sean says, "It never will Wallace, but when ah overheard yie speakin' wie young Moray there a moment ago, ah feel ah should say somethin' else to yie that may help yie better with yer black thoughts."

Curious, William enquires, "What do yie mean Sean mòr, what is it that yie have to say to me?" Sean replies, "Well son, ah know that this might be difficult for yie to hear, and maybe for you as well young Moray, but some folk who speak about ma reputation, well, they say that ahm a wee bit heavy handed on occasion, and that ahm no' too keen on treatin' ma enemies wie' very much decorum…" William exclaims, "Heavy handed…?" Both he and Andrew laugh heartily; then William says, "Sean mòr, ah don't want to be makin' this difficult for 'you' to hear, but yer reputation about the land is that your nuthin' but a ruthless murderin' savage big bastard, who never shows any mercy to none, and that you and yours only ever take prisoners just to be torturin' them and then skinnin' them alive, and all just for yer amusement."

"Really?" Exclaims Sean mòr, "Well there yie go now, recognition at last." William and Andrew look at each other bemused and in amazement. After a moment's mirth, William enquires, "Are you serious Sean mòr, do yie really believe that folk think yer just heavy handed?" Sean replies, "That's a moot point now that yie've made ma day Wallace.

What I really wanted to say to yie is, yie can be spendin' yer life as a victim to be moapin' and moanin' about everything that yie should o' done or what could o' been, or yie can live life like me, wie no worries or cares as a witness." William exclaims, "As a witness? What the fuck are yie talkin about?" Andrew says, "Ah think I know what yer talkin' about Sean mòr, ma Dá had said something similar to me just before I left to go and fight as a squire in the low-countries." Sean mòr says confidently, "There yie go Wallace, young Moray knows what ahm talkin' about."

William shakes his head; then he gazes for a moment at the tough battle-scarred features of Sean mòr, he then glances at the young man's features in Andrew, although they are both more than a generation apart, they both have a barely perceptive spectre in their eyes. "What ah mean to say to yie is this," continues Sean mòr, "what happened to you and yours over there at Invergarvane, it will sure no' be the last time yie see this kind o' barbarity up close and personal wie yer kinfolk, what ahm here to tell yie is this, yie can either be a victim and let it eat away at yie if yie survive for very long, or…" Andrew interrupts, "Or yie can live yer life as a witness, meaning, that everything you see and experience may deeply touch your heart, but bein' o' the witness mindset, it will keep your wits whole and free from feelin' any guilt." Sean mòr sits back a little, then he slaps his big hand down on Andrews back, he says, "Ah couldn't have delivered it better ma'self. Well said there young Moray." William enquires, "But what do yiez mean, live as a witness?"

"Listen to me Wallace," says Sean mòr, "whatever yie think o' ma reputation, one thing you do know is, ah have a very big family, a clan that's loyal, proud, and most important, they're mostly still alive… and ah'll tell yie the main reason for that, it's because o' livin' ma life as a witness, in that, ah never will dwell on what ah'v done, what ah'v seen or what ah'v had to do to survive, nor do I have any regrets about any o' the decisions that ah'v made, be they good ones or on the very rarest o' occasions… a bad one. And remember this too, no matter what age yie are Wallace, never forget that everything yie do in life is an important lesson, don't never stop learnin' for it's vital for yie to grow ever smarter from, that is if yer wise enough and clever enough to be seein' it as such. Aye, even though ah might o' made a few bad decisions here and there in ma life that maybe cost me some of ma' bonnie fightin' sons and daughters, anything less or for me to be worryin' about any bad decisions that ah made, would surely have meant many more o' ma kinfolks would o' met with an early grave, for it's ma' job and ma duty as a father, a clan chief, call it what yie will, to see to the very survival o' all o' those who depend on me being there for them; and leavin' them a proud legacy to follow, that's what livin' as a witness does for yie."

"He's right Wallace." Says Andrew.

"That I am." Agrees Sean. "And that's because ah believe everything in life's trials and tribulations is as the Aicé has meant for me, meanin' what I witness is for me to make sure that what I've experienced never happens to me or to mine, and yie cannae be doin' that as a victim. What I 'm supposed to do wie that knowledge is learn from it and 'make sure by whatever means are at my disposal, those terrible things I see as a witness, as ah said before, never ever happens to me or any o' mine. It's the best way to survive in these uncertain times Wallace. What I do is make sure that folk who would be ma enemy, fear ma very name if they ever try to cross me, for if they do, ah will surely kill their fuckin' sheep, goats, horses, chickens and ther' cattle in front o' them first, then ahl take great pleasure in spendin' a long time killin' their whole fuckin' family in front o' their very eyes too, and then, I'll kill them." William exclaims, "Ahm no' sure what yer tryin' to say Sean mòr, it sounds like a madness?"

"Ach ah don't expect yie will," replies Sean, "for ahm aware yer a wee bitty slow on the uptake… But some day soon yie will, ah can see that it in yie. I've watched yie since we first met, yie have a good and a kind heart, but what's comin' for us all must surely turn yie into the very thing yie hate, just for you and yours to survive. Yie must be much worse by deed and reputation than yer enemy could ever be, so that those who would strive to wrong yie; will always fear yie. That's why yie must always think o' yerself as a witness, never a victim. Fuck me, in ma long life ah'v seen so many good men like you who became victims to their own thinkin'; blamin' themselves for this and blamin' themselves for that, then they go and fuckin' kill themselves when it all becomes too much for them. Listen tae good advice Wallace, if yie ever think like that, don't be killin' yerself, go kill somebody else, yie'll feel much better for it."

Once more, William and Moray stare at Sean mòr, almost in disbelief; then they both start laughing.

"What's se' fuckin' funny?" enquires Sean; then he too laughs. "Ah hope yie get ma meanin' in all o' this young Wallace, for like ah said, yer enemies must fear yie bad, and ah mean, really fear yie… and more than just in any battle, they must surely fear yer very reputation, that to cross yie will make yie strike them and theirs asunder in ther' beds, and with such a cruelty and retribution, so much greater than they could ever imagine, for ah tell yie this in all sincerity Wallace, if yie don't do what ah say, you and yours will soon become more dead and forgotten victims to this up and comin' storm we'll soon be havin' wie the English." Morrison mòr approaches them, "Fellas, we won't be landing at Invergarvane, there are too many English ships patrollin' about the coast n' longshore, we'll be skirtin' the coast o' Kintyre instead, then heading up into the northwest Clyde estuaries, that's where yer backup drop is supposed to be, and you Wallace, yer uncle Ranald will be waitin' there for yie, and you Moray, you've to head North to Avoch with big Rob." Sean says, "Right yie are Morrison mòr. Am away to let ma Gallóbhet know what's happenin." Sean stands up, then looks at William; he says, "You two young fella's mind what ah said." William and Moray acknowledge Sean mòr as he walks away.

Early next morning, the Blue Angel Birlinn's sail into the mouth of the river Clyde and follow the rugged northern shore coast. Soon, after having skillfully avoided any contact with roving English warships and various piratical approaches. Morrison mòr's small fleet nears to their destination and ship's landings in the sheltered mouth of An Gearr Loch, near to the Ros Neimhidh s' Rhu narrows on the Càrdainn Ros. A few miles northwest of the Dumbarton castle, the three Birlinn's sail close to the long shore landings to deliver their precious cargo to waiting horsemen of the Lennox. Moray says, "That's Sir John Stewart, the Mormaer o' Lennox." William replies, "Aye, Bishop Wishart told me Stewart would supply us with men and horses. He also said we're to meet with him when we get back at the Bishops Palace east o' Glasgow."

The keel of the first Birlinn begins to scrape the gritty floor of the long shore, Stephen calls out excitedly, "C'mon Wallace, lets get our feet on good auld Scottish soil again. Sure now boys, isn't it a great feelin' to be had headin' homeward to be seeing our nearest sweetest and dearest. They must be sorely aching for our foin company." Stephen jumps from the gunnels of the Birlinn, but his feet catch a gangrope and he falls over the side of the Birlinn into the freezing cold sea. Everyone on the Birlinn cheers and erupts into laughter as the second and third Birlinn's of MacDougal and Ruaidhri slope up the shore beside them. William and Moray rush forward and lean over the gunnels on the larboard side of the Birlinn to laugh at Stephen, but they can't see him anywhere. Stepping forward, William leans further out and grabs at a sail rope, slips, misses the rope and falls over the side into the freezing cold Clyde waters beside Stephen. A second roar of approval and laughter goes up from all three Birlinn's. Morrison mòr growls, "For fucks sake, I sail nigh on a week avoiding marauding English ships and feckin' pirates, but those two may as well have asked me to deliver them personally to the English garrison, the noisy young eejits…" Torrance, standing beside MacGilchrist says, "They're drunk."

Rob laughs heartily as he pulls young Andrew Moray to his feet, he says, "This one here is no' much better." Morrison mòr curses, "Be getting those drunk bastards away from ma Birlinn's MacGilchrist and be damned quick about it, ahm no' in much o' a mood to be waitin' about, ah don't want to be cornered here by any English ships with ma arse stickin' out into an' Gearr loch." Torrance laughs aloud, "Would yie look at Gormlaidh…"

Rob looks towards the stern of the ship to see Gormlaidh affectionately embracing a pile of wolfskin brats, smiling, while occasionally sweeping back his long thick tightly curled tresses as though preening himself for a lover's tryst. Rob says, "C'mon Torrance, we'd better be getting them all off the Birlinns before auld Morrison mòr here sails away with them still aboard, for yie know what he's like." Torrance, himself well stocked up on craitur, gazes at MacGilchrist, he grins then says, "Dyie think we should just leave them on board? Ah would love to see the look on all o' their faces if they woke up on some wee island on the edge of the world, with nuthin' but Morrison mòr's hairy arse'd crewmen and a flock o' curious puffins for company." Rob sighs, "Tempting as that may be, let's get Gormlaidh and Moray ashore first, then help me to fish Wallace and Stephen out o' the Clyde."

Rob and Torrance soon manage to get the motley band of bonded brothers landed safely ashore. William and Stephen have partly sobered up, caused mainly by their shocking cold experience of being in the freezing water, they sit down on the beach shivering beside Moray and Gormlaidh, who are still in a drunken stuper.

"J,J,J,J,J,Jaezuz..." shivers Stephen. "WALLACE..." barks out a commanding voice. William squints his eyes and looks up to see who is calling out his name.

"Get on your feet Wallace. What kind of condition do you call this when you're on important business concerning the future of Scotland's estate?" William cups his hands over his eyes to see who has called out his name; he exclaims, "Ranald... True Tam." He staggers up to welcome them, while trying to pull Stephen to his feet at the same time. The two friends stand swaying in front of Ranald and true Tam. William looks around and notices Moray sitting with his head in his hands. Gormlaidh is beside him, still fast asleep. William tries to rouse them, "Get up Moray... for fucks sake, ma uncle wants to talk with us." Moray stands bolt upright with his hands covering his face; then he moans, "Oh my feckn head."

"What are you thinking about boy?" snaps Ranald, "Scotland is in turmoil, folk are starving to death all over our land trying desperately to survive, there are English patrols everywhere... and you are all blootered with drink?" MacGilchrist returns with some of his men and throws skinfulls of freezing ice-cold water over the drunken friends.

Ranald scowls at them, but he can hardly contain his humour, for he's not laughed in a long time, and he knows only to well, that as a youth, there are occasions when you can easily miscalculate the amount of raw craitur one could drink... and stay conscious. Ranald says, "William, you must be coming with us immediately. We ride for Glasgow on urgent business and we've no time to be standing here. There was another meeting of the great council of Glasgow, and much of it about you. Anyway, they have agreed for the third and last time, to grant you a pardon..."

Trying to focus, William exclaims, "Me... another pardon?" Ranald replies, "Aye, it would seem that the English governor De Percy, is willing to grant you this one last opportunity to redeem yourself, otherwise..." No further words are needed to convey the seriousness of the statement.

Ranald then turns to speak with Andrew Moray... "Hear me well young Moray. I need you and your Gallóglaigh to go with MacGilchrist and Stewarts men across to the Lennox and then on up to Strathearn, once there, more men of the Moray will be waitin' for yie. From there they will escort yie back up to your homelands in Avoch. And as for the rest o' yiez... Torrance, when we get north o' Ayr, you get all the Gallóbhet gathered together and return to the Laglan camp. I want yiez all to wait there with William while I attend a great meeting o' the Chiefs and Nobles o' Ayrshire with this new English Governor, and after that yiez can all go back to the Wolf and wildcats." William exclaims, "Am ah no' supposed to be meetin' with bishop Wishart?" Ranald replies, "No, yer going straight to the Laglan."

"Awe naw uncle," sighs William, "I'm so feckn tired o' travellin' and I've no' slept in days, no' the Laglan please, I just want to be going back to Marion and ma wee Mharaidh; for I've no' seen them in sic' a long time, then I just want some peace to be sleepin' for about a week." Ranald, True Tam, Sean mòr and MacGilchrist furtively glance at each other, un-noticed by William or the others. Ranald says, "William, you give Torrance a hand to get Stephen and Gormlaidh mounted, we must be leaving at once, now get everyone ready to depart from here." True Tam says, "C'mon Wallace, I'll give yie a hand to get your friends on their horses." William exclaims, "Tam… What are you doing here?" True Tam laughs, "I'm here to stay with you while the two councils are confirming you've gained yer pardon, for even though yie will likely be getting' it, it's no' guaranteed yet, so we need yie as far away from any English as possible." Hayde arrives with horses for the hapless friends to mount. William shouts across to Moray, "Are you no' coming with us to see Brannah?"

"Aye, fuck Avoch…" says Moray, now sitting precariously on his horse, he calls back to William, "Hold yer horses, Wallace I'm coming wie uze."

Ranald glances at Rob, who shakes his head forlorn, then he says quietly. "They don't know yet do they?" Rob replies, "Thankfully not, but they must be the only ones in Scotland who don't." William overhears the conversation and enquires, "We don't know what?" Ranald realises William has overheard him and thinks quickly to avoid giving him the true devastating answer, he says, "C'mon William, we must get you Stephen and Gormlaidh away from here as soon as possible, we have many miles to move in just a short time." As William pulls himself back onto his horse, he hazily attempts to hold on to the saddle horn, then, still determined, he enquires, "So tell me uncle, what is it we don't know yet?" Ranald replies, "Ach, it's just that our entire family lands from south Ayrshire all the way up to the Ynchinnan shores, has been sequestrated as surety by the English for your good behaviour, and I may add, not just now, but also in the future." William looks down and shakes his head, he groans then says, "Ahm so sorry uncle…" Ranald says, "Yie have nothing to be sorry about, I just need yie to get a grip o' your wits son, for I have information regarding the resting place of ma dearest Margret." William's humour quickly vanishes when he hears the words of Ranald. The nightmare reality of what happened to his foster mother and his families murder at the hands of the English, come flooding to the fore in his mind. He rubs his eyes, and a semblance of thoughtful concern appears as he focusses on Ranald. He enquires, "What information is that uncle?" Ranald replies, "Wishart has had ma dearest Margret interred in consecrated ground up in Dunfermline abbey, but she's buried in an unmarked grave for fear of further desecration. One day soon though, when you're up at your late uncle's land in Kilspindie, you can take the opportunity to pay your respects. The prior will show you where her sweet ground lies."

William nods solemnly as Ranald continues, "I've given Hayde all o' the details that you'll be needing, as he appears to be the only one o' yiez who's not drunk. When yie do sober up, he will pass you all the information about where to go and who it's safe to speak with up at the abbey."

Appearing to sober up somewhat upon hearing this news; William dismounts once more and goes over to help the men trying to push the bull framed Gormlaidh back onto the horse he has just fallen from. Ranald nods for Sean mòr to help William while he has quiet words with Rob. "It would seem it's right enough William or Moray have no inkling of what's happened down in Lanark to the Braidfuite's then?" Rob replies, "None know, well, none other than Sean mòr, one of his men knew and told him, but then Sean approached me and spoke of what he had heard, luckily he hadn't the heart to pass that news on to Wallace and Moray." With a grim countenance, Ranald says, "They'll all find out soon enough though, so we must be ready to contain them when they do, especially William there, for he has caused us enough trouble with the English, we must be ready for him. I know that you'll contain young Moray, I'll have Sean mòr, Torrance and Stephen…" True Tam says, "Wasn't Stephen's sweetheart defiled too?"

"Aye, that she was." confirms Ranald. He looks up to the sky, then looks at true Tam and Rob, he says, "We must all try to do what we can to thwart their impetuous reaction, too much is now at stake for them to be allowed to seek revenge just yet, they must be guided by unseen hands. Now, we must leave here immediately, for I'm already late in attending the Sherriffs council and court in Rosbroch. I have been summoned to appear before the new English governor, Sir Henry de Percy to try and explain why the Sherrifdom of Ayrshire and my lands should not be confiscated from when I last stood bond for William. And after his last incident down in Ayr, I reckon I'll be lucky to keep my head."

Rob replies, "I'll keep close eye on Moray and sway him away from any trouble Ranald, but when he does find out, there will be no' much more that I can do to stop him." Ranald says, "I understand, it's when William returns to the Wolf and wildcats and finds out, that's when our problems will really begin. Who knows what'll be his reaction and that of Stephen too? It's certain they will surely seek a bloody vengeance. I'm sure glad that Sean mòr is with us, for he and William have struck a bond by Cruathnie oath. Otherwise, I think there would be a bloody uprising way too soon." Rob enquires, "But isn't that what Wishart wants, for Wallace and Moray to raise hell with the English in the two far corners of Scotland?" Clenching his fists, Ranald replies, "I don't know if that's what he really wants Rob. But he has myself and others convinced that it's what Scotland needs, if we are to raise the guardian army successfully to fight back against the English before it's too late. It would appear that Wishart and others, have something very particular in mind for both William and Moray in what's about to unfold." Rob sneers, "I don't like this at all Ranald, it's sounds to me more like that the Moray and Wallace are to be sacrificial lambs in some luckless venture, and I will tell yie this now, I'll not stand idly by and watch them giving up their lives to feed the ravenous blades of the English, simply to be gaining time for treacherous nobles to make their mind up what side o' the crib they lay upon." Ranald replies tersely, "You think that I do not feel the same as you MacGilchrist?" Rob growls contemptuously as Ranald continues, "Rob, I have to think that Wishart's plan will work, for it's the only plan we have. If we do nothing, we'll all be dead soon enough, this way we may at least die on our feet."

"So be it," replies Rob, "but I tell yie Crauford, many of our kinfolks are no' happy about this situation at all." Hayde calls out, "We're ready to leave..." Rob leans from his horse; then he says quietly to Ranald, "Freedom or death Crauford, freedom or death..."

MacGilchrist turns and leads Moray and his men away from the Lennox northward towards the Troiseachan Mountain passes, where they know it will be safe from English spies or Patrols going through the heart of that wilderness, another wild and untamed mountainous part of Scotland, smaller than Galloway, but just as feared by the English for outlaws, Brigands, fantastical demons and evil spirits. Sitting on his horse and watching them leave, Ranald is torn between thoughts of William and Moray being used in a game of lethal politics, for his heart is with William and his family as his kinsman. Also, the burden of shame he feels that no one has yet told William of the rape and murder in Lanark. He is distracted when seeing the long Lennox procession halt; then he sees MacGilchrist turn and gallop back towards him. It's not long before Rob pulls his horse to a halt beside Ranald.

"Crauford…" says Rob. "I cannot be party to this mischief any longer. In all good consciousness I reckon that Moray and Wallace deserve to know the truth, and I'm honour bound with Moray as we are kin." Looking just beyond the burly chieftain, Ranald sees that William, Stephen and the Gallóbhet are meandering towards them.

"I do understand what yie are saying Rob," replies, Ranald, "my heart agrees with yie, and I don't doubt your word to faithfully discharge your duties as kin to young Moray there, all that I may ask of you is to yet hold your peace with Moray, only as far as his return to the Avoch." Rob says, "I will endeavor to do this Ranald, but I cannot stomach not telling them. Listen, I must leave yie now, for I cannot look young Wallace there in the eye. I'll hold my peace with Andrew till we are nearing Avoch, but then I'll be telling him of Brannah's troubles. So fare yie well ma friend, till the next time we meet." Rob canters off and stops a moment to converse with William. Ranald speaks with Sean mòr, "I beseech you Sean mòr, I must have your bond as a father and as a Chief, that you will say nothing to William about what happened to the Braidfuites in Lanark town." Ranald sees William and Stephen are gaining closer, Sean mòr sees it too, he looks at Ranald as time drains quickly away.

"Yie reckon so?" says Sean mòr, "Then I'll be deferrin' to your better judgment as his kinsman Crauford, but never ask such a thing o' me again, for it cuts deep into ma black heart where none have ever touched before. I'll be keepin' my true peace from young Wallace there, but, ach well, you have my word on oath." A few moments later, William and Stephen, looking a little shamefaced, approach on their horses.

"I'm sorry uncle…" says William. Ranald smiles, "Naw William it's fine. Come on now, lets get movin' over the back o' the Campsie hills and get away from the sight of anyone and make our way back home. When we reach the eastern edges of the Whangie and Cortmalaw moor, I'll be leaving yiez to cut down through the Gargunnock drove roads to settle things with the councils in Glasgow then Rosbroch. Sean mòr will escort yiez to the Laglan, once there, I need yiez to wait just a wee while longer for the pardon to arrive. When yie get word from me that it is safe for yiez to travel, you all can move safely on through to the Wolf and wildcats."

Sean mòr approaches William, carrying two heavy-looking bags in each hand. He stops beside William and thumps them both down on the rump of his saddle.

"What's in those two bags?" enquires William. Sean mòr replies, "That's your share o' the English siller we took from them robbin' English bastards down in that Chester place." William exclaims, "But, they didn't rob us, it was you who…" Sean mòr growls at him, "Shut it Wallace, ahm a fair man. And before yie open yer big mouth, Moray has got his share for him and his; Morrison mòr, Ruaidhri and MacDougal got their fair share for them and theirs, now this is your fair share for you and yours, that'll be the end o' the matter Wallace."

As Sean mòr walks away and mounts his horse. William grips the two bags of silver and laughs; he turns and looks back at Stephen, who is smiling at something else. Stephen points behind them, curious, William turns to see that Gormlaidh, Torrance and many of the Gallóbhet are all fast asleep in their saddles, Stephen grins, "They've gone and tied all their bleedin' horses together nose to tail, so that none o' them would wonder off while they slept... ingenious." William looks at Ranald, reassured and feeling satisfied to be returning home. He says, "I reckon there will be one big happy ceilidh waiting for us when we finally get back home to the Wolf and wildcats." Ranald and Sean mòr glance at each other; knowing William will find out soon about the terrible events in Lanark, and then they must try to limit the likely damage that will be caused when he seeks bloody retribution by the blood tax. Nodding knowingly to each other, they turn their horses and lead the weary Gallóglaigh on their long journey home….

Forge o' Joppa

A laborious and uneventful trek, takes Wallace and the Gallóbhet through remote mountainous tracks above the glens of the Lennox, then they move on down to trail along deserted drove roads across the hazardous Whangie moors, not stopping untill they reach their first destination, a few miles west of the Cummin clan fortalice of Cathair Cheann Tulaich, where Ranald and true Tam leave to continue their journey to Glasgow for the Greater council meeting, then on to Rosbroch for the Sherriffs conference. A little while later, from their position in the Gargunnocks the Wolf and wildcat Gallóbhet, with Sean mòr's Dregern, are relieved to see in the farthest distance, the rolling hills of high Kilmaurs, from there they know that by sunset on the following day they will be nearing the Laglan woods, and soon after that, they will be home safe and in the arms of their loved ones. The motley group ride with fortitude on their weary journey, taking the most uninhabited and hazardous backcountry routes, in order to avoid meeting up with any roving English patrols. Unfortunately, a sight that is becoming ever more commonplace, is the sporadic collections of small Balloch's, Clachans and Obhain's that have been annihilated. The smell of rotting flesh and the sight of bleached white carcasses of men, women and children, many of whom are left where they had been murdered, deeply affects the marauding Gallóbhet, reminding them of the same brutal savagery that had taken many of their own families during the Pact conflict, especially survivors of the Ceàrdannan massacres. They see quite often, the broken remains of wretched people, grotesquely reduced to bizarre mosaics of scattered bones and broken skulls, having provided a gluttonous feast for the carrion corvus and wild beast. In other places they meet many orphaned children appearing as living skeletons, emaciated and barely surviving in the remote wilderness, they stand in rags, freezing and begging desperately for food, but the Gallóbhet have neither food nor nourishment to offer or distribute, occasionally they slaughter one of their horses to feed some of the larger groups they find. Their long somber day continues, with everyone taking sleep-naps in their saddles, untill dusk lowers the nigh-time curtain.

When the falling of darkness fully envelops them, a palpable sense of relief follows, for everyone is well aware that the English much favour the light of day or the sense of security given from a blazing night brazier for their sense of safety, whereas the Gallóbhet are born, bred and educated to favour the dark of night, with only the lanterns of the moon and stars to show them the way. By the time the Gallóbhet hear the distant tolling of the midnight bells, they are entering the Clyde glen basin, then they pass over a shallow river crossing, not far from the lower Strathaven pass.

By early morn, they approach the sinister and treacherous Mauchlynn moorland, where Sean mòr leans from his horse and shakes William awake in the saddle.

"So, your back with us again then Wallace?" William groans as he sweeps his long-matted hair away from his face, "Feck me Sean mòr, I've got a belter o' a sore head and one achin' body, but I'm glad to be headin' homeward."

Sean mòr laughs, "Ach, ah don't know, you feckn youngsters nowadays, yiez have all been sleepin' on yer horses all feckn night and day, while us auld fella's have kept up the watch to be keepin' yiez all safe from harm..." William smiles as Sean mòr continues his morning lecture. "For fuck's sake Wallace, when ah was about your age, ah could stay seated in ma saddle for weeks without..." William interrupts, "Look Sean, look away over there in the distance, isn't that smoke comin' from the auld forge o' Joppa?" Sean mòr squints into the distance, looking in the direction William is pointing. He curses, "I can't see a fuckin' thing; for me eyes are fuck'd for seein' a long way away." Faolán and Stephen ride up beside them and also peer into the distance. Faolán says, "Aye, that's Joppa all right, but some fool has a smokin' fire goin'"

At that moment, Hayde and the point outriders suddenly appear, galloping towards them at speed. As they pull up beside William and Sean mòr, Hayde, though breathless, says, "There's a couple o' strange fella's sittin' down in the auld Joppa forge, we couldn't tell who it was that's in there and we didn't want them to see us by chance, so we thought it better to come back here and tell yiez what we saw..." William says curiously, "We passed Joppa just a few weeks ago, no' long after the English had ridden through and had murdered everyone down there, so ah reckon we know that it cannae be anybody from hereabouts?" Stephen says, "Well it's none o' our lot for sure, for we wouldn't be letting the English aware we were there wit' a smoky bleedin' fire goin' on." Hayde says, "It's like ah said, we couldn't tell for sure who's in there, but their no' just feedin' the fire, it looks like it to me as though their tryin' to work up a good heat in the auld smithy forge itself?" Sean mòr laughs, "Well then me dainty ladies, why do we not satisfy our curiosities and go down there to find out who it is? Besides, they might have bags of siller with them, and if they do..." They all begin to laugh; then they say as one, "It's yours..." For the first time since they left the Lennox, everyone laughs heartily. Gormlaidh says, "What if it's a ruse that's been set by the English to lure us folks into an ambush?" Stephen replies, "Well me foin' friend Gormlaidh; lets git going down there and see, for I'm bleedin starvin.'" Gormlaidh says, "Did you no' hear what ah just said?" Stephen replies, "Sure ah did, and I said, lets git goin' for ahm starvin'"

Everyone laughs again as more of the Gallóbhet gather to talk about the smoke rising from the forge of Joppa. Gormlaidh, confused by everyone's apparent disregard for his concerns, says once more, "Ah'll ask yiez all again, what if it's the feckn English setting a trap for us?" Sean mòr replies, "Gormlaidh, if they've got my siller, it had better be a big fuckin' trap to be stoppin' me from getting it..." Stephen says, "Well Sean, if it's a bleedin trap right enough, lets be killin' them all anyway." William looks at his erstwhile friends and laughs, he says, "That's what I like when ahm riding about wie you fella's." Stephen enquires, "And what is it you'll be likin' about it all then?" William replies, "Ah'll tell yie Stephen, most normal folks would be thinking if it was an English trap waitin' for us, they would be wanting to be finding the quickest route away from the place, likely goin' in the opposite direction, but naw, no' you lot, half of yiez want ambushed so yiez can kill all the English for a feed, not thinking se' much they might just be thinking the same about us, and the rest of yiez don't seem to mind getting ambushed, so long as they have siller yiez can strip from them after yiez kill them." Sean mòr enquires, "Aye, and your point is?"

Thinking Sean is joking, William laughs heartily, but he soon notices that he is the only one that's laughing. Sean mòr enquires once more, "Then you tell us Wallace, is there any other way to get our siller n' grub that I don't yet know about?" William shrugs his shoulders. "Fair enough, so what's the plan then?" Sean mòr sneers, almost cynically he replies, "C'mon Wallace and ah'll explain ma plan to yie, now let's get movin' for the Joppa forge, we'll ride on in there and see what's going on. If it's an English ambush, then we kill them like ah said, there, that's the plan."

"What?" exclaims William, "are we no' going to make up some sort o' a sane plan of approach?" Sean mòr pulls his horse around swiftly then he replies tersely... "Wallace, Joppa's about a mile away from here, if the English ambush us, we kill them; that's the fuckin' plan, have yie got that? Now c'mon, lets get goin' for ahm more certain than ever that those bastards down there have got ma siller." Glaring at William, Sean mòr nimbly turns his horse and gallops off towards Joppa. William Shakes his head again in utter disbelief, he exclaims, "There's about forty of us here, we know that the English will no' patrol with less than a hundred o' a squadron around these parts, and it's fairly likely that we could be riding right into an ambush as Gormlaidh said... and the plan is, we just kill them?" Gormlaidh quips as he mosies away. "Well Wallace, we could wait here till they've brought some more soldiers up in support, if yie are thinkin' that there's no' enough o' them down in Joppa?"

William looks over at Stephen to gain some moral support, but the doughty Irishman simply shrugs his broad shoulders and smiles as he too passes by while following Sean mòr's lead. He calls out to William, "C'mon Wallace, git a move on me fine fella, or yie will be missin' all the Norman bleedin' fun down there." Williams watches his friends mount up and ride on after Sean mòr, Faolán pulls up beside him, she says "What are yie waitin' here for Wallace, an invite?" she then canters off with Eochaidh and Fiónlaidh following close behind on their hablars before William can reply to her. As more of the riders pass by, William looks around to see that they have all now gone and he is sitting alone, for the Gallóbhet have followed Sean mòr and are fast disappearing into secretive tracks that will lead them through the Mauchlynn moor to the Joppa forge. William thinks to himself… *'Am ah just witless and gone to some mad place or is this some feckn fucked up world I've just woken up in, maybe it's the curse of Morrison mòr's lethal craitur?'*

Laughing heartily to himself as he canters along after his companions, he thinks that he is likely to be as mad as the best of them, with the absolute exception perhaps of Sean mòr, who apparently excels in the logic of analytic insanity, to which, William knows that he is now a hungry, eager and very willing pupil. He also knows that he has much to learn from this ignoble warrior… the feared brigand chief, Sean mòr MacDhuibhsídhe, great spawn of the dark spirit. Following on quickly, William soon catches up with the Gallóbhet as they stealthily move closer to the Joppa forge. He canters past everyone till he finally rides in beside Sean and enquires, "Sean mòr, seriously, tell me, what if there really is an ambush waiting for us down there, what will we do then?"

"Jaezuz," replies Sean, "ah'v fuckin' told yie twice already Wallace, if it's a trap we kill them, for if they have a plan, we're already a plan ahead o' them wie our own counter-plan, can yie no' see ma logic?" William appears confused. Sean continues, "Fuck me; listen up Wallace, if it's a trap, we might lose one or two, hmm, maybe a few more than that, but we will know for certain where the trap is then set,"

"This cant be right Sean mòr," says William, "tell me the real truth." Sean pulls his horse to a halt then speaks firmly, "Aye, ah'll tell yie the real truth about what's really goin' on Wallace. Ah know yie've experienced for yourself these last few years, all o' the cruelty that's been forced upon us, you, me and most o' the common folks of Scotland. Everyone here that rides with us, has seen such terrible sights, even yestreen on our way here an' up to this very day. Wallace, we've all suffered a great loss o' our own kinfolk through murder, massacre and starvation, so naw, no more pullin' our beards or cooryin' low to the usurper's lackeys to avoid any trouble, for it still amounts to fuck all in the end but the slaughter o' our people. Well, I will tell yie this truth Wallace, I've had enough, we've all had enough, no more of this subjugation, no more ah say, ahm no' backin' down nor hidin' away from the English on this, the sacred land o' ma ancestors. If am gonnae die, then it'll be goin' head on in and taking out as many o' them there English fucks and our own arse-lickin' nobles as ah can, and well long before they put me down. There, do yie understand now, do yie, do yie finally get it?"

"Aye." replies William, "Ah reckon I'm really gettin' it now Sean mòr." Sean spits out the words, "Well, you'd better be gettin' it Wallace, if yie need any more convincin' just look around yie at all o' them that's here with us, they all carry the same shared outrage and a need to do something, can yie no' feel it?" William mumbles, "Aye ah can sure feel it." Sean continues, "And of course, yie were right when yie thought earlier that it's a fuckin' madness for us to be ridin' in blind to Joppa, but we've all fuckin' had enough Wallace, Jaezuz ahm fuckin' ragin', so it's no fuckin' more ah tell yie."

William is slightly taken aback, he thinks long and hard on Sean mòr's raging explanation, but curiously, it really sits well in his own mind, then what Sean just finished saying… that makes even more sense. Sean mòr sees William's expression and adopts a more thoughtful approach. "Listen to me Wallace, do yie hear me fine when ah use ma humour, do yie listen to the way ah talk tae people? Well ah'll tell yie, that's all just a front, an honest front, but a front nonetheless, ahm gonnae say this to yie as well, because ah know that yie'll likely understand. Ahm well aware yie may think that ahm witless, reckless, maybe yie even think that am mad in the head when I chose to make this move on Joppa, ah mean, who in their right fuckin' mind would knowingly ride into an ambush, especially when yer certain to be outnumbered at least three-to-one… right?"

"Nobody would do that?" replies William. Sean continues, "And do yie think that nobody could ever fool yie Wallace, naw, no' you with such a fine education and a gifted awareness yie profess to own, right?" William replies, "Aye, ah reckon that's right too?" Sean continues, "Well, if you're se' fuckin' clever, what are yie doin' sitting here wie me preparin' to ride into an ambush and likely to be killed, for something that makes no fuckin' sense at all?" William is slightly flummoxed, he replies, "Because it's you…" Sean laughs then says, "Aye, but it's 'what' because o' me? Is it that yie think that I might pull off something big, despite all common sense and against all the odds?"

Suddenly William understands what is going on with Sean mòr, he realises that he has been talking to him in a way that True Tam, his uncle Malcolm and wee Maw used to speak with him, even his father Alain during those long nights of storytelling. Now inspired by Sean mòr's words, William replies enthusiastically, "Because ah really believe in yie Sean mòr, that's why ahm here waitin' to go in with yie." A broad grin sweeps across Sean mòr's face, "Exactly, that's ma point. Now you listen to me Wallace, and yie had better be listenin' well and good; If Stephen or Faolán there, yer closest and smartest friends, had proposed the same kinda pointless plan that I proposed to yiez all earlier, yie know, about attacking Joppa for grub and siller that we don't really need, yie would have questioned them and tried to talk them out of it, but when yie questioned me, ah gave yie such a fucked up reply, yie accepted it wie no more questions… yet here yie are, committed to following me anyway, even though death may be moments away in a probable ambush, and for what really, some triflin' siller and some grub? Not a fuckin' chance, this is your future am explainin' to yie Wallace, how yie see me, this is how everyone sees you. Accept this Wallace, yie have a natural gift o' leadership, ask any o' these fella's here, they would follow you onto death if yie asked them, even ma own kith and kin would follow yie now. Fuck, even I will follow yie if yie choose to lead us?"

"You would follow me?" gasps William.

Sean mòr looks into the soul depth within William's eyes before he replies. After a moment he says, "Aye Wallace, I would follow you. For yie are like a son to me and a brother in arms… and a fine father of men, feck, yer like ma very own dearest kith and kin… so you lead us and we will follow." William is completely taken aback with these words of Sean mòr; he enquires, "Why would anybody want to follow me, even I don't know who I would be fighting for, other than King John. So why do you not take the lead Sean mòr, since you have a vision of what should be?" Sean laughs, "Ach Wallace, ah have ma reputation to think o' first, but you, yie really don't realise the reputation you have amongst the common folk o' this land, do yie? I mean, most folk from Galloway and all the way up to Dundee, they think that you're Scotland's fuckin' savior. Listen son, ahm aware that yie have gotten much more credit for the things yie haven't done than for the things yie have done, but are yie just goin' to wander about the place till the English finally nail you and yours to a fuckin' door, like what happened to your dear auld Dá and everyone in glen Afton, for they will if yie don't make a stand, make no mistake about that." William enquires, "But what do I do, for am yearning just to be back with Marion and…" Sean exclaims, "Wallace, get this intae yer fuckin' skull will yie, the only way for you to really be protecting Marion and everyone else that yie love and care about, is to be the leader o' men that we all know yie to be. Rally the folks o' Galloway, and together we'll make our land as it once was, a proud kingdom in its own right, for we know the English fear the land o' the Dál Riatans, Ceardannan and Gall-Ghàidhil more than any other part o' Scotland. You call out everyone to yer standard Wallace; for ah tell yie now, they will surely come."

"Sean mòr," says William, "even if I thought I could do the things yie ask, I wouldn't know where to start?"

With a broadening grin, Sean replies, "Don't you worry yerself about that Wallace, for circumstance will provide a start for yie. The English have already begun to wipe us off the face of this earth as yie well know, and they will no' be stoppin' till they nourish their fields with our dead flesh and bones." Thoughtful of all that Sean has said to him these last few days, William is still curious about one last piece of his own puzzle. "So why are yie really telling me all this Sean, what's the real reason yie have to be fillin' ma head with all these notions about raisin' an army and rebuilding an ancient kingdom that's fallen to history, there's so much more to yer words than just the music o' yer delivery?"

Sean mòr looks at William intensely, there is something in Sean's eyes that intimates he is about to reveal a truth of truths, and William can sense it.

"Wallace, ever since the death of good King Alexander, Scotland is failing, we've been cursed by a terrible avarice inflicted upon us by two-legged rats, spreadin' their deadly plague o' murder upon us that'll surely kill us all in the end. It was both your folks and mine yesterday, the country folks we saw this day, and nigh on the morrow, it will surely be our very own children, and there's nobody that's gonnae save us from the greed of our own fuckin' nobles and the ravenous fuckin' English but ourselves. They both thirst for everything we lowborn Scots have left to give; then they will kill us or bind us into slavery and take our women as whores. That pairing o' bastards is as a plague o' biblical fuckin' locusts son, and soon, only a few of us will be left alive for them to feast upon. Wallace, the sooner yie realise what yie must do, the better it will be for Marion, your wain, and all o' the folks who look to you to lead and protect them, for come the day, yie will surely be leading the army of the people, Scotland's army son, yie can be certain o' that. And ah don't give a fuck whether yie like what ah say next or not, but by the honour and glory o' Magda mòr, the divine Aicé in her glorious wisdom brought our paths together, and ah will be by yer side all the way."

"Ah do hear yie Sean mòr," says William, "ah know that the Gallóbhet are se' proud of their honoured place to be directly in front o' the king in times of war, and I know for sure how well earned that coveted honour is, but for us to take on the English army, and for folks to be thinkin' that it's to be me leading it, that's just a fantasy Sean, naw, we wouldn't never stand a chance against them..." Sean says, "Naw, ahm no' talkin' about taking on the whole English army, we would never do that, what ahm sayin is, we link and spread all o' the Gallóbhct n' spar's throughout Scotland where an English Lord or sheriff resides and any Scots noble who's in the pay o' Longshanks. We make it well known that their names are high on our own death lists, and at any time, should they raise a finger o' hurt in their shire, they are dead men walking. By any means we will kill, murder and massacre every fuckin' one o' them; their families too, then we simply disappear back into the forests. Terror Wallace, terror is as much a weapon to be striking down our enemies as havin' an army at yer back. Once the blood tax has been paid in full for what they've done to us in this land of ours, then if they persist, we become dedicated hunters o' men Wallace, kill their families down in England if needs be..." Sean continues, "it's the only way, take it from me for I should know, a good leader will soon tame these Sudrons who've made their murderous fuckin' cuckoo's nest up here in Scotland."

"So, tell me this truth then Sean mòr," enquires William, "why don't you lead us?"

This direct question causes Sean to smile, almost innocently. "Wallace I will tell yie the truth as to why no'. Many who don't know me, aye they would fight for me, only because they fear ma very name; but given the opportunity, they would flee the first chance they got. But for you, there are many common folk o' Scotland that would fight for you because they love yer very name, for it gives them hope Wallace, where there's no other who gives them that hope, no' even their priests. What yie've done already may seem like nuthin' to you, other than actions yie had to take in order for yie just to survive. But to many others, yie represent a man o' their own kind, who is fightin' against overwhelmin' tyrannies for what yie believe in, simply that o' yer family. In the minds o' the common folks who ever hear yer story son, and there are many, yie are fighting for their families too, for yie are no' a nobleman that's se' distant from their ways and understanding o' life, yie are one of them, yie are one o' us. Wallace, ah beg yie, if yie really do want to live in peace, then an all-out bloody war is what yie must prepare for. The English, along wie our own fuckin' nobles, they must no' just think it, they must really believe it to be true and fear it. So, for reasons unknown and wherever this journey may take us, yie have ma oath from me and mine, that we are with you and yours unto death Wallace." Sean mòr extends out his hand… "Unto death, brother." Without hesitation, William readily accepts the hand of brotherhood extended by Sean mòr, he replies, "Unto death brother…"

At that paradigm moment, they instinctively know something naïve, fragile and wholly resistant has finally been broken in the youthful spirit within William. Their conviction and senses are now welded together in a pure spiritual and primeval place, born from all that has gone before them in their lives, clearly shaping their loyalties and faith as proud freeborn Céile Aicé warriors, fighting for the earth of Magda mòr.

"Well Sean mòr?" enquires William, "are yie ready for me to lead yie onto death without question?" Sean replies, "Aye Wallace, of course, no more fuckin' around, just fuckin' do it, that's how the Duibh Sìhd have always fought in battle, get goin' hard, fast and then pile straight in and don't stop till they're all fuckin' dead, or we are." William laughs, for he is no longer bemused by Sean's crude logic, nor anything outlandish he may say or do… "C'mon Wallace or we'll be late for our very own sui mortem." They both laugh heartily at the humour, then spur their horses on, leading their loyal Gallóbhet. Soon, they all pull to a halt within a hundred yards of the old Joppa forge. For a while they wait, watch, and consider their next move, William thinks of his last visit to Joppa, when they found the ravaged body of his friend old Jop. He then reflects upon what had happened at the nearby Sundrum fortalice, where he had to set to the shining fire, the mortal remains of his kinsfolk, auld Duncan Wallace and that of his family too, along with all of the families of Sundrum murdered by the English. He also thinks about when he was on route to warn his uncle Richard at Riccarton about the death lists… and the bizarre fight with the Englishman lord Longcastle nearby. His thoughts are suddenly broken when Hayde and the two scouts return with new information. Sean mòr gathers all the Gallóbhet together a few hundred yards from the Joppa forge, with the exception of the scouts watching the location intensely. Hayde accurately relays an account of what they have seen. "Yiez will no' be believin' this, but there's some young English knight sittin' down in there, he's a' cookin' and a' vittlin' wit' a right scrawny big beggar."

"An English knight in the Joppa forge…" ponders William, "Ah wonder what he's doin' in there, could yie see?" Hayde replies, "They're just sittin' around a big glowin' fire at the smithy forge, eatin' talkin' and drinkin'. There are no traps and no English troops anywheres that we could see, ceptin' those English that are away over at the Sundrum fortalice, and that place appears to be stoutly garrisoned now." Sean mòr enquires, "Why didn't yie just cut their fuckin' throats and be done with it?" Hayde replies, "Ah'll tell yie why Sean mòr, cause they fellas were no' just speaking the English tongue, but in the Galloway Ghaeltacht too, I could tell by their accents. And the rough lookin' big beggar, a swear that he has a northern-Irish accent."

The surprise amongst all the gathered Gallóbhet is palpable. William enquires, "An Englishman that's speaking in the auld Beurla regarde tongue… and wie a Gall Ghàidhil twang too, that's no' possible, are you sure he isn't a Scots knight?" Hayde replies, "I didn't know there were any decent Scots knights left in Scotland, never mind any in Galloway? Besides, it's definitely English colours he's wearing… Ach, I don't know, but there's somethin' feckn odd goin' on in there, that's why we didn't kill them Sean mòr. Ah thought it best that we'd better get back here and ask you what we should do?" Sean mòr walks to his horse and mounts up, he says,

"I'll go down there right now and ask the bastards straight, where's ma siller, then ah'll kill them." At that, Sean mòr spurs his horse forward. Everyone scatters to mount and follow Sean mòr's lead. The Gallóbhet arrive in a storm of horses and surround the Joppa forge. As everyone dismounts and makes an approach, William follows as Sean mòr brazenly barges straight through the doors into the darkened forge and announces himself to the two strangers.

The low red glow of the forge fire causes hellish shadows to flicker on the faces of the bearded Gallóglaigh, with their scars, ruddy faces and accoutrements of amber and finger bones woven through long greased tangled hair weaves, a sight that would petrify the most courageous of men. The knight simply looks up, but he appears disinterested in the arrival of these savage looking warriors, then he looks back at the forge and begins to sup gruel from his bowl. He speaks without lifting his head up, "So, you're Sean mòr... Why are you here old man?" Before a blustering Sean mòr can react or reply in any way or reach out to smite the young knight down; William calls out, "JOP?"

Everyone is surprised and looks at William curiously as he barges in through the open doors of the forge, past the Gallóbhet and Sean mòr. They are even more astonished when William and the apparent Englishman, greet each other with a warm embrace and great affection. "Jop..." exclaims William "Feck, what are you doing here?" Stephen comes in through the doors and walks over to stand beside the two friends, he says, "Jop me foin young fella, now isn't it good to be seeing you here instead of an angry English ambush?" Jop replies, "Aye, it's good to be seeing you fella's here too." Sean mòr curiously approaches the obvious friends. William introduces them, "Jop, this is Sean mòr, chief of the MacDhuibhsídhe and Dregern Gallóglaigh. Sean mòr, this here fella is Gilbert de Grimsby, ach but we all know him as Jop, we're old friends from wainhood, this is his auld fathers forge." Sean mòr appears confused; he sniffs the face of Jop then enquires, "What the fuck is an Englishman doing sitting in auld Jop's place then? Have you got a death wish Englishman, for ah'll sure oblige yie right now?" William says, "Hold on there Sean mòr, Jop is as Scots as you or me, this was his father's smithy, just give us peace for a wee while and ahl explain it all to yie later." Sean mòr appears relatively satisfied, then he enquires, "You got any siller about yie Jop?" Before William or Jop can reply, Sean mòr raises his hand in a friendly gesture, "Ach away, ahm only jestin' with yie young fella." Sean mòr turns to set watchguards on perimeters and orders everyone else to rest awhile and refresh their vittals.

Meanwhile, William can see that there is great distress etched on the face of his old friend, he says, "Ahm truly sorry to be meeting with yie under such sad circumstance ma friend. Ah must tell yie, we know what happened here to yer dear auld folks." Jop replies, "Aye, that's why ahm come home Wallace, I must tell you though, that my mind is in a dark place right now, for I know that I must dwell on this great evil awhile before I respond in kind."

"What will yie do?" enquires William. Jop replies. "I'll go through my sources and find out exactly who did this to my family, then I will deal with them by taking the blood tax." Suddenly they hear a scuffling noise nearby, coming from a dark recess of the forge, the Gallóbhet quickly come to arms, but Jop holds his hands up and speaks calmly, "Come out Fawdoun, your safe enough." A tall burly looking young man slowly appears from behind some water barrels. "Wallace, Sean mòr," says Jop, "this here fella is Fawdoun. I met him wandering about the place when I first arrived. He's been bringing me sustenance and looking out for other survivors of the Joppa massacre. He's also been tending to my auld folk's sweet ground." William and Sean mòr acknowledge Fawdoun, then Sean mòr calls out, "Listen up awe yiez bastards, vittal the horses then go git some rest, we leave here by last light." The Gallóbhet slowly disperse to make a brief camp for vittals.

"Jop, your father..." says William, "we buried him away up on the hill o' your ancestors." Jop replies, "I know yie did, Fawdoun here saw you, he doesn't talk se' much and has no care for strangers, that's why he didn't reveal himself to you. He told me where my father was buried, placed him by my dear mother's side. Wallace, I must thank yie for the care you showed to the body of my folks." William says, "Ah'll be thanking you Fawdoun, for your thoughts and kindness towards ma friend and his kinfolks."

Fawdoun nods in respect. Jop says, "Fawdoun here found some survivors from around the Sundrum way, they told us about all that happened over there, a terrible business." Jop continues, "You fella's cannot be staying here though, for there's a baggage train and large Garrison troop of a few hundred men coming up from Carlisle, I reckon they'll be hereabouts in two days at the latest. Their foragers will be spreading out ahead and hunting well in advance within a ten-mile radius of the main body, they'll surely find you fella's here if the garrison at Sundrum don't find you first." William enquires curiously, "Where's this baggage train heading for... Glasgow?" Jop replies, "No, they're heading with all of lord de Percy's personals in train to garrison Ayr castle." William looks at Stephen, "De Percy, there's that fuckin' name again." Stephen replies, "You're bleedin' right. If we had enough fella's here, we could trap and capture him, then we would find out the bleedin' truth of it all." Everyone is surprised at Stephen's comment. Jop says, "De Percy is in Lanark at the moment, then he's going to Glasgow, there's no use in thinking that just a few of you could trap him, far less capture him, he's too well guarded by his loyal retainers." Sean enquires, "Then who's bringing over the train?" Jop replies, "Lord Fenwick, I think…" William and Stephen are immediately alerted to hearing the name. "Fenwick," exclaims Stephen, "Wallace, he's the fella that murdered Malcolm and young Sandy at Loudon hill. This could be our opportunity to claim our blood tax too." Jop enquires, "Who, Fenwick?" William replies, "We met some hunters who witnessed Fenwick and some other knight called Cressingham flay ma uncle Malcolm to death over at the Loudon hill." Sean comments, "Wallace, why don't we hunt the hunters. Let's hunt down all o' those who carry those death lists." William enquires, "What do yie mean?" Sean mòr replies, "We make a list o' English marked for death, then we make sure the English finds out about it, on our list could be Fenwick, if this is the bastard who causes yie so much pain, then put him top of our list? It will sure let them know how it feels."

William looks at Sean almost in amazement, "Sean mòr, you just make me wonder?" Sean appears almost embarrassed at the compliment; then he continues true to his persona. "And there will sure be some amount o' siller in that baggage train ah'll wager. This could be the opportunity we've been waitin' for." William ponders for a moment, then he replies, "Maybe your right Sean mòr, but If we're going to do this, then I'll make up a plan and will match it with yours Sean, between us we will win a war of our own." Sean replies, "That's right fine by me, and if we agree, which we will, then let's share all o' the contents of this baggage train amongst all o' us." There is a great murmur of approval from everyone in the Joppa forge. William enquires, "Tell us Jop, how many troops would yie say will be travelling with such a train as this?" Jop replies, "I reckon between one, maybe two hundred all told, that would be normal, but most of them will be veterans of great experience though, too much I think for well-meaning but untrained fella's such as yourselves." Stephen says, "Why not send riders out in every direction to gather as many as we can to the call?" Sean enquires, "Aye, but where would we be settin' this trap for everyone to meet in the first place, and we'll need them there damned feckin' quick wherever it's gonnae be?" Everyone sits awhile, thinking of all the possibilities.

"Loudoun hill." exclaims William, "No matter how many we draw to the cause, we'll still likely be outnumbered, but the Winny Wizzen drove road that passes by the east foot of the Loudoun hill, that would be perfect, it's about half a mile long, narrow and with dense forested steep braes on either side... we could trap them in there, if we could cause a landslip from the side o' the Loudoun, it would force the English tight, and if we block both ends and we control the braes, there would be no escape, for that's the only way through to Ayr, and that's the way they'll be coming. Even if we can raise half o' their numbers with our own hunter bowyers, we could really catch the bastards cold." Sean mòr grins, "Well said there young Wallace, now that sounds like a proper plan, this is what ah'd call yer opportunity."

"There are a lot of 'ifs' in that proposal of yours Wallace." says Jop. William enquires, "Jop, will yie help us with your knowledge o' what the English tactical reaction would be in such a trap as this?" Sean mòr enquires, "Aye Jop, what would you do, will yie help us? Fuck young fella, in fact, why not come with us? The English have murdered your family too... Jaezuz, how the fuck could you have ever fought for them?" Jop sighs, "Sean mòr, I thought that I fought for a good Christian king against enemies who would kill us all for our beliefs. Never did I ever think for a moment, it would be my own people who would be on the receiving end of such tyranny. And the answer to your question is yes, I'll help you, and after we have done this deed, I am going to seek out all Scots nobles in the English court who are prepared to fight back and drive these English usurpers out of Scotland. And yes, as you are well aware Wallace, I have more than enough knowledge of English tactics and battle strategies to arrange a fine trap for them at the Loudoun hill, for I too know it well." Stephen says, "We have to do this Wallace, this is the first time we will be striking back at them, instead of always being the recipients of their bleedin' good-will." William agrees, "You're right, let's get goin' to the Loudoun and prepare the land."

Everyone's spirit rises at the thought of finally striking back at the English after years of oppression and murder. Sean mòr laughs and says, "The only fly in the craitur for you Jop is, ah think yie'll be hard pressed to find any living nobles in Scotland that are prepared to fight and risk losing their lands and wealth." Jop replies, "Find them I will my large Gallóbhet friend, for I have in my possession the rampant lion standard of good king David, as was passed on to King Alexander. It was good Alexander himself who presented it to my father after the battle of Largs. The best of them will gather to the Royal Rampant Lion."

"The Kings very own war flag?" exclaims William, "Do yie mean the one that was flown at the battle itself, by Lord Scrymgeour?" Jop replies, "The very same."

"The Lion o' Scotland..." says William almost in awe. "I'd stand and fight beside you with my bare hands beneath those colours Jop." William continues, "Sean mòr, will yie call everyone to gather in a circle just outside the forge, we need to discuss this move to attack the English at the Loudon, we all need to be agreed upon our intent, for there won't be no second chance to get this right. We'll get the message sent out to our known supporters as fast as possible and for others to join us."

"Wallace," says Faolán. William says, "Ah know yiez are leaving us here to go down to Dun Reicheit to be with yer families Faolán, I wouldn't ask yie to stay, but..." Faolán cuts through William's sentiment, "We're stayin Wallace; this is our fight too. Now, here is what we can do for yie, the Gallóbhan have a way of making sure the English scout riders and those foragers that were mentioned earlier, are dealt with. Let us ride on ahead and we'll deal with them in our own way, a way that'll make sure that no news ever gets back to the baggage train regarding our presence." William nods in agreement, "Then get goin' Faolán, our only enemy now is time." Faolán says, "Ahm stayin here by your side Wallace, as soon as we know your plans, I'll send Eochaidh and Fiónlaidh to raise all o' the Gallóbhan right away. They'll make for our nearest border outposts then send out relay riders from there to every part of the auld Gall-Ghàidhealaibh kingdom, then they'll meet with us at the Loudoun by morn," Jop says, "We should go now too." William replies, "Aye, let's get packed and get goin', even if it's nightfall when we get there, that will still be time enough to sight out all the perimeters o' the land over there and prepare our strategies, that's if we gain enough support by the time we're ready to attack. If we don't get enough support by the time that wagon train arrives, then we're gonnae be prepared to trap the next train."

Suddenly a watch Gallóglaigh comes rushing into the forge, he says, "There are squadrons of English cavalry and foragers preparing to leave Sundrum by first light o' the morn, we'd better be moving right now, for we're directly on their route." Sean mòr enquires, "Ah must ask o' yie this

Jop... This baggage train coming up north from Carlisle? will this de Percy fella be sendin' his siller with it?' Jop smiles then he replies, "Aye, and plenty of it there is too Sean mòr, including armour, weapons, food and many other fine things to keep his lordship in luxury. Lord Fenwick is..." Sean mòr immediately turns and calls out to the Gallóbhet, "Mount up." Sean mòr looks at William and Jop then says, "This here fella called Fenwick, he has my Siller. So if you want him too Wallace, he'll be ripe for the plucking, for you're right, he must pass the Loudoun hill if he is makin' for Ayr, and yer right again, that's where we will have him, well, you can have him, I just want ma siller, and I may add, if we get there before nightfall, on the way there we can formulate Jop's martial plan and strategy then carry it out to the letter, if that's all right by you Wallace?" A surprised William queries, "To the letter Sean mòr?"

This newfound face of Sean mòr amuses William, Jop and everyone nearby.

"Aye, to the letter." Replies Sean mòr, "As much as yie all may think o' me as brave and heroic to a fault, Wallace here knows that ahm also a strict adherent to discipline, aye, but only when required." Then he winks at William, who knows well enough now the strategy Sean mòr uses to instill humour in the soul of each and every individual that would otherwise fall to nervousness or stress. The urgency, grit and determination of the Gallóbhet mounting their horses and preparing for the oncoming conflict, stirs the blood of everyone. There is an air of electrifying excitement amongst the usually stoic and dour Gallóbhet. William mounts his horse and looks at Jop and Fawdoun, he enquires, "Are yiez comin' with us then?" Jop needs no second invitation as he and Fawdoun rush to mount their horses. Soon they pull up beside William, Stephen and Sean mòr, "Wait," says William.

"Sean mòr, can yie spare two men to take a message up to Crosshouse for me?" Stephen says, "What's to do Wallace?" Sean mòr enquires, "Aye, what is it are yie thinkin' o' there Wallace?" William continues, "I want to get an urgent message sent up north to Andrew Moray, I want to be letting him know what we are plannin' down here… if anything happens to me across at the Loudoun hill, then I'll want him to be lookin' out for the safety o' Marion and the wain for me. When he weds Brannah, he'll be all the kin that I have left that's in a position to protect both her and the wain to keep them safe from the English." Stephen enquires, "And how are yie goin' to be doin' that then Wallace me boy?" William replies, "There are doo's up at ma uncles that belong to lord Moray. When your riders get up there, Ranald will likely be still in Glasgow at those council meetings, tell yer riders to ask for big Seamus Mackay, he looks after all the fine birds up there, he'll know what to do with the message."

Sean mòr calls out for his Gallóbhet outrider scouts to attend him. William quickly writes down two small notes and passes them over. Within moments, both Gallóbhet outrider scouts are spurring recklessly through the early evening for Crosshouse.

A few hours later, at their camp at the Loudoun hill, William and the commanders are discussing tactics, when Sean mòr approaches. "Ah'v just sent outriders away for ma bonnie Dregern Gallóglaigh and all o' the dispossessed folk they meet that can fight, ah'v said they're to join with us at the Loudoun hill as fast as they can muster." Faolán says, "Our riders will already be on their way down the west coast to do the same Wallace. Many will respond to the call, they may not come as one, but come they will." William says, "Aye, I've sent word into the Wolf and wildcats too." Stephen says, "So Wallace me boy, we're finally going to strike back at the bastards?" William replies, "Aye, we sure are, so let's get workin' on the Loudoun hill, for we've plenty to do." Everyone disperses to fulfill their given tasks, leaving William and Stephen alone, its then that William explains fully the conversations he has had with Sean mòr." Stephen, grinning as he wraps loose horse reigns tightly around his fists, says, "This has been a long time a' comin' Wallace." William sighs, "Aye, it's maybe been too long though Stephen, ah'v bided ma time deliberately, unsure about what to do if am bein' honest with yie, maybe because o' what happened at Invergarvane, ah dunno, but ahm thinkin' that if we don't do what we need to do now, then we're all well and truly fucked if we don't." Stephen grins, nudges William then winks at him, he says "Ah sure hope that our bonnie lassies have some undiscovered before now patience beyond belief Wallace, for ah'll be tinkin' to me'self we'll have much o' the explainin' to be doin' when we get back." William sighs, "Feck me Stephen, ahm not sure what welcome we'll get, though ahm sure Marion is goin' to kill me when we do get back."

Unexpectedly, Sean mòr approaches them with bowls of stovies, he hands them across, then he asks William a question, "Well Wallace, is this circumstance showin' itself to us by the grace o' Magda mòr, or is this just an opportunity?" William sups some stovies, then he lifts his head to look at the Loudoun hill, appearing to be embraced by a backdrop of an infinite svelte-like black heaven, infused by countless quicksilver stars. William says thoughtfully… "Circumstance or opportunity?" he smiles confidently, "Sean mòr, it's both…"

The Iron Briar Patch

On the banks and braes of Loudoun hill, the Gallóbhet have worked feverishly all through the night, digging and building traps for both horses and men. They continue their hard labours, while constructing their ambitious plan to ambush the English wagon train, now closing in on the densely forested surroundings. Knowing that they are heavily outnumbered, maybe even as much as three or more to one, does not deter the Scots from their zealous labours of causing a vast rock slip to spill from the east side of the Loudoun cliff face, in order to narrow even further, a section of the main traveller's route known locally as the Winny Wizzen gully. This ancient drove road passes below the Loudoun hill and is used as the only safe route to Ayr town coming from the southeast, then running northwest directly below the remains of an ancient frontier fort and series of defensive ditches, strategically built above a narrow blind curve on the drove road, making this particular location the most suitable site for a well-placed and concerted ambush against a much superior force.

Faolán's scouts are tasked to hunt down any outriders from the English train, while others ride fast to the Wolf and wildcat camp for more re-enforcements. Sean mòr has also sent riders out to his lair of the Dregern Gallóglaigh to bring back all warriors who could fight. Yet, despite the grit of the Gallóbhet, William knows that his small band of Scots are well outnumbered, and the English are more than a match for any fighting force in Christendom, no matter the fearlessness and fighting skills of the opposition. He also knows he needs more fighters of experience for this type of warfare if he is to have any chance of succeeding. But something tells him this is the right time, the right place. Meticulously, William surveys everything, the terrain, the woodlands, the Loudoun hill itself; he continually studies the pass, the surrounds and again the iconic hill, assessing where everyone is to be positioned. Suddenly he has a gut feeling that something is very wrong; something potentially catastrophic is missing in the overall picture for him.

Sean mòr enquires, "What's with yer face lookin' se' sour Wallace, does your bowels shift on their own at the thought of the coming days work?" William replies, "Naw, it's no' that Sean mòr, but I do know that what we're doing is no' going to be good enough. Blocking the front o' the train and then the back, piling rocks and flights down on top o' the English trapped in the middle, this will no' be enough, there might be too many to completely trap them, they'll maybe just as easily break out, then what, do we run, do we stand and fight? You tell me Sean mòr, what would we do then? For the English are no' fuckin' stupid, far from it, if we're going to do this, we've got to do it right... but there's just one last piece that's still missing for me and tearin' away at ma gut."

"You have no spears Wallace," says Jop, "if you are foolhardy enough to be taking on English cavalry, renowned as the finest horsemen in Europe, you'll have to fight them on foot, and for that you will need long spears to give yourself a glimmer of a chance. Slinger stones, rocks, arrows, bolts and bravery will ne'r be enough, believe me, I know how they fight, I reckon we'll be vastly outnumbered too, maybe we should really think this through and perhaps withdraw till we can at least match them in numbers." Sean mòr booms, "Give us our spartaxe and we won't need any more men Jop, for ah'll cut ma way through the bastards like the shite they are." William shakes his head forlorn, he says, "For the raw unquestionable bravery of you Sean mòr and all of the Gallóbhet, it cannae never be doubted, but courage will not be enough. The last time I tried this, I lost many friends and only I survived. I'll not kill my own people and do the work for the English myself… I just need time to be thinking this through." William sits on his hunkers and looks all around the terrain once more, desperately searching for something to give him hope.

"Don't be thinkin too much Wallace," says Sean mòr, "remember what ah told yie the other day, too much thinkin' can also be yer downfall, make a fuckin' decision."

After a while, William says, "Maybe this was not such a good plan after all and I agreed to this too quickly without enough rational thought, I was too easily spurred on by my own thoughts of vengeance and also by you Sean mòr, with your righteous convictions." Suddenly he notices something so simple, it convinces him immediately that the impossible could be possible, and Sean mòr may get his wish. William stands up, "Sean mòr, call all the Ceannards here to me now… I've had a thought." Sean, Jop and Stephen look curiously at their friend; something in the energy emitting from William, satisfies all of them he may have a thought worth listening to. Before long, all the Gallóbhet Ceannard stand in a circle beside William, eager to hear his plan and thoughts. "Stephen," he says, "send thirty o' our men into that lodge-pole coppice over there, and as fast as they can do it, cut down as many o' them that must be at least fist girth width and a length that takes two men to hold, and cut three or four poles for each man, then get the Gallóbhet to use their axes and dirks to needle point the narrow end of each lodge-pole, Stephen enquires, "What's yer plan?"

"My plan?" says William, "My plan is that there's got to be two men to handle each pole, we get them to angle the thick end of the pole into the earth so there's no give, when the English horse charge at us full tilt, which I reckon will be between twelve to fifteen abreast, we'll wait till they're almost on top of us and unable to stop, then, on my signal, the pole-men are to lever up the poles with the sharpened ends to the front, aim the points between the underbelly and throats of the charging horses, for it'll cause each horse or rider to be impaled or unsaddled, at that moment, our bowers are to power loose two or three flights into each man. When the poles are used, drop them and step the men back a pace to pick up the next pole, then do the same for the next charge, when all poles, horses and men are downed from the first few charges, they'll become fine obstacles for slowing down any further charges, which there will be, for slowin' them down will make them real easy targets for our slingers and bowyers." Jop says, "That may just do it for both their heavy and their light horse Wallace, trust me, I've examined the terrain around us, with the numbers we may expect to be here and will likely be attending upon the train, this is the one moment in time and the right place that this overall plan could really work for us."

"I knew it," exclaims William, "I knew that there was something missing, and I reckon we've found it... Stephen." Immediately Stephen moves away and speaks with some of the men, who turn and run at speed to carry out his orders; then he returns to the circle. Jop smiles, then he says, "When more waves of the English knight chargers rush forward, they'll be well hampered by the first waves we fell, that's good, and by leaving the first poles all asunder, this will definitely slow down the following charges and cause them to traverse the fallen knights and horses, if they don't, they'll be forced forward by following chargers and will slip and lose their footing on the bodies of their fallen companions and horses from the first attacks. And the lodge-poles, they'll easily get tangled about the horse's legs and hooves. It'll be absolute bloody chaos for the English knights down there, riderless horses will panic and be desperate to escape any way they can, but they can't, that'll add to the uncontrollable confusion for the English soldiery, and it'll be another source of great injury."

William grins as Jop speaks, for the English respect Jop as a master battle tactician, and equally as important, he knows all the tactics of the imperial English war machine. "Down inside the Winny Wizzen gully," says Jop, "once the English have spent their horsemen, by blocking them in simultaneously front and back, it will be their downfall. For there is nowhere for them to run, if we can muster enough bowyers placed along both the close flanks of the pass, the English will be leaderless and in complete disarray, it's only then and how you plan to use all your wits that will decide the outcome in the end." William ponders, "You said leaderless?"

"Yes," replies Jop, "Fenwick will most likely be travelling in the middle of the train, he will never be expecting an ambush, he won't be prepared." Stephen says, "Perfect, then me foin fella's, with all their men and foin horses bein' brought down and those big feckn poles scattered all over the bleedin' ground, it will sure cause mayhem amongst the English knights, and with them there so tight packed, our archers and slingers must be usin' everything at hand to launch a relentless fusillade upon them, even to be throwin' big fuckin' rocks at them." William says, "Just one more thing… I want all of our archers, spear-chucker's and our crossbowyer's to hurl everything they've got at their front-rank captains on foot, but first they're to take down their lead knights of distinction, all of them, all except that bastard Fenwick, he's mine." Sean mòr declares, "Aye, and all his gold and siller, its mine… eh, ours." Everyone in the circle laughs at Sean mòr's unique gesture of sharing 'his' newfound booty. The sound of laughter coming from the commanders, offers great inspiration to the men and women still frantically working the Loudoun hill to make it all possible.

"Wallace," says Jop with a broad smile, "I'm thinking that you may now have more than just a glimmer of hope this day." William grins, "So much more than hope Jop, as more folks arrive, we have over three thousand arrows and bolts already with us here, and the Gallóbhet are second to none at close quarter bowery, with three flights from every archer aimed at every knight and their foot-captains, I reckon our odds gain greatly before we get into them with sword, hammer, axe… and a vengeance."

"What do yie want me to do?" enquires Torrance, William replies, "Torrance, ah need you to put the order out for the Ceitherne to make sure there's enough cairns of throw rocks and sling shot placed all around the prominent heights of the Loudoun. Make it to affect that the smallest stone has the power to stun, stove or kill. We don't have fancy weapons like the English, but if we use what we have wisely, a rock in the face well struck, will match the most delicate of fancy ten-pound English maces." Torrance laughs, for his size and power he is a devastating slinger, William has witnessed the killing of many Normans at the hands of Torrance and his able slingers many years before in Ireland. Torrance says, "Ah can see that Stephen's men are downing the lodge-pole and sharpening the end points, and now yie're wantin' me to fetch the rocks off the Loudoun to the front line. Well, any man who brings nature to the defence of his land, has ma heart racing to get goin'... I'll prepare a stone feast the likes o' which these Sudrons will have never swallowed afore." Everyone laughs at the gallows humour, then Gormlaidh says, "What about this for a thought then Wallace, why don't we lay oversize boulders strewn all about the drove road, just big enough not to really be seen as an obstacle, but when they try to canter or charge over them, and ah'll make the spacing ever closer goin' forward, this will surely bring the horses down as the rocks beneath their feet roll or trip them?" William grins, "Do it Gormlaidh." William says, "Naw wait... Dig wee holes too, about knee deep."

"What, dig what? queries Gormlaidh, "dig holes?" William replies, "Aye, dig wee holes, knee deep. Dig them in between or behind the rocks and boulders, if the horse's miss the boulders, then the holes will be a nightmare for them as they trip, tumble or spook." William continues, "Stephen, I need you to gather at least a quarter of the crossbow bolts from all o' our Gallóbhet, bind them up as crows-feet, I want yie to stake them in the ground between the holes and the rocks, spreadin' them about as yie come forward towards our front line, do it in such a way that no man can walk fully through your iron plantin' without his foot getting' pierced through. Stake them ahead of the rock feast, no wait, start an arrow-head planting in there first, just a little way inside the rock feast, and make sure that all the arrowheads in front of us are slightly angled back towards the horse's legs or up into the soles o' their hooves, then plant the bolts after that." Stephen replies, "Pierce the frog and planter and yie kill a horse's heart. Aye Wallace, and I'll cover up and hide away all the heads with hair-grass, plant and fern too." Sean mòr grins, "Ah really do like yer style Wallace, rocks and holes, arrowheads and bolts, and that's before they reach us, and when or even if they do, it's a grim business to be put upon the poor auld horses. Yer head is sure on right this fine day Wallace, though we've no' got real crows-feet (Caltrops) with us, these make-do crows-feet o' yours will do us fine. Seven fingers and me will help lay down such a magic carpet, the feckn English will each be needing to be ridin' fuckin' Pegasus to make it cross our fancy iron briar patch."

Everybody laughs at Sean's humour, a much needed and welcome interjection from the heightened sense of excitement mixed with trepidation felt by everyone.

Those nearby hearing the banter are invigorated by a sense of timeless pride, feelings most ordinary men and women in extraordinary circumstances, will never experience nor ever understand in a lifetime, unless they have ever prepared for imminent battle. "I must warn you about something curious," says Jop, "There's a phenomenon that's present before a battle, that can overtake even the most experienced men of war that I think that yiez should know about." William enquires, "Aye, and what's that?" Jop continues, "Well, this might sound a wee bit witless to hear, but trust me, it happens. Sometimes even when men are directly ordered to simply walk in a single file, it can become the most confusing order if not delivered precisely and with a confidence in the outcome." William nods, for he knows this to be true from instinct and past experience. He also understands the importance of making all of his orders clear, concise and simple.

Sean mòr enquires, "So what's your point then?" Jop replies, "Every man and woman here this day, must obey their commanders without question or any delay, that, with the courage of the men and women who trust in their Commanders to carry out their given duties to the letter, is the only hope that this battle strategy will work."

Torrance enquires, "So, yie mean that we should beat down any who would show the slightest hesitation to obey our commands?" Jop replies, "Aye, or kill them immediately if needs be. Once we accept our duties to our Warlord, then nothing, and I mean absolutely nothing can be allowed to break with the chain of command, or all will be lost. On this we must be all agreed without favour, if not... then go home, for you're not prepared for war, nor ever will you be." William says, "Jop's right, though it sounds like we're just changing one oppressor for another, our own command, but for this to work, we only have one chance... are we agreed?"

Everyone nods positively that they will do what must be done. Sean mòr enquires, "And who's this Warlord yie speak about Jop?" A chorus of laughter erupts again... then they all look at William.

There is no reaction from William as he studies the faces of men and women who have witnessed all the cruelty that any man can inflict upon another. He ponders for a few moments, then he says, "Before now I would have told you all to fuck off, for I'm not your whatever yiez think I am. But I will say this to all of you here and now, from the youngest Ceitherne who stands with us on the Loudoun hill, to the trust you have all placed in me, by your faith in my judgment to win this day for us.... yiez can all call me whatever the fuck yiez like, for that title so dearly yearned by some, many perhaps, is to me of no greater merit than the unknown soldier who does not baulk nor hesitate on the front-line. So, I'll do my duty by you fella's this day, will you all do yours by me?" Everyone gives a great rousing cheer. William smiles wryly, for he was expecting some resistance to his impromptu outspoken thoughts of leadership, even though the coming battle is still causing an air of uncertainty to flow through his mind. Stephen slaps him on the shoulder and says, "Well me newfound Warlord of the Wolf and wildcats, what's to do for us next?" William replies, "Wait Stephen…" Turning to face his 'commanders,' William enquires, "You all know what you have to do, are yiez all well ready to do it?" Everyone replies positively and clasps each other's hands with an iron grip of fortitude, then they begin dispersing to ready the final pieces of the ground plan for the approaching English baggage train. William says to Sean mòr, "Prepare our combined force Sean mòr, tell them this is the one chance to strike at the English and to do so without mercy, no quarter, for it's the only way to ensure that we win this day." Sean replies, "Aye Wallace, you're right there for sure, I'll give everyone the order, no mercy, no quarter."

"Stephen, Gormlaidh?" says William, "I'm going to say this once more to yiez, Stephen, I really need you to make double-sure that all of our bolts are well placed in the ground and pointing straight up to pierce the frog. Make it so that the English horse will be virtually on top of our men at the front before their knights realise what's happening, if they see the bolt or arrowhead traps too early, they may avert and regroup, you have to make fuckin' certain that it must be too late for them to turn away by the time they realise it. Plant our flanks too, so that not one single English knight can charge up the verges to reach us without impaling the hooves of their horse." William continues, "Gormlaidh, I want you to make sure that all the barbed hunt arrows are buried deep in the ground notch-end first, be certain the points are all facing in the direction of the incoming English horses, for we need to catch their forelegs as they run into them, with something as simple as a keen sharpened arrowhead, angle it right and it will shove up hard and easily rip into the horses legs and tear their ligaments, veins and tendons. I need it to be that the charging horses hit the rocks and holes first, arrowheads next; then the bolts last, all placed like a welcome path to our front where the lodge-pole men will stand firm. Once those first knights are fallen, we'll have that one chance we need." Stephen and Gormlaidh confirm their orders, then they leave to inform their Ceannard. William continues; "Sean mòr, I reckon that the length of the Winny Wizzen might no' just be enough to trap the English proper, some may escape, or they might try to outflank us coming from the rear, I need you to make sure all of our crossbowyers sighted above the English, are covering everything from the middle, so that they may sight front or rear at will. And make sure our longbowyers up in the old fort ditches, are prepared to launch a relentless broadside into any flanking movement, otherwise, keep a torrent ready to loose at the English vanguard when they're almost on top of us at the front, it's imperative for ma timing they keep a sharp eye on our front ranks, when their leading squadrons strike our pole guard…"

"It's called a schiltrom," says Jop, "That's what you call it when you place many spearmen together in a tight defensive block, a schiltrom."

Sean mòr laughs, "Aye, that sounds about right Jop."

"So Wallace?" enquires Torrance, "where else do I come into all o' this?" William replies, "You stand beside me to ma left with the north-face schiltrom. When the pile-up of horses and knights so thickens at our feet and Hayde securely seals off the English retreat at the back end, when the time is right, Jop, you take over as the commander of the north-front with ma kith and kin, I'll lead half o' our Gallóglaigh down their right flank, you Torrance, lead the other half of our Gallóglaigh down their left flank, once past the crows-feet, bolt and rock feast, we turn and get into the middle o' them to block any more o' the English coming forward."

"And what about me?" enquires Stephen, William replies, "Stephen, you're wounds are still well fucked from the Dunbar battle, so this is what I want from you and Gormlaidh, I need all o' the Irish Gallóbhet to bide their time, ah know it will be difficult just to be standing watching, but yie must wait till Torrance and me outflank the English to hit them hard in the centre, I'll try to give yiez a signal, if no' then wait till the fighting in there is at its peak, that's when I'll need your braw fella's to run down the braes and get right into them, I want it to appear like your a fresh force arriving to back us up. We need to get all o' their soldiers and cavalry well trapped, not one of them should be able to escape. And one more thing, just before I lead our folks into the fray, before ah leave, Sean mòr, you're to take the Dregern Gallóglaigh away from the north-face, traverse the back of the Loudoun well out of sight, then join the fight with Hayde and seal off the back end of the Winny Wizzen, then I need you, Hayde and all your men to fight forward to meet with us in the centre."

Sean mòr says, "This sounds feckn good Wallace. The hardest thing to defend against, is when you're caught in a trap and being attacked from all sides at different times." William replies, "Exactly, they won't know for certain at any time that they outnumber us, for their heads will be so busy spinning like spindle-spools and looking all directions at once." Sean mòr's piercing eyes light up, "Ahm likin' even more yer way o' thinking Wallace. So me boy, yie want me to leave and then attack the rear o' their baggage train wie' Hayde after we've stalled them up here at the front, but just before yie leave to hit them from both sides in the centre?"

Upon seeing William grinning, is all the confirmation the notorious Dregern Gallóbhet chief needs. William continues, "Sean mòr, initial success for us depends greatly on Hayde being able to force the wagon drivers and followers up into their rearguard, to cause them as much chaos as he can. When you join with Hayde, I need yiez to wipe out the English rearguard, do what you need to do to achieve this, use your finest hablars, spearmen and spartaxe warriors. It's vital that yiez must be creating much of a slaughter back there, take no prisoners, none, for I need the English to believe you're a fresh force that's coming in at their rear with veteran reinforcements. Then, with Torrance and me attacking their centre, and with Stephen and Gormlaidh attacking from the hillside flanks, they won't know what the fuck has hit them." Sean mòr grins with glee; then rubs his massive, calloused hands together.

"What's up Sean mòr?" enquires William, "Yie look as though yie've found a King's ransom, and yer keeping it for yourself." Sean replies, "Wallace, yie could o' sprung from ma very own loins, such is the joy you gift to me auld black heart. Consider your commands done, really well fuckin' done…" William smiles, then he continues, "One last thing I need to be heard sayin'. I want all o' the young Ceitherne bowyers and slingers to be standing behind me. When we fuck the English both back and centre, those left at the front wie Jop, must make sure the English can no longer move forward because of their own fallen from the, eh, the Schiltrom…"

Everyone smiles as William continues, "Stephen, Gormlaidh, when the fight initially opens up and before yie leave, I need yiez to command our young Ceitherne butchers and meat skinners to be huggin' each flank nearest to our front line, while we hold off the English host. When and as soon as the English knights start to fall, it's then yiez send in our Ceitherne, yie know what to say to them, they have to get in there fast, do the business, then get out just as quick, they must be out before the next English charge falls upon us." Gormlaidh replies, "Those youngblood Ceitherne butchers and meat skinners are all orphans from the Pact massacres Wallace, they'll know their tasks and will relish an opportunity to carry them out, wie a vengeance." William nods then he says, "Again, when the time's right, I'll be leavin' yiez to flank then hit the bastards hard in the centre with Torrance, that's when you Stephen and you Gormlaidh move to the higher flanks to do yer business, Sean and Hayde will lead the rear force, and you Jop, you'll command and hold the north face... Are we clear?"

Everyone roars in rousing agreement.

"This is a good plan Wallace." says Jop, "You'll have the English knights and commanders in total disarray by us fighting them on all four fronts..."

"It's more than that I'm hoping for Jop, there may yet be a good return to our call, for I see there's fightin' folk and others arriving all the time, and how many is yet to arrive from the Wolf and wildcats and Dregern? But even so, when Stephen and Gormlaidh appear on the field. I want it to appear as though they are our last flush, but it won't be, Faolán's Gallóbhan will be waiting to make a final charge on horseback to get straight intae them and take out as many of their mounted horse that's left standing."

William pauses to look at the stern faces of his commanders and Ceannard, then he says, "There is one last but vitally important thing that I need as a constant, and this is to you Stephen and you Gormlaidh in particular, I need yiez both to be watchin' the charging knights closely at all times, when you see their horses are not on the charge towards us, I need yiez to make damn sure that every single spare bolt, flight and slinger brings down their archers, for they'll no' have any cover... and if those lethal bastards manage to get a grip and regroup, they could thwart everything we've planned so far, for they're deadly archers and fierce killers with those longbows." William enquires, "Are there any questions from yiez?" Everyone grins, but they make no reply, for the men and women of the proud Gallóbhet chieftains and Ceannard Garda, are all well contented with William's plans, communicated back to him more by line of sight, than any words they could ever find to say. William bows his head in respect of that, and all reciprocate, whereupon the circle quickly breaks up and everyone eagerly sets about their given tasks in preparation for the forthcoming battle, with a renewed sense of vigour and enthusiasm.

"Faolán?" says William. "Aye Wallace," replies Faolán "what is it yie require o' me?" William says, "Will yie walk with me Faolán, for I'm needin' to defer here to your better judgment." Faolán enquires, "What's bothering yie then Wallace?" William replies, "I understand that if I'd said anything back there that wouldn't have any chance at all, then I reckon there's only you, Sean mòr and Jop who have the experience o' worth that would have pointed it out, but yiez didn't..." Faolán says, "It is a real good plan Wallace, really good, though much of it may depend on who and how many rallies to our call, but if we can rally even half the numbers the English have into the play, then what you propose can be done, ah have faith in yie Wallace, so have faith in yourself." William is surprised by the unexpected compliment and also her advice, and though he doesn't show it, he still has nagging doubts.

"I want you to thoroughly analyse ma battle plan Faolán, find any faults or flaws, then come back to me as soon as yer ready with your own thoughts. Also, I need to know what yie think is the best play most suited to your own command structures and way o' fightin' for I need you to have complete command o' your own force o' Gallóbhan and all o' their personal Ceitherne..." For a single moment, Faolán looks at William curiously, but before she can reply, William says, "Faolán, I know o' your history, I've seen you command in action, and remember that day down at the plains of Dalry, well my respect…" Faolán interrupts him, "Wallace, yer plan is like Sean mòr sez, and he's a master o' the trap, it's a real good one under the circumstances. We all knew in our hearts, that some day we would have to strike at the English before we are all slaughtered, like those we love who have gone before us, well, that some day is now this day, so I'll take your words with me, then we'll talk later."

At that, Faolán walks away, but it is not the forthcoming battle to the fore in her mind, she knows she must speak with William soon about what happened in Lanark to the Braidfuites, and the defilement brought upon Marion, Brannah and Brìghde, though something is telling her now is not the time, but she is not sure. The usually stoic and decisive Faolán, is torn about what she should say and when she should say it. Watching Faolán as she approaches her Gallóbhan commanders, William, completely unaware of her troublesome thoughts, thinks that the Gallóbhan Aicé has no real sense of the soaring confidence she has inspired in him by her words. After a few moments deep in thought about the forthcoming confrontation, William turns to scan the ambush location once more, believing that now they have a real fighting chance. As he looks up to the Loudoun hill, William sees a signal coming from lookouts, indicating that there are horsemen fast approaching.

The signal simultaneously calls for everyone to get into his or her strategic position and well hidden from sight. Jop and Stephen watch the grit and pitch everyone is applying to William's plan, his attendance seemingly has been in every part of the Loudoun hill, creating a feverish excitement amongst the Gallóbhet, complimenting the adrenalin that is coursing wildly through the veins of everyone. This adrenalitic energy surges through all the Gallóglaigh on the Loudoun Hill like a lightning strike, pulsing and charging their very souls. As everyone disperses to their given positions, Jop speaks with Stephen. "I could see that Wallace has a natural ability of employing a very precise battle strategy Stephen, when I listened to him earlier and heard all that he had to say, I do believe that he offers us more than just a workable plan, I reckon that if we can bring enough men to the cause, and soon, then I believe our chances to win the day are more than fair. It would also seem that his ability of seeing in his minds eye the martial geometry required for the fight, has all of the Gallóglaigh captain's and their men in high spirits too." Stephen replies, "Aye, he's a real good man Jop, and yet here was me thinking all o' this time, that it was goin' to be you who would be laying out what our plan was to be, you with all o' that fine knowledge and experience bouncing about that head o' yours?"

"I would have done so," says Jop, "but Wallace there, I actually believe that he saw much more than I did. And for no real experience in the fine arts of war, what he has given already to this coming fight, is much more than just a chance that we may win. By enthusing everyone to do his bidding and if they do it well, I believe we will surely win so much more than just this day." Stephen looks up at the Loudon hill, then he says. "I believe in him like a brother Jop, I reckon everyone here does." Jop says, "It would seem the only fellow needing convincing of that, is the man himself."

Smiling wryly, Stephen replies, "He will Jop, for he has a blood tax to collect." As Stephen and Jop go about their duties, the Loudoun hill soon appears as a beautiful scenic wilderness where no-one can be seen, as the Scots retire into their hidden positions, prepared for the fighting to come.

Birds sing, butterflies and bees flutter about the heads of flowers, cows can be heard yawning away in the distance, any other day would see this transformation as a scene from the garden of Eden. But for everyone who waits for the English to approach, it also creates an impatient nervous eternity in each individual's thoughts, their minds race, thinking of what they will do, how they will do it. Nerves and pulsing excitement, fusing with the absolute reality of gruesome wounding or death, heightens everyone's senses.

Suddenly, the lookout who had signalled a few moments earlier, is now indicating that many horse riders are fast approaching and about to appear. The tension is heightened when many horsemen suddenly come storming over the Loudoun hill behind William and the waiting Gallóbhet. A great cheer goes up when they recognise Kerlie appearing at the head of about one hundred well-armed warriors riding in behind him.

As the heavily armed squadrons of fresh Gallóbhet arrive, William takes in a deep breath of refreshing air, then he notices dismounting with all the new arrivals, his kinsmen Adam, Richie and Simon Wallace, with the three sons of Sir Richard Wallace, who have also come to do battle. He also sees alongside them, his old friends Cleland, Robert Boyd and more of his kinfolks, the Wallace's from Galloway. Accompanying all these Wallace chieftains is Eddie óg, who is already dismounted and running towards him, wearing a great oversized hauberk with his léine sleeves flying freely in the wind. William notices Eddie óg is clutching a bulky hemp sack. "Ah'v brought you this uncle…" exclaims a breathless Eddie. William takes the sack from Eddie óg and opens it. A broad grin sweeps across his face as he pulls out his grandfather's old battle helm. William smiles, then he scrimmages Eddie óg's hair by way of thanks. Kin and friends alike all warmly greet each other in the old fort remains on the braes of the Loudoun hill. William is jubilant upon seeing this gathering of his own kinfolks too, all willing and able to stand and fight against English tyranny. Many of the other Gallóbhet are also joined by their kinfolks, sending their already heightened morale soaring even higher, then William notices some old friends approaching him.

"Kerlie… Blair, you're all here too?" exclaims William.

The friends warmly embrace each other and vigorously shake hands as Sean mòr approaches with a grim countenance, "Wallace, the English baggage train has been spotted no' se' very far from here." Then Sean mòrs face breaks into a big grin. "Wait, there's more, for the news just gets even better, the feckn English don't have any outriders or point scouts to be seen. It looks like Faoláns Gallóbhan have taken well care o' them." William exclaims, "Fuck, are yie sure about this, so where's the main body now?" Sean mòr replies curtly, "Of course ahm fuckin' sure Wallace, anyways, they're all travelling from the direction of the southeast and comin' directly towards us, apparently they're prancin' and preenin' as though it's a summertime fair, with their bright flags and bunting a' wavin' wie' all of them dressed se' fancy coutered in bright clothes. And get this, they're only wearing their shiny fuckin' state armour… the feckn eejits, their no' wearing full battle armour."

"How many do yie reckon is in the baggage train? enquires William. Sean mòr replies, "Ah dunno, ma scouts said there must be about three hundred or thereabouts?" There's a long pause then Sean mòr continues. "We've got what, maybe two-hundred or so, but all o' us are fit, fine and itchin' for a good fight at last…" William exclaims, "Fuck me, at least three hundred o' them yie say, that's still heavy odds for sure, bigger than ah thought… How long do yie reckon we have to prepare before they get here?" Sean mòr replies, "About the same time as it takes to roast a fat chook on a slow burnin' fire ah would reckon." William immediately calls for all the Ceannard and chiefs to gather once more to confirm their plan of attack. All the new volunteers are distributed as per their skills to each section of the little "Army." Kerlie and his fresh warriors from the Wolf and wildcat camp, run fast about the Loudoun hill, carrying and distributing bundles of the feared long handled spartaxe, long-darts, javelins and ring-spears, placing the weapons where they would be picked up and best used. William watches the reinforcements in awe and in admiration, for many of them are wounded survivors from the battle of Dunbar; some are obviously still in pain from their healing wounds, but as they all finally disperse into their battle positions, another small group of riders approach from the west of Loudoun hill.

"Faolán..." exclaims William. Fifty of Faolán's fighting Gallóbhan come riding fast and foot-sure along the high goat road towards the old fort. Immediately upon their arrival, they quickly dismount. William sees that Faolán and her fighting women are all bristling with light weapons, horse-bows, short ring-spears, javelins, long-darts and in particular, their notorious short curved hand swords and the notorious sgian cuartha they use in close combat.

"Wallace..." says Faolán. As the two friends meet, they warmly embrace, then Faolán pulls away and places a hand on William's shoulder; unusually, she pulls him close in a tight embrace. William looks over her shoulder at Blair and Stephen, both shrug their shoulders curiously, as Faolán is not known for her affectionate embrace of any man. William pulls back and looks into her eyes. For the second time since they first met, he sees the absolute beauty in Faolán as a woman, there is something he feels emitting from her that is exquisitely feminine, rather than the warrior, but there is also something else there too, something is wrong. Faolán also studies William, for she knows in her heart what she must say to him. William speaks first, "Faolán... I would be honoured if you have thought of our plans for this day, if you think them right, then place the Gallóbhet where you believe they would fly best. Ever since the day I stood in your Sparr on the hillside of Saint John's plain, I learned vital lessons from you, and I truly understood as much that day about the disciplines of a battle plan as I've ever gained by experience in my lifetime." Faolán is caught off guard by William's thoughtful compliment; she is lost for words, but she quickly regains her composure, then she replies, "Wallace, I would be honoured to stand by your side this day with my own Sparr, for its now time for Eochaidh Gunn and Fiónlaidh to deservedly come to the fore and lead the Gallóbhan. It is they who must now converse with your Ceannard."

Faolán falters, William notices something is wrong, but then she says, "Wallace, I have words that I must surely be parting with you." William looks deeply into the eyes of Faolán, but she averts her eyes to look for Eochaidh and Fiónlaidh. Sean mòr knows in his heart what Faolán is about to part to William. He walks over, then he says, "Faolán, I'll tell Eochaidh and Fiónlaidh of our plans." Faolán nods, then Sean mòr, Eochaidh and Fiónlaidh leave to discuss the placement of the Gallóbhan on the Loudon hill.

"What is it that ails yie so Faolán?" enquires William. But Faolán does not yet reply, instead she turns away and glances at Stephen, who is also curious as to her demeanor. She says "Stephen, Wallace, will yiez walk with me awhile to where we may talk together, alone, for I have something that I must be telling to yiez that you both should know." William and Stephen look at each other, quite bemused, but they obediently follow Faolán till they are far enough away from any who may overhear, then they sit by the Irvine burn that flows gently past the Loudoun hill. The watching Gallóbhet don't need to hear the words that are being spoken, for such is their acute reading of body language, they already know all the detail responsible for Faolán's unusual behaviour. The three companions sit together awhile, with only the sounds of birds singing in the treetops and the gentle babbling noises coming from the tributary of the river Irvine, flowing gently on its way to the Irish sea.

Sean mòr returns and stands with John Blair, Jop, Torrance, Kerlie and Eddie óg. He speaks with John Blair, "Do yie know what it is that Fallon speaks about Blair?" John Blair replies, "Aye Sean mòr, sadly I do…" Torrance enquires, "What is it, what has Faolán to say to them that must take Wallace and Stephen away from their course of thought and duties?" Sean mòr shakes his head. Blair puts his hand to his chin, as everyone is now focussed on the little group, watching closely every little detail of their body language. Gormlaidh joins the waiting commanders. He enquires, "What's happenin', what's Faolán sayin' down there to Wallace n' Stephen?" Sean mòr simply shakes his head forlorn once more, then he says, "News o' Lanark's bad tidings."

"What's that?" enquires Torrance, "what bad tidings?"

"Fuck, that's right," says Sean mòr, "You two were on the boats to fetch Moray, yiez wouldn't know." Torrance looks at Sean mòr and Blair, "What th' fuck is happenin', what don't we know, what is Faolán sayin' to Wallace and Stephen?" No one says anything, eventually Sean mòr replies, "Young Brian Braidfuite has been hung for sedition by the Sherriff of Lanark and the English soldiery also tortured Sir Hugh beyond any repair, and ah have to tell yiez this too, the fuckin' English soldiers have plied much rapine upon

Marion, Brannah and Brìghde." Torrance and Gormlaidh are both visibly shaken by this unwelcome news, Torrance exclaims, "Fuck naw…" Blair says, "Aye, and there's more bad news, Wallace and Marion have lost their unborn child, then Brìghde lost her and Stephen's unborn a few days later. When I was in Lanark just a few days ago, I found out that Brannah had bled out from her ordeal and had passed away soon after, aye, it's bad, bad times for us all…"

No-one has any words to say as they look down the hill to their three companions. "Is it Brìghde?" enquires Stephen curiously, Faolán replies, "I must tell you of Marion, Brìghde and Brannah, for no man who knows of this, dare speak these words to you both, for I and only the Gallóbhan could tell you of such things."

For everyone that's watching the scene play out down by the old oak tree, time appears to stand still as they wait patiently for something to happen, anything that will break the tension now building up amongst the gathered warriors standing on the Loudoun braes. After a few more tension-filled moments, both Stephen and William stand up and look despairingly at the sky. William clasps his hands behind his head and walks away from Faolán; while Stephen simply sinks to his knees and squats, showing no other signs of reaction to what Faolán had just said to them. Everyone watches William closely as he walks over to a great oak tree to look up at the boughs and branches. Sean mòr says, "That's the tree where Wallace's uncle Malcolm was flayed alive then murdered by that bastard Fenwick." Stephen walks across the glade and puts his arm around William's shoulders. Faolán walks over too; then they appear to console each other. Eochaidh appears and rides over towards them, dragging a spare horse behind her. She halts and speaks with Faolán urgently, who quickly mounts her horse, then they both ride off at speed, leaving William and Stephen alone with their thoughts, while news of Faolán's report quickly spreads throughout the little Scots army gathered on the banks and braes of the Loudoun hill. Suddenly two scouts come galloping at speed up the drove road of the Winny Wizzen. Strategically they avoid all the traps set in place for the English chargers, it is not long before they pull to a halt beside Sean mòr; they dismount quickly and speak with him urgently. Sean mòr turns to look down the hillside at William and Stephen. He calls out to Eddie óg, "Ride fast on your hablar and be tellin' Wallace that…" Eddie óg impatiently waits for Sean mòr to finish his sentence, he enquires brusquely, "Tell Wallace what Sean mòr?" with his deep black piercing eyes, Sean mòr scrutinises Eddie óg; then he mutters, "Go an' tell Wallace that Fenwick and the English baggage train, they are nigh upon us…"

Winny Wizzen

Under the shelter of a broad leaf forest canopy, an idyllic little waterfall flows into a naturally formed pool, before overflowing and disappearing into a small river. Four young women, appearing to be not much more than in their twentieth summers, bathe and cavort naked in the pool, splashing water and laughing without a care in the world. One of the women, seemingly tired of the frivolity, gets out of the pool to sit at the waters edge, there she begins to lather creamy cur na ré into her skin. Curiously, she hears the bray and whinnying of horses nearby, she silently signals to the others, who pause their gaiety and look around the dense forestry to source where the horses may be located, then they notice a short distance away through the trees, a young knight and four squires, all sitting mounted and entirely motionless on a forest pathway. The five horsemen appear to be smitten and in awe as they gaze down upon the nakedness of the four young women, who glance at each other and simply giggle.

The horsemen are quite taken aback by this unexpected moment of Elysian serenity; they smile at each other knowingly, then they begin to walk their horses slowly down towards the poolside to where the young women stand, thigh-high deep and naked to the world. The young Knight and his squires pull their horses to a halt beside clothing that's been carelessly discarded by the young women, who are now modestly attempting to hide their female charms, but as the women turn away, they continue to eye-tease their newfound guests. The young woman kneading with the cur na ré, smiles at the knight, who smiles back by return. He takes off his helmet and looks to his friends, then amusingly, he turns and winks at the women, they all smile when they see his exotic bronzed Teutonic features.

A younger woman in the pool speaks out to the handsome knight. "Why sir knight… you've caught us so unexpectedly in all of Gods grace, with us as naked now as the very day we were born."

The young knight, tall with a toned physique, dark smoldering eyes, long silken jet-black hair and a well-coiffed wispy beard, quickly dismounts and throws his reigns carelessly over a nearby bough, then, grinning with delight, he slowly removes his heavy riding gauntlets and proceeds to walk confidently down towards the pools edge, whereupon he holds out his hands with an obvious chivalric kindness of intent, demonstrating to the young woman who had spoken to him, that his actions hold no threat towards her, other than to assist her safely out of the pool. Freely, the lubricious girl abandons all modesty as she slowly sweeps her long auburn tresses away from her face; she reaches out, as their hands touch, their eyes meet… Instantly a spark of intense excitement courses between the two young strangers, as though both are long-familiar lovers attending a forbidden lustful tryst. The handsome young knight eagerly leans forward and helps her from the pool.

Once safely on the riverbank, she immediately pulls him close to her nakedness, whereupon she sensually presses her lithe body up against his. The young knight looks joyfully up towards the light blue skies, then feels her warm sweet breath gently caress his neck…"Oh, Mon diue, douce jeune femme."

exclaims the handsome young knight, "Mon pauvre cœur endolori…" The young woman appears surprised. She quips, "Aha… so uze are all bein' Norman fellas are yiez?" The young knight replies, "No m'lady, we're English." Smiling, he continues, "But I shall say this to you my pretty, this moment can only be for the language of love." Giggling, the young woman reaches out and begins to stroke his long jet-black silken hair with the back of her fingers, all the while gazing alluringly into his eyes. The attraction is highly charged between the two, then, with a cheeky smile, she deftly unties his braies and gently slips her hand inside to caress and encourage his manhood. Meanwhile, the young knight's companions are eagerly scouring the nearby woodlands for any more beautiful nymphs, who may be hiding away in order to protect their modesty, but they find no others.

Returning their gaze towards the pool, they see that the two young women still in the pool, quite unashamed in their naked beauty, wade across to a shallow dip in the riverbank then climb out, they then wander playfully towards the Englishmen, sauntering around trees, stroking boughs and branches with an air of absolute sensual abandon, akin to mischievous woodland sprites as they approach the mounted squires. The appealingly sybaritic young women begin to stroke and caress the horse-leathers and firm saddle horns of the squire's horses, arousing and teasing the Englishmen with affectionate and inveigling little glances. One of the young women flashes her dark hazel eyes at a handsome squire in particular, she giggles then she places a finger gently to her lips: intentionally seducing the squire with her willful sensual movements. The squire becomes a little flushed and is obviously ensorcelled when he notices that two of the women are now holding each other passionately, then they lightly brush their lips together in a long and sensual kiss. Another woman twirls her flame-coloured tresses seductively then she runs her fingers slowly down to and over her erect nipples, she speaks in a sultry voice to one young squire, so obviously taken by her beauty.

"Why Sir knight, does our base nakedness and feminine wiles stir a manly fire within your loins? Is that what's causing you to flush so with such hot-blooded desire, or it may be that you have a yearning to be pleasured while seeing me this way?" Stammering, the squire replies, "I… I'm no knight m'lady, I'm but a lowly squire…" The young woman laughs heartily; she looks up at the squire and says to him, "That's good to hear me fine young squire, for I sure am no lady."

The apparent consternation of the squire amuses the young woman as she reaches up and strokes the inside of his thigh, she sees that her sensual taunts are causing his cheeks to flush with colour. His blue eyes, fair complexion and locks of long blond hair protruding from his helmet, inspire the young woman to reach up and lightly stroke his face. The squire tentatively leans over and gently cups her breasts; the silken alabaster texture of her skin, sends waves of intense pleasure surging through his body. Though he is still a little nervous and apprehensive; he looks to his friends, who eagerly urge him on. The squire deftly removes his helmet and smiles at the woodland sprite, while she displays quite openly an expression of intense excitement and anticipation. As he prepares to dismount, a gentle mist of blood gracefully falls upon the face of the young woman, as a hunt-arrow pierces the squire's eye and exits through the back of his skull, simultaneously another arrow skewers the side of his head, tumbling the squire silently from his horse, the young woman reaches out, grabs and keeps a firm grip of the horse's reigns, while whispering zip, zip-zipping ripples of a deadly arrow fusillade flies overhead, immediately striking down the other three English squires. More flights of arrows are mercilessly burying themselves deep into the Englishmen before their bodies hit the ground. Suddenly, as though appearing from out of the very trees that shelters them, Gallóbhan' rush from their hides and begin to stab and slash at the wounded Englishmen about their eyes, throat and groin, ripping at them like frenzied wildcats with their infamous sgian cuartha, the claw-like curved daggers of the fearless Gallóbhan.

Meanwhile, the knight standing by the idyllic whirlpool is stunned by the speed of what has happened. He mistakenly moves to shelter the young woman he is with from what he believes to be brigands and robbers, he turns to protect her, only to be viciously slashed across the neck by a sgian cuartha held by his naked lover to be, simultaneously she pulls firmly on his genitals as her blade sweeps down and easily slices everything off at the base of his stomach… For a moment, he simply stares at her in utter disbelief, she smiles back at him coyly; then, with the sgian cuartha in her other hand, she mercilessly slices deep across his throat to open up his jugular. The young knight can only gasp blood as he desperately grabs at his throat. In vain, he tries to plead with the young woman for help, but she is devoid of any empathy or a scintilla of emotion. His expression is now more of shock than disbelief as he gazes at his own blood pulse-spray outwards. He glances pathetically at the young woman, for a brief moment she looks into eyes, eyes that cry out by terrified expression, "Why…"

The horror-struck knight looks down at his bloody groin; he shakes his head in despair as he staggers forward then falls to his knees on the riverbank. The woodland sprite simply watches him in silence as he gets up and stumbles about, desperately trying to flee. He turns from her and tries in vain to scramble away and escape from this hadean nightmare, but his throat and groin are painfully pumping away his lifeblood, weakening him and causing him to stagger about clumsily. Distressed and gasping for air, he reaches out to lean against a tree then glances at the young woman with his confused pleading eyes. Suddenly two arrows strike him high in the chest; another rips straight through his jaw and embeds into the tree beside him, he staggers forward and tumbles into the whirlpool. More Gallóbhan appear and quickly drag away the bodies of the dead Englishmen deep into the woodland undergrowth, some still twitching in their death throes. Two of the naked women pull the dying young knight out of the bloody pool and drag him away into the woodlands, while another Gallóbhan gently hushes all the spooking horses; then they too are disappeared, all the while, the woodland stream babbles and murmurs as it tumbles gently over water-worn stones and boulders, slowly washing away the blood expended from the young English knight. Soon, the idyllic pool becomes crystal clear once more. Noticeably, the harmonic cacophony of nature's musical innocence returns to the small theatre of bloody murder. Birds begin to sing their choral song as leaves rustle in synchronicity high above in the treetops.

The beautiful glade of sprites in the ancient forest basking serenely in the presence of the Loudoun hill, returns to its paradisal peaceful place in nature's order, as though the unfortunate Englishmen had never ever existed.

Suddenly Faolán rides in and halts beside the four naked women. As she passes over their war garb, she enquires, "A fitting end for the Sudron's Fiónlaidh?" A satisfied Fiónlaidh smiles then she replies, "Any other time and that handsome young knight could have made for some great lusty breedin'... Eochaidh, what dyie think?" Eochaidh curses while pulling on her léine, "Fuck them all dead." She spits on the ground, "I hate every single one o' those English bastards for what they've done to me and mine." Fiónlaidh says, "It was the best way to get all of them quick Faolán, we did it fine and well to make sure that we secured everything they carried with them." A Gallóbhan dressing nearby, smiles and says, "I enjoyed that, but why the naked play?" Faolán replies, "A fair thought, we could just as easily have had them caught cold in an ambush, but if even one had been allowed to escape or if a horse had gotten loose, that could've potentially warned the English o' our presence hereabouts, then they could o' prepared themselves and everything would have been undone, but to offer most men the opportunity to make love rather than war…"

"Fiónlaidh, Eochaidh," continues Faolán, "before we get back to the Loudon hill, you and your Ceitherne must go through all of those Englishmen's clothing, satchels, purses and saddlebags, they're likely to have been carrying important information for that de Percy fella' to Ayr town that we could use. Be thorough, go through everything, for it's vital that you don't miss anything at all." Two of the young Ceitherne who had been bathing with Fiónlaidh and Eochaidh earlier, bring forward two large black cobs. Just as Fiónlaidh and Eochaidh are about to mount, another Gallóbhan comes riding fast into the glade and pulls up beside them. Almost breathless, "Faolán," she gasps, "I've got an urgent message from Wallace, he says that he needs you by his side… right now, the English baggage train is gaining real close to our positions." Before departing the glade, Fiónlaidh issues orders to the younger Ceitherne to ransack everything the Englishmen wore and carried with them for any useful information. Faolán and her two loyal companions turn their horses away quickly then spur to ride fast and furious; they then traverse at great speed through the dense Loudoun Forest, meting out harsh encouragement upon their horses, till finally, they arrive by the side of Wallace and quickly dismount.

"Faolán," says William, "the English train will be here soon; did yie get to any of their scouts?" Faolán smiles at Fiónlaidh and Eochaidh, she enquires, "Did we get any scouts?" Fiónlaidh grins then replies, "Aye Wallace, we sure got them." Faolán turns to speak with her two faithfull Ceannard, "Fiónlaidh, Eochaidh, you have drawn for us the first blood tax o' this day, let it no' be your last. Now it's your time to lead our Gallóbhan and Bhàn Sìhd into battle as their Aicés... this is my gift to you."

Eochaidh and Fiónlaidh reply simultaneously, "Our lives are our gift... to you all."

Without further ado, they both hastily mount their horses then spur at speed towards their given positions behind the craggy braes of the Loudon hill. Faolán stands beside William with two of her young Ceitherne, while another takes away her horse. She enquires, "What's your plan Wallace?" William replies curtly, "We wait..."

Stephen, Blair, Sean mòr, Torrance, Gormlaidh, Jop, Faolán and two of her Sparr, now stand sentinel beside William, blocking the narrowest part of the drover's road that passes below the braes of the Loudoun hill. Silent and patiently they wait, akin to statuesque heroes from some mythical fable, all the while remaining extremely focussed on the blind curve of the drove road, less than a thousand paces ahead of them. A piercing shrill warning is heard breaking the silence, like a hawk calling danger to a laying mate, signalling that the English train has now entered the Winny Wizzen. "Soon, it will begin..." whispers William. John Blair utters nervously. "I... I'll pray for us." Torrance quips, "Yie'd be better prayin' for the fuckin' Sudrons Blair, for it's them that's leavin this earth, no' us." Stephen says, "I'll be thankin' yie for that Blair, but I'll be prayin' me'self to the most divine o' mothers, our bonnie Magda mòr. For it's herself now to be lookin' after us, holdin' and protectin' us in her bosom, that we may all be warm bloodied by the end of this day..."

William, almost oblivious to the various deity prayers being said all around him, watches the drove road intensely, while he unconsciously strokes the scales of the dragon's back on the apex of his grandfather's war-helm. Then, almost religiously, he slowly places the helm on his head, letting the steel jaw-guards fall gracefully over his cheeks, the spine guard offering comfort to the nape of his neck as the bronze browed nasal guard lightly brushes the tip of his nose. He shakes his head to settle the helm, but he leaves the chinstraps hanging loose to avoid strangulation, in the event that he is later caught by the helm from behind by any adversary once battle proper has commenced. Methodically he takes his longbow from his back, then he pulls arrows from a clutch that he'd stuck in the ground in front of him earlier, next, he knocks a long flight then he hangs three loose arrows between the fingers of his draw hand. He pulls the bowstring taught, raises the bow high and then tests to full pull, as do all the Gallóbhet commanders... and fifty Ceitherne behind them.

Every bowyer, having now prepared and flexed for maximum pull and loose, eases up on the taughtness, then they all stand down in their given positions and wait patiently for the English train to appear. Sean mòr glances at William; he sees there is a fierce but grim determination in his eyes while he keeps a wolf-like focus on the curve in the road ahead of them. He also sees in him the same spirit of character as that of his grandfather as he remembers him, when he himself had stood next to Billy Wallace as a young

Ceitherne in the Garda Rígh, King Alexander's bodyguard at the battle of Largs. Sean mòr gazes confidently at William, who appears no longer to be an indecisive young man, he sees him now as a true warrior of immense tenet who stands regally poised before him, intense, with a ruthless air of conviction that supports every inch of his tall, powerful and muscular frame, complimenting the air of a confident and inspiring Gallóbhet chief... a true Warlord.

Sean mòr also senses that Wallace is completely emotionless, cold and calculating, with ice for blood and a hunger to kill, seething with a hatred unmatched and unseen in him before now, such is his reaction to all that has gone before him. Sean mòr has no doubts that the terrible tidings brought to him from Faolán, will cause William to fight with the same mighty grit and tenacity as that of his namesake, grandfather Billy. Sean mòr's thoughts turn away from his young Warlord; then he too focuses intently on the same bend in the drove road as all the others. He gently runs his thumb over a unique pattern of notches carved into the six-foot hardened ash shaft of his spartaxe. The few who had ever seen his ancient spartaxe and lived to tell the tale, could easily have mistaken the intricate knotwork patterns finely etched into the wood, as a work of art, but for Sean mòr, each miniscule notch keeps an intimate record of every head he has taken with this fearsome weapon. Sean mòr grins, for he knows that by the end of this day, there will be many more notches to whittle into his spartaxe ash.

The silence is broken again when a second hawk like warning signal is heard.

Tense moments pass by... then the Gallóbhet get their first sight of the English, when a squadron of light-horse scouts come meandering slowly round the bend in the drove road, blissfully unaware of Wallace and the Gallóbhet waiting ahead of them. After a few eternally long moments, the cumbersome looking vanguard and main body of the English baggage train slowly begins to appear, following on behind the forward light-horse squadron, all unwittingly hemmed in by a dense dark woodland and extremely steep banks of the Whinny Wizzen, with the gentle Irvine burn meandering below.

The English baggage train of De Percy rumbles onwards, confident and without a care.

Impressive is the vanguard as it rides six abreast and endless columns deep, with brightly emblazoned pennants and banners faintly billowing on the end of erect lances. Each quicksilver lance-tip glints in the early afternoon sun, as does the light armour and helms of the soldiers and knights, so gaily complimented with gloriously colourful and ornate coats of arms on their tabards, shields and caparison quarters of their steeds.

At first, the English vanguard don't notice the Gallóbhet standing further up the drove road blocking their path, for the appearance and war-garb worn by the Scots, with their heavy dun brown and ochre-coloured brats, dark green léines rusty chainmail hauberks and their drab-brown battle jacks, renders them all but invisible in their natural woodland habitat. The leading squadrons of English horsemen are nearing Torrance and Gormlaidh's well-prepared and laid out 'Rock feast and iron briar patch' when they get their first glimpse of Wallace and the Gallóbhet commanders, waiting a short distance ahead of them. They notice that Wallace and the Gallóbhet are all standing motionless and simply staring at them, successfully diverting English eyes away from discovering the buried crossbow bolts and back facing arrow heads, so well constructed and concealed by Stephen of Ireland, Gormlaidh, Sean mòr and Hayde's men.

"HALT…" calls out the point commander, but the English column continues to slowly file round the long bend in the road behind him, packing them tightly together. The knock-on halt eventually flows back, slowing down then finally stopping when the entire baggage train is within the near half-mile length of the Winny Wizzen gully. The English commander Lord Mableton, calls out, "You there… move aside." But there is no reply from the Gallóbhet. Irritated, Lord Mableton looks behind him, only to see the entire English train is packing ever tighter together. He turns around and calls out once more to the sinister looking band who are momentarily, and successfully, blocking the old traveller's road north.

"You Scotchmen… clear the road, or by the saints, you shall suffer for this delay."

Once again there is neither a reply nor any obvious movement apparent coming from the stoic Gallóbhet, who remain defiantly blocking the road in front of the English host. Lord Mableton is immediately concerned, while his English knights look at each other quite bemused and somewhat entertained by this very unusual interruption to their otherwise uneventful journey. Curious, they begin to point at the Gallóbhet, who remain resilient and unmoved, so quaintly dressed in their earthy antiquated armour. Many of the English begin mocking and laughing at them. Mableton speaks to his squire, "Quickly, I need you to ride at speed, go and tell lord Fenwick that the main highway to Ayr town is being blocked by a band of wretched Scotch Brigands." The squire immediately turns his horse and sets off at speed to find Lord Fenwick. William calls out, "Englishman…" Lord Mableton replies curtly, "Desist this foolishness you filthy brigand, and I shall ensure your death is a swift one, but if you dare continue to defy my lord Fenwick and I any longer, on this the king's highway, then I shall personally make sure that your death will be a long and a pitiful business." William ignores the threat from Mableton and calls out to him, "Sir knight, I want you to inform lord Fenwick, that I am here to kill him and him alone, but I may be of a mind to let you all go free to tell of this day. Now you sir knight, you and all of lord Fenwick's men... look all around you and be sure to look well Englishmen, I want you all to savour everything that you see here, for if you do not hand over to me Lord Fenwick and then turn around and go back to England, I swear to you all, that before this day is done, you will all remain here... as dead men."

Upon hearing William's bizarre declaration, the nearest squadrons of English cavalry and soldiers laugh heartily, but lord Mableton and his experienced veteran knights, immediately begin to scan the surrounding woodlands for any signs of an ambush. They meticulously scrutinise the dense woodland, then they look up to the fern and gorse covered braes of the Loudoun hill, still keenly observing, but they see neither Gallóbhet, Bandits, Outlaws, nor any apparent threat to their body of men.

"Scotchman..." calls out Mableton.

"Englishman... my name is William Wallace." Lord Bormand, sitting beside Mableton, speaks to him very briefly; then Mableton calls out again... "So, you're William Wallace are you? A cowardly brigand, thief and murderer by all accounts, a waylayer of innocents." Mableton laughs, then he calls out to William, "That insolent head of yours will earn us many a pretty silver merk from our lord this day, especially when we place it on a meat platter for his hounds to merrily feast upon." William grins as Mableton continues, "Wallace, cannot you see, we here number over five hundred brave English yeomen and chivalric knights of lord Percy and good King Edward. Even if your numbers that are so obviously hidden away from the sight of us are a thousand or more, you are sorely outmatched in wit, strength and in any of the necessary skills of battle. You are naught but a band of cowardly thieves, robbers and murderers. And these supposed curs of yours, who may well be hidden from the eye as I expect, but look you now Wallace, they may no longer even be there, upon seeing our might and strength of arms under the sacred banners of our sainted Lords."

The English soldiers and knights continue to laugh and guffaw at the mere thought that a hidden band of 'Scotch' brigands and robbers, may now have deserted this fool Wallace who stands before them. But the mockery and laughter from the English host and the words of lord Mableton, have no obvious nor any apparent effect on William or his little group of Gallóbhet, for they continue to stand defiant and unmoved.

"Over five fuckin' hundred..." exclaims William under his breath. He speaks almost in a desperate whisper, "Sean mòr, can't your scouts no' fuckin' count?" Sean mòr replies, "Naw, ah never said that they could count, did ah?" Jop says, "It's too late now to do anything Wallace, even if we make any attempt to flee, they will simply ride us down..." Lord Mableton calls out, "Well Wallace... what is your will?"

Rather than reply to Mableton, William simply nods towards Sean mòr, who slowly raises his spartaxe... then suddenly, from all around the Woodlands, braes and crags of the Loudoun hill, hunting horns being carried by each and every Gallóbhet, begin their shrill staccato blasts, immediately startling all the horses of the English vanguard and causing many of their riders to lose control when their steeds start kicking, bucking and rearing, all the while the Gallóbhet horns continue blasting their ear-piercing tones.

As immediately as the shrill hunting horns have peaked reverberation in nerve-shredding chaotic unison, Sean mòr once again raises his spartaxe... they stop.

For a few tense moments, there is an eerie silence in the Winny Wizzen gully, then, just barely audible, faint sounds of awful screams and the clash of what sounds to be a battle, can be heard coming from the far and distant rear of the English baggage train. The hunting horns of the Scots had signalled to Hayde's Gallóbhet slingers to launch a lethal attack on the baggage wagons and their guards, with non-stop torrents of deadly slinger missiles, bolts and flights, all aimed at the heads, rear-end and back legs of the knights horses to bring down their riders, also the Gallóbhet target the draught horses that pull the wagons, in order to thoroughly block the southeastern end of the Winny Wizzen and stop the English host from making any successful attempt to counter attack or to break out of the deadly trap. When all of the English rearguard horses are brought down, the Gallóbhet led by Hayde, move quickly under the cover of the missile fusillade and launch a deadly Spartaxe attack. Immediately they begin to cut bloody swathes into the lightly armed train guards and drivers, tactically pushing any of the survivors forward and up into the rear end of the English vanguard. Hayde's Gallóglaigh show no mercy and are fast completing the first part of the trap set by Wallace.

As the fighting at the rear of the train intensifies, the English are unwittingly caught in the extremely claustrophobic confines of the Winny Wizzen, and there is no escape. At the front of the train, Lord Mableton is beginning to realise the full extent of what is happening and the seriousness of the situation the English are now in, potentially disastrous if he does not take counteraction immediately. He looks to the men closest to him and calls out, "Will someone bloody well bring Lord Fenwick to me, now…" Mableton turns and then glares at the Scots blocking the road in front of him; while he waits for his men to bring their horses back under control and lord Fenwick to arrive. It's not long before Lord Fenwick gallops through the tightly packed ranks of the English soldiery and halts beside Mableton.

"Why have you halted here Mableton when the rear of our baggage train is obviously in difficulty? I cannot believe that you are sitting here idly by and parleying with this rabble of savages in front of us. My God man, have you lost your bloody wits, why on earth do you not ride these rapscallions down immediately?"

"But my Lord," replies Mableton, "this is a trap. It is certain that should we now go forward, it would be naught but folly. We should ride both hillsides and outflank this brigand Wallace and his curs."

Suddenly Fenwick slaps Mableton across the face with his gauntlet, "You fool, of course it's a bloody trap; I can see that for myself can't I?" At that moment, Gallóbhet slingers now appear from either side of the woods then they run fast to take up positions behind William and the commanders. At their feet, well hidden from view of the English host, lay the sharpened lodge-pole. A shrill horn blasting far behind William, causes both he and the Gallóbhet to look round quickly, then much to their relief, they see about fifty fresh mounted Dregern Gallóbhet arriving from Sean mòr's camp in the west, they are galloping at speed, bristling with weapons and soon pull to a halt. They then quickly dismount behind Wallace's small schiltrom, there they consolidate for a brief moment then divide and rush to settle on each flank in battle formation, with hunting bows, flights and javelins aplenty, all without a word of command or an order given, for they know their place is beside their chief, every man woman and Ceitherne knows their duty. Fenwick enquires, "Mableton, what are those ungodly and extremely filthy looking creatures doing standing over there? And what do they bloody well want?" Mableton shakes his head in dismay, then he replies, "It is somewhat outrageous and quite unthinkable their demands my Lord?" Fenwick is mildly curious, he enquires, "Then do explain yourself sirrah, what is it they want?" Mableton, slightly hesitant and unsure of how to really explain William's demands, pauses for a moment, then he replies, "My Lord, these men, they are felonious Scotch outlaws, and their leader is a well-known Brigand chief by the name of William Wallace, that is who now stands before us. My Lord, he does make so bold as to say that he will kill you this day and all of us here too, if we do not turn and go back to England. He also says that he may set us all free if we hand you over to him." William watches intensely the murderer of his bond father Malcolm; his outrage is tested to the limit not to run at Fenwick and kill him now. Lord Fenwick laughs upon hearing of Williams demands.

Mableton glances at his nearby veterans, he sees their demeanor is fraught, for they are aware of the danger, yet Fenwick appears to be completely oblivious to the true nature of the devastation and carnage being wrought at the rear of his baggage train by Hayde and his Gallóglaigh, though Fenwick is somewhat amused by what Mableton has just said. Fenwick enquires, "Wallace, hmm… that name, it does sound a tad familiar to me. Do tell me Mableton, where have I heard that name before?"

Aghast, Mableton replies, "My lord, I have no idea?" Fenwick sighs, "Oh well then, you just toddle along there and tell that creature Wallace or whatever his name is, that these brigands of his must surrender to me immediately and I may spare some of them. Though I must say, I am rather curious to meet with this odd-looking fellow who would dare to defy me. But should he choose not to surrender to me personally; then I require you to ride them all down forthwith, spare none of them the hoof and lance… Wait, perhaps you may kill all of them except Wallace, I may let him go free, after some jollies with him of course." Mableton replies, "But my lord, I fear…" Fenwick exclaims, "What… you fear? You cowardly dog. When this day is done, you shall have something very tangible to fear sirrah, now advance and be done with it."

"Yes, right away my lord," replies Mableton, "I shall deal with them immediately."

"Be sure that you do," replies Fenwick. He continues, "I shall now retire with lord Bormand to the rear of the baggage train to see what sort of nuisance is going on back there. Now Mableton, I insist that you eliminate this rabble before us, or there shall be dire consequences for you." Mableton replies, "Yes my lord, just let me try once more to get these Scotch to surrender, then I shall attend you to the rear of the train." Fenwick replies, "Oh well then, if you must, go on then but do hurry up." Mableton turns and calls out to the Scots one last time, "You there, Wallace… I know not if you are simply a drunkard or just a witless fool, but my lord Fenwick here does offer you very charitable terms if you surrender. If you do not, then we shall simply run you down, then all that shall remain of your roguish existence will be under the hooves of our horses."

Upon hearing Mableton's 'charitable' offer, causes the small band of Scots to laugh out loud in response. William soon replies, "You there, Fenwick, you and all your men should hear me well, that I William Wallace, do warn you now, that there will not be one of you Sudrons left alive here after this day is done…" For the first time since they met, there is no longer any more laughter or mockery coming from the English host, especially with the fearful noises coming from the unseen rear of their train, almost half a mile away behind them.

"What did that filthy Scotch savage just say?" enquires lord Fenwick. Mableton replies, "I'm not quite sure my lord?" Fenwick glares at Mableton, "Then what are you waiting here for you cowardly fool? Attack them… attack them now. I want you to kill them all."

Mableton replies, "At once my lord."

Nudging his horse to walk-on, Mableton rides at a leisurely canter towards the front of fifty knights to take up his position front and centre. Once there, he spurs his warhorse deep in the flanks, causing the steed to rise high up on its hind legs and flail its mighty war-hooves. Immediately upon landing, Mableton turns and spurs his steed into a forceful canter directly towards William and the waiting Gallóglaigh, quickly followed in a perfect 'V' formation by all his knights of the first squadron, riding five abreast and ten deep. They spur-on to a paced gallop and gain more speed, then together in absolute unison, they all lower their lances with disciplined conviction. The force, power and the weight of the English horses, causes the ground beneath the feet of the Gallóbhet to vibrate ominously. As the English horse gain closer to William and the waiting Gallóbhet, the English knights begin to group ever closer together and ever tighter, in order to completely obliterate the Gallóbhet when impacted by a solid wall of warhorse bone, muscle, cold steel and then trampled underfoot by the iron-shod hooves of the English' horse, but, just as the front ranks of English chargers are closing in upon the small Scots force, the front horses begin to run into and over Gormlaidh's prepared rock and hole traps, tripping up and turning away many of the horses from their given path, causing the English charge to lose its momentum. Upon clearing the first obstacle of rocks and holes, Mableton's mounted knights quickly regroup and force forward on a power gallop, but almost immediately, the leading front ranks of horse's have their legs penetrated and ripped open by the razor-sharp barbed arrowheads that penetrate easily through muscle, cartilage and a vast network of veins, bringing many of the proud horses and knights down.

Those riders who do make it through the second trap, strike the third trap by tramping down a force of weight with such kinetic power upon the sharpened iron bolts, it drives them deep into the soft plantar in the hoof, directly connected to the horse's heart, causing the horses to violently rear and tumble, throwing their riders to the ground. The horses following-on behind, upon seeing and sensing the very real danger that lays ahead of them, and also hearing the horrific almost un-natural screams of other tortured horses, instinctively try to avoid the unseen traps, but they are too late as they too begin to run over the vicious crows-feet, driving more of the sharpened iron-points deep into the sensitive frog of unfortunate horses that also rear and fall, violently throwing more of the riders to the ground in front of the waiting Scots, there they are quickly dispatched by deadly spears and flights. Immediately, many small groups of William's skinner and butcher Ceitherne, who have been hiding nearby, suddenly appear from both flanks of the dense woodland and run out at speed in front of the Scots front-line to enter the fray with a vengeance.

"My God..." exclaims Fenwick, "What on earth is happening up there?" The disastrous failure of the initial English attack is stark. Fenwick is appalled as he watches the Ceitherne youngsters running over the prostrate bodies of his fallen and injured knights, frenetically slicing and slashing viciously at English throats, pulling open helpless knight's helm visors, then plunging inside repeatedly with their long needle-sharp daggers to pierce through eyeballs and into brains. Others are stabbing in a manic frenzy at unprotected groins or into the vulnerable under-arms of the fallen knights, then just as quickly, upon hearing a single hunting horn blast, the Ceitherne run away again at speed to safely gather behind Wallace and the watching Gallóbhet, who are stoically prepared to repel the next English cavalry onslaught, now coming at them at great speed. At the last moment, William signals to his bowyers on both his flanks and to others hidden on the braes, who now begin appearing upon his command, they immediately loose deadly tracer arrows into the flanks of the leading chargers, striking down many of the English knights and their horses.

The surviving knight's quickly rally under Mableton's experienced command and charge again.

Gaining almost to within striking distance of the Gallóbhet, they affix and focus their lances directly at their chosen targets, all the while, charging forward at great speed with dauntless and grim determination. At the last moment, when the English chargers are almost on top of William and the Gallóglaigh, upon his signal, the Schiltrom lodge-poles are pulled up from the ground and immediately impale the leading horses, throwing their riders at the feet of the Gallóbhet or into the path of following horses and are cruelly trampled to death by their own knights. Any of the grounded English knights who do survive this initial calamity, are soon to be dispatched by the Ceitherne, who run out once again and begin stabbing and slashing all the knights as they lay where they have fallen. The remaining English knights quickly regroup and charge once more, riding hard and fast with lance's fixed on track. Mableton gains to within yards of reaching William, when suddenly his horse is skewered by two lodge-pole deep in the chest, the sharpened hardwood pierces the horse's heart, causing the steed to collapse and throw Mableton near to the feet of Sean mòr, who grins and immediately raises his spartaxe. The hapless Mableton raises his hand, pleading desperately for his life, but it's too late, Sean mòr scowls then brings his mighty spartaxe down with such a force, it easily slices between the fingers of the upturned hand to exit at the elbow then cut cleanly through the neck of Mableton, decapitating him instantly.

Sean mòr grabs Mableton's head by the hair, steps forward then boots the bloody head high into the air and back into the midst of the melee, much to the chagrin of the late Mableton's surviving knights.

Lord Fenwick is greatly perturbed by what he sees. He calls upon lord Bormand, his second in command, "Lord Mableton has disgraced us all before the King's standard, send in our heavy destriers to clear away and kill all of those Scotch curs. And when you are done Bormand, I want you to bring Wallace to me, for that cowardly dog by Judas, I shall make that Scotch beast suffer greatly for this disgraceful state of affairs." Bormand brings forward his finest knights and the heavy destrier warhorses of the English cavalry. These riders are Longshanks' chivalric knights of distinction, trained for war from birth. When coming of age, they chose a specific large stallion from a particular breed for lifelong companionship and tutorage in the arts of total war. These enormous horses are bred for conflict from foalhood and are the cream of England's war machine, much feared throughout Christendom for their prowess, fearlessness and daunting abilities in the midst of battle. The mounted Destrier knights set to formation, positioning themselves slowly and with definite purpose, then they walk-on. The formidable ranks of English knights close their visors in unison. At the ready, they raise their lances and begin to canter towards the waiting Scots, for these chivalric knights, this brigand band from their king's new 'shit' province, who would dare to challenge the might of Edwards ruling elite, is going to be naught but leisurely sport. These particular English knights could not conceive of anything else, as they have never experienced defeat in any battle or any campaign during all of their long years serving Longshanks, from Acre in the Holy Land, Ireland, Wales and France to the fields Flanders. Proudly, Bormand leads forward the mighty Destriers into a precision charging formation, when all are prepared, they then proceed to canter forward to a three-beat gait, all the rider knights are now shoulder to shoulder, ten abreast and ten deep. One hundred experienced veteran knights of England, ride on with great confidence and determination towards Wallace and the waiting Gallóbhet.

As the English knights gain closer, they soon find out that their way is greatly hampered by many wounded or dying men and horses from the earlier advances. By callously Ignoring their own wounded or injured colleagues, the regal knights of past distinction riding their grand imperial war-horses, mercilessly forge on with no regard, trampling underfoot with their massive iron shod hooves both the wounded and dead. They drive relentlessly forward now at a heavy four beat canter. At about one hundred yards, the English knights then up speed to a heavy determined paced gallop, proceeding to a full gallop, it is only then that Bormand lowers his lance, as do the following knights.

More Gallóbhet, hidden till now on the lower braes of Loudoun hill, suddenly appear on either side of the charging English flanks and launch a torrent of arrows into them.

Volley after deadly volley from the hillside Gallóbhet, strike deep into the flanks of the charging knights and war-horses from both sides of the gully, bringing many of them down. At the same time, William and his own Gallóbhet pull and loose deadly tracer volleys directly into the front ranks of the charging war-horses, bringing even more of them down, others stumble and fall over the boulders, arrowhead and deadly crows-feet bolt traps. Those that do reach Wallace's schiltrom, fail to penetrate the Scots ranks and are mercilessly impaled by the lodge-pole of the Scots, or ruthlessly dispatched by the Gallóbhet archers, slingers and crossbowyers, then, at close quarters, by the Gallóglaigh spartaxe and brazen Ceitherne.

As English footsoldiers arrive to support Bormand's now depleted command, close fighting rages into bitter and brutal hand–to-hand combat. William sees that unhorsed armoured knights now on foot, fight bravely and courageously while trying to break through the ranks of the packed schiltrom, but they are no match for the savagery of the lightly armoured Scots. During a brief lull in the fighting directly in front of William, he glances knowingly at Sean mòr, who immediately raises his spartaxe, signalling for his nimble fleet-footed hablars to be brought forward.

Sean mòr and William again make signal eye contact with each other; then Sean mòr and his fierce Dregern Gallóglaigh quickly mount their hablars then ride away at great speed and over the Loudon brae. Once out of sight of the English host, Sean mòr's Gallóglaigh traverse the west side of Loudoun; circumnavigate the great hill and then move on down to the rear of the English wagon train. There they join in with Hayde's attack to carry out their strategic duties to fight forward, in the hope of meeting William's wolf and wildcat Gallóglaigh in the middle. Fenwick is enraged, before him lay dead or dying, almost two hundred of Longshanks and lord De Percy's prize cavalry and soldiers. As he ponders over what he should do next, he is informed that a Scots commander has be seen fleeing away from the field with his men: Fenwick grins, for he mistakenly thinks that Sean Mòr's Gallóglaigh have deserted Wallace.

A ranking knight arrives and halts beside Fenwick with extremely grim news.

"My lord, the Scotch are completely destroying our rearguard and are now fighting their way forward, I fear they are trying to reach this position… I do believe if we tarry here much longer, then all may be lost." Fenwick appears almost in a panic. "My lord?" enquires the knight. "What are your commands?" But Fenwick ignores the question; for he is looking directly at William and is chilled by the very sight of him.

The screams and sounds of battle coming from the rear of the baggage train grow ever closer: convincing Fenwick that he is about to make the right decision.

Sensing Fenwick's hesitation. William calls out to him… "Fenwick, surrender to me now, and you may live." But with Fenwick's inability to make a decision and his mind panicking and in absolute turmoil, he spins his horse around in manic circles, knowing that whatever is happening at the rear of the Winny Wizzen, ensures he could not go back in that direction. For a few brief moments, there is an unnatural lull in the fighting between Wallace's men and the English at the north-end pass of the Winny Wizzen. During this lull, William calls out once more… "Englishmen, hear me well… if any of you Sudrons wish to leave the field this day and return to England, you may leave here now and go there in peace, then you may tell your friends that I, William Wallace, will no longer tolerate nor suffer English injustice imposed upon me and mine upon our sovereign land. Should you choose by your own folly to remain here, then we will surely oblige you unto death." This time there is no mocking and jeering from the English ranks. Lord Fenwick desperately looks all around him; then much to his dismay, the Scots renew their attack by launching relentless volleys of arrows, javelins, bolt and slingshot, striking down many of his soldiers and knights all around him. Fenwick stands up high in his stirrups and calls out for all his horse and foot soldiers nearby, to follow him and charge directly at William, for he believes that if he could break through the small number of Scots who are completely blocking the north exit at the head of the Winny Wizzen, he could flee to Ayr town and then he will bring back many re-enforcements to capture this insolent Scotchman, William Wallace.

Fenwick grabs at his lance and raises it proudly high, then he walks his horse forward towards the waiting Scots, followed at a pace by all of his remaining cavalry, yeomen and any footmen not fighting as rearguard. Fenwick pauses a moment as he looks along the bloody road of battle directly at William; he hesitates when he perceives the look in William's eyes. Suddenly his courage begins to fail him, which stalls his intent. Again he ponders over what he should do next, while all around him his men are being brought down in ever-greater numbers by the deadly rain of missiles fired down upon the English by the Gallóbhet.

Suddenly the lethal volleys of arrows, bolts and missiles stop. For a brief moment, Fenwick thinks that he sees an opportunity to strike out. He quickly spurs his horse and immediately sets to pace gallop directly towards William.

Relief from the pause in the deadly Gallóbhet fusillade, raises the spirits of the English chargers, yeomen and footmen. They take great heart as Fenwick spurs his horse on from a pace gallop to a full charge, he leads his men through the mangled pulp-like remains of his first three attacks, to finally ride down the Scots. Just then, Fenwick sees ranks of Gallóbhet from the Wolf and wildcats appearing from the woods and then more of them already charging down both sides of the Loudoun braes to stand resolute behind their chief. Fenwick is now determined to finish this disgrace once and for all. He tilts his lance and rides directly at William, but the carnage in front of him hampers his run. Fenwick's horse instinctively jumps across the bodies of men and grounded horses, but when attempting to clear a flailing horse, Fenwick's horse has no earth to land upon and digs its hooves into the guts of the wounded horse, slides and crashes to the ground, throwing Fenwick from the saddle.

As he struggles to get back on to his feet, Fenwick is quickly surrounded by thirty of his finest knights and yeomen. Seeing Fenwick so close, William looks at the ground and sees a double-handed 'boar-sticker' longsword lying nearby. He throws away his bow, steps forward, picks up the sword then stands the point in the earth; the pommel is level with his nose. He grips the hilt firmly just behind the pommel, then he places his other hand forward of the quillons behind two large protruding 'Teeth' a few inches up the blade… He is about to launch himself at Fenwick when he hears a great cheer rising from all the Scots warriors in the vicinity of the Loudon hill. William looks round and is almost dumbfounded when he sees Jop has unfurled the Kings war flag of Scotland, the red rampant lion of King Alexander.

"Take them now," calls out Jop, "Wallace, we can take them." William replies, "We wait Jop, when there is only a few o' those English horse' left… we're going in." Long moments of tension pass between Fenwick, his guard and William's Galloglaigh, then William sees that only a dozen or so of the English horses are left standing. "Now is the time Jop…" shouts William. Jop proudly steps forward, raises then he waves and flies high the Rampant Lion and shouts out at the top of his voice… "A WALLACE…"

A great impassioned roar arises from the Scots all around the Loudon hill and in the Winny Wizzen gully; the guttural roar is quickly accompanied by the shrill sound of the Gallóbhet hunting horns, enthralling and inspiring every Scot with these base tribal and national symbols. Psychologically, the raucous outpouring un-nerves and severely unsettles the English. Suddenly the Scots charge on masse, William and his Gallóglaigh race down the right flank of the English host, while Torrance leads his men down the left flank, then, at the given moment, both William and Torrance change direction and lead their men directly into the centre of the English host from both sides, immediately the fighting at the north face of the drove road becomes a brutal no mercy bloody affray. More of Fenwick's bodyguards quickly surround him; then he is brought another horse that he quickly mounts.

Fenwick and his men can hear all around them the horrific screams of his dying men, then, much to his horror and dismay, he sees coming down from the woodland flanks hard and fast, the mounted Gallóbhan, led by Eochaidh and Fiónlaidh. The Gallóbhan charge fearlessly straight down the hillsides and headlong into the English ranks, all the while throwing their long-darts, loosing arrows and skewering Englishmen with their deadly ring spears. Others throw out their grappling hooks deep into the melee to pull Englishmen from their ranks or to rip through the shoulders and neck flesh of those who would try to resist. Smaller much nimbler Gallóbhan and their Ceitherne quickly dismount then run fast and tumble or dive underneath the stomachs of the Destriers, while dragging the keen edge of their sgian cuartha behind them, spilling the great warhorse's guts to the ground. Amidst the carnage and bloody chaos, the screaming of wounded, dying men and horses become as loud and unsettling for the English as the incessant crescendo blasting from the Gallóbhet hunting horns. Fenwick, while desperately seeking a way to escape, suddenly notices that Wallace and his men are now fast approaching him. He immediately sends his bodyguard forward to stop them. On seeing this sudden movement by Fenwick's guard, William and Torrance's Gallóglaigh change their pace to run full speed towards the English lord.

Within mere seconds, both sides crash into the English ranks, brutally stabbing, slicing, slashing and bludgeoning without any thoughts for mercy nor for any quarter to be given. The ferocious and savage close-combat fighting is to the death, and there is not one soul from either side who averts from their given duty. William and Stephen fight together like lions, as do their bodyguard. Slowly and methodically the Scots begin to push the English back.

All around William and Stephen, Englishmen drop, either mortally wounded or dead, victims of the deadly archery from Faolán and her Bahn-Ceitherne, female bowyers who are dedicated to put three arrows into anyone who would be a threat to their chief. As the battle rages on, for many, their feet no longer touch the ground as there are so many dead and dying underfoot, in the tightly packed confines of the Winny Wizzen. Amidst the bloody fighting, William is suddenly shoulder charged down by Gormlaidh, as he falls to the side, a sword strikes downward, missing William's head by mere inches, but it strikes Gormlaidh's left arm, almost sheering it from his body. William instinctively spins about and brings his blade down swiftly upon the assailant's sword arm, cutting it clean through above the elbow; William quickly jerks the blade forward, smashing the right quillon of his long sword deep into the eye socket of the Englishman, he then turns at great speed and decapitates the unfortunate assailant with a backswing. The ferocity of the fighting keeps up at a formidable pace, untill William is about a hundred feet away from Fenwick, suddenly just John sees something is wrong, he yells out above the chaotic sounds of battle, "Wallace go back, it's a trap, it's a trap for you…" but William cannot hear just John's call, for in the heat of a close combat battle, deafness closes the ears of the warrior as the focus of the fight is so intense and beyond the ken or understanding of those who have never experienced such things.

Knowing the deadly risk of exposing himself, just John clambers up high onto a large boulder and screams out at the top of his voice while waving frantically, desperate to gain William's attention. "Wallace… go back, get back, it's a trap…" Fenwick sees just John; he points and screams out to his archers, "Kill him…" Two bowmen step forward, aim and loose two tracers, in a mere second, two deadly thin bodkins easily pierce just John's hauberk, striking him deep in the chest just above his heart… just John stumbles forward while grabbing at the arrows in his chest, trying to pull them out, then he topples from the boulder into the mass of the affray.

Suddenly William notices that the English are backing away from him, but too easily. He curses when he realises that he and is men are now completely surrounded. Like a fool, he hadn't seen it coming. William glances at Gormlaidh, Faolán, Stephen and Torrance; he sees that they are all completely saturated in blood and bloody gore. Gormlaidh's left arm appears to be hanging by a thick strip of skin. Faolán has two arrows stuck high in her shoulder and a crossbow bolt sticking through of her thigh, blood runs profusely from beneath her helmet. Stephen is bearing many deep scars and appears completely drained and exhausted, for he has still not gained back to full strength from serious wounds he received at the battle of Dunbar, and Torrance is slashed badly about the head and has arrows in his back and legs. With few of his guard left standing, William calls them all to quickly group into a defensive circle.

The proud Gallóbhet glance at each other during this lull in the fighting immediately around them. William looks above the heads of the English surrounding them and can see the scything spartaxe action of Hayde and Sean mòr's Gallóglaigh, hacking their way towards him. He could see too the archers and ring-spear warriors are continuing to pour relentless fusillades of deadly missiles of all descriptions into the English flanks from the braes of the Loudoun hill. But William knows that Sean mòr will probably not get to where they now stand in time to save them.

With a determination to kill or be killed, William knows by experience, that to offer up his life to be taken, for whoever mistakenly comes to claim his life; is close enough for him to remove the opportunist's head, no matter the cost to himself. To sacrifice yourself for your comrades is not what most would do in battle, as the instinct for self preservation is too overpowering, but William thinks, *'If they want me, they can fuckin' have me.'* This is also the mettle of his trapped Gallóbhet comrades.

Fenwick observes that he now has Wallace and his small group of Gallóbhet completely surrounded, and vastly outnumbered. He feels his confidence return and is now assured of taking the head of Wallace, the notorious brigand chieftain. *'Better still'* he thinks, if he could capture this brigand, then he can make good an escape from the deadly carnage and bloody frenzy fast approaching him from the rear. With Wallace as his prisoner, Fenwick begins to congratulate himself, thinking of the accolades and satisfaction to be gained by capturing this notorious outlaw. He thinks too of how Wallace's capture will bring him great prestige and rewards from lord Henry de Percy, perhaps even from Longshanks himself. Fenwick calls out…

"Take Wallace alive."

Gripping his longsword tightly with both hands, William raises it high above his head, inviting a killing strike from any of the Englishmen now surrounding him. One soldier springs forward to take advantage, but William swings the sword blade down with such a ferocious torque, it easily cuts through the soldier's face, spraying brain, blood, bone and teeth asunder. Another Sudron lunges at William, but he is instantly decapitated as William brings his sword round on a backswing. No other English soldier has the courage to approach William as he hews his sword in great arcs, cutting heads and limbs from all in his path as he begins to drive forward towards Fenwick. Inspired by William's courage, the fighting erupts once more with a greater passion than ever before, unexpectedly, Stephen, Faolán and the surrounded Gallóbhet launch a furious attack upon the English.

The sudden ferocity and determined prowess shown by the surrounded and outnumbered Scots, catches the English by surprise. William, Stephen and the others begin to press home a great slaughter by taking the momentary advantage. Hunting horns sound their primeval clarion calls behind William, he turns quickly and sees Jop proudly flying high the red and yellow lion Rampant as more Scots, fresh to the battle, now appear in great numbers over the braes of Loudon hill, led by his Ayrshire kinsmen Adam and Richard Wallace, he watches as they charge down the braes at great speed with valiant war cries, straight towards him at the centre of the battle. Instantly this has an effect on both Scots and English alike. The dismay and confusion on the face of Fenwick is noticed by his men, who are becoming demoralised by the ferocity of this renewed Scots attack... and by the lack of leadership from Fenwick.

Hunting horns blare once more, signalling a rapid forward movement by all Scots on all sides of the English column. The influx of fresh warriors with their ring spears flashing, their spartaxe and long-swords cutting deep into the English ranks, soon changes the dynamics of the battle centre. Upon seeing this new and invigorated force fighting towards him, Fenwick calls to fall back, only to find he is now trapped against a back wall in the gully of the Loudon hill. Knowing that they are now completely trapped and surrounded... the English retaliation and fight-back is brave, bloody and formidable. Adam and Richard Wallace fight their way forward ferociously to within striking distance of the English surrounding William, while Fenwick realises this renewed attack by the Scots has finally closed off any escape route to save himself. Panicking, Fenwick issues conflicting orders and throws the remaining English at the north-end of the Winny Wizzen into total disarray.

The Scots meanwhile, follow up their advantage on seeing the English falter. William signals to the braes Gallóbhet, who have been launching the fusillade, to rush forward and attack all along the English flanks where they too fight with courageous intrepidity. William resumes swinging his longsword with devastating effect, slicing more limbs from bodies, splitting skulls and dashing brains from any who dares to come near him. He is becoming untouchable in the eyes and hearts of the virtually leaderless English soldiery, now being harried on all sides by the Scots, causing utter disorder and striking fear in the heart of every one of Fenwick's men. Wallace and his companions fight on with a renewed vigour and incredible resolution, while Fenwick has all but lost control, caused by his indecision and by the Scots laying waste to the English with increasing bloody slaughter. Fenwick becomes ever more alarmed when he sees William cutting a swathe directly in front of him. Occasionally, the two adversaries catch sight of each other; it is then that Fenwick clearly sees for the first time, the real savage hatred in William's eyes. Fenwick looks to his flanks then to his rear, anywhere to flee from this madman, but all he sees is his beloved troops disappearing beneath a sea of flailing bloody swords, ring spears and spartaxes.

The ambush has now become a vicious and brutal no quarter bloody fight for survival. Fenwick is paralysed with fear and trepidation, conscious of the vengeance and retribution he will face if the Scots capture him. He continues to reign his horse around in circles, looking to flee anywhere and any way he can, but the walls and mounds of dead and dying English knights, squires, yeoman, soldiers and horses, surround him in a deep thick mire of blood and gore. Wounded horses kick out and scream pathetically while trying to raise themselves up as the fighting rages on.

Fenwick is mortified when he sees the Ceitherne jumping over dead or dying horses and pulling at the English knights trapped below, these blood-soaked young boys and girls, barely in their teens, are hacking and stabbing his proud men to death. Fenwick turns his horse away, but instinctively jerks back when he sees Wallace swinging the long sword directly at him, but the blade inadvertently strikes an English soldier on the side of the head, lopping off the top of his skull and deflecting the blade of Wallace away from its intended target. Before Fenwick can regain his thoughts, Adam Wallace of Riccarton drives a ring spear into the guts of Fenwick's horse as Robert Boyd runs at him at speed then jumps from a large boulder and topples Fenwick from his horse. Boyd quickly grips Fenwick by the throat and pulls him to his feet, but both of them have no purchase standing on thick bloody gore underneath their feet, causing them to slip and fall over. As they roll about desperately fighting each other with their bare hands, Adam again grabs Fenwick by the throat and drives him backwards while pulling his visor open wide, Boyd pulls a dirk from behind his back then he pushes the dirk into Fenwick's face, cutting him deep just below his eye. "I yield I yield... Please don't kill me..." screams Fenwick. Instantly, all around Fenwick, English soldiers, battle shocked, drained and thoroughly exhausted, also stop fighting where they stand and beg to yield for mercy, they begin dropping their weapons to the ground in a bid to surrender.

"NO..." yells William as he runs and leaps over Fenwick's dying horse, shouting, almost screaming in a frenzy; "Don't fuckin' kill him..." Stephen and Faolán arrive by William's side. They are almost unrecognizable, as is William and every other Scot, for they are all covered in layers of blood, brains gore and mud, as are most of the English survivors. Both friend and foe alike are now virtually indistinguishable from the butchery in the Winny Wizzen. The fighting in the immediate vicinity of Fenwick has stopped in its entirety, but the vengeful Scots are now in a frenzied bloodlust, as this sudden yielding by the English cannot be accepted. For the Scots, it's impossible to stop now, as many still have the primeval will to collect their blood tax.

English combatants, who foolishly thought to lay down their arms to surrender, are brutally forced to kneel on the ground, but instead of mercy, they have their throats cut or brains dashed. Many other English combatants who witness the killings, plead and desperately cry for mercy, but none is given. Every Scot who fought this day in the shadow of the Loudoun hill, has an experience or been the survivor of an atrocity perpetrated upon themselves and their families by the English.

Looking around the bloody carnage, William notices that many of the wounded English prisoners from the north face of the Winny Wizzen, are now being dragged away down by the blood-red Irvine water, there they are tied up, bound to trees, then being used by the eager young Ceitherne to ply their first real kill with a ring spear, a vicious weapon where the needle point of the spear goes in through the flesh of the body, the skin pushes the tip-ring back to release coiled strips of tempered metal that splay apart, tearing the unfortunate victims innards asunder. William and Stephen, both realising that they are now standing in the bend of the drove road through the gully, look towards the rear of the English column, they see there that any English attempting to surrender, cannot satisfy the vengeful bloodlust of the Scots led by Sean mòr and Hayde, forcing the demoralised English survivors to renew a desperate fight for their very survival. William quickly rallies his Gallóbhet then he leads them hard and fast into the southern flank of the remaining English defenders, who are now fighting desperately to thwart the bloody onslaught from Sean mòr's Dregern Gallóglaigh coming at them from the southeast end of the Winny Wizzen.

The intensity of the fighting heightens as the savage and brutal battle renews, with much killing on both sides, The remaining English soldiers of Percy's Northumbrian yeomanry are extremely tough and battle-hardened veterans, they fight on with an equal ferocity to any Scot, but soon, their axes, swords and halberds are no match for the passionate wielding of the ring-spear, sword and spartaxe of the Scots in their manic frenzy for English blood. The fighting at close quarters becomes so bitterly intense, that most can no longer hold weapons that easily slip away from the grasp of blood-soaked hands, the grips are now much too slippery from the saturated blood, sweat and minute globules of human fat to grip, rendering them virtually useless. Such is the reality caused by the closeness and barbaric fight for survival on both sides, they begin to tear and claw at each other with their bare hands, grabbing at each other's throats, ripping mouths, ears and gouging eyes, felling with rocks, almost hopeless, almost pointless is the fighting now, but both Scots and English alike continue to kill with nothing but a primeval fury, causing more to needlessly fall…

The singular difference deciding the outcome between the two opposing forces and giving one side the final edge, is the Scots desperate lust for retribution at all costs, including a conviction that they are all prepared to die to claim their blood tax.

As the fighting rages on, William and Sean mòr's Gallóbhet continue pounding into the English trapped between the two forces of Scots on the road of the Winny Wizzen. The prancing preening pomp and confidence of the Englishmen who faced the Scots earlier in the day, is now well and truly gone. They are completely leaderless and they are fighting by any means they can to survive and try to escape imminent slaughter. The remaining English troops continue to fight desperately, they no longer have any choice, for it is kill or be killed, with each individual searching for any way to escape, as it is now every man for himself. William, still in the midst of the fighting, is struck a glancing blow on the side of the head, he turns and swings his longsword instinctively and with such an almighty ferocity, he slices deep into the mid-waist ribs of a young English squire, cutting him almost cleanly in two. Sensing another strike closing in on him, he deftly turns to bring his long sword down directly upon his foe's head, but he finds himself looking directly into the eyes of Sean mòr, who holds his spartaxe at the ready, prepared to deliver the same execution by return.

Seconds pass by as they both stall from delivering the mortal blow, for it is only the eyes that are plainly recognizable, such is the blood and gore that cloaks them both in entirety. Sean mòr slowly lowers his spartaxe then rests on the heel of the shaft. Wiping his dry mouth, Sean mòr says, "We've won the day Wallace… we fuckin' did it." William stands with the long sword still held above his head, staring back in disbelief at Sean mòr, who grins at him inanely, his white teeth and the whites of his eyes are unusually bright against the blood splattered mud-caked skin of his face.

Sean mòr says, "Wallace… ah tell yie, we have really won this fuckin' day." William slowly drops his long sword and looks around at the absolute carnage.

The road and braes of the Loudoun hill appears as though every inch is covered in blood, gore, dead men and horses, both Scots and English alike. The screams of captured English soldiers being brutally tortured and executed or murdered, now replace the previous sounds of battle. Stephen, completely exhausted, rests on his knees, he says, "We bleedin' did it Wallace, we fuckin' well did it." William slowly takes of his grandfather's helm and immediately feels the sweet cool and soothing breeze refreshing his head and face. Exhausted, Faolán sits on the ground and takes off her war-helm too, her hair is matted and soaked with blood and sweat, both that of her enemies and also her own. Jop approaches, "Wallace we've captured a few notable knights and squires, where will we take them to hold for ransom?" William ponders, "What?" Jop repeats the question as William squats and watches the sporadic fighting and chase of the new hunt, fleeing English soldiers. William answers his friend, "There are no sanctimonious priests calling for piety and mercy here this day Jop. We Scots have a need to vent our pain upon the English from losing our loved ones, for what Jop, tell me? Let all the people seek uncompromising retribution upon any English that they find on our land, it is their right, for 'No prisoners' is the fate of the ordinary freeborn Scot, isn't that the law of the English. Blood tax is the law of the Scots." Jop shakes William, "What about the prisoners Wallace?"

"Hang them all..." replies William firmly.

"But..." exclaims Jop as he looks curiously at William, "it's chivalric to ransom them Wallace, we may raise a small fortune to support our cause with these men."

Glaring at Jop, William replies in anger, "It wasn't chivalric when Fenwick flayed Malcolm alive on yonder tree over there was it? It wasn't chivalric when the English skinned alive and nailed my father Alain, Mharaidh and my half sister wee Caoilfhinn to the front doors of our home in Glen Afton... or boiling Stephen's family alive as a bloody stew. What about Ach na Feàrna, Sundrum and Kilspindie or then the bastards hang young Brian Braidfuite, and they rape our women... kill our children?"

Jop cannot find a reply as William continues, "And what about your own mother and father Jop, what about them? Was it chivalric to have your mother defiled to death or your father tortured then roasted to death above his own forge?" Stephen speaks out, "Wallace is right Jop, none of us fought here for wealth, nor are we here to be ransomin' them there English bastards... fuckin' hang the lot of them I say, and even that's too bleedin' good for them." Jop turns to Kerlie, but he is in agreement, "Hang them all Jop, fill the tree boughs that line the route to Ayr... or cut their fuckin' throats, do to them tenfold what they've done to our own loved ones." William replies almost in despair, "I have tried Jop, the glorious Aicé knows that I have tried. I have tried so fuckin' hard to keep my peace with the English, but it appears that peace to them bastards appears as a bloody license to do as they will, to be raping, torturing and murdering any and all with impunity, well, no more Jop, no more talks no more negotiations…" Jop nods his head, he understands now as most others already know, that this coming war with the English will be like no other he has ever experienced.

"Strip the English dead… or alive," says William, "then hang all of them from the tree boughs of the Loudoun and let our own orphaned young one's tear at their flesh with anything they like. For the English, they come at us and employ total war upon a realm at peace, well, now they will reap the seeds of a war that they have sown. When their friends come here to collect what is left of their dead, they will know that they should leave our country or they sure must never fall into our hands alive, for I will take a lifetime by slowly killing each and every fuckin' one of them." William's thoughts then turn to Marion; he speaks to those close enough to hear, "Stephen and I have to be leaving for Lanark, for we must go to be with Marion and Brìghde."

Sean mòr speaks, "Take a troop with yie Wallace, there might be a few o' the Sudrons that fled who may still be armed and making for Lanark, and yie can be sure news of this day's fine work will be flying round Scotland quicker than a hungry hawk skydiving its prey." A Dregern outrider comes riding in fast from the southwest side of the Loudoun hill. He quickly dismounts and runs up to Sean mòr. He says, "We've captured thirty–odd wagons, all laden with wines, luxuries, medicines, vittals and yie will no believe this Sean mòr, but there are great iron-strapped chests that are just full of silver and gold." Jop enquires, "What else did you find?" The outrider replies, "There's also loads o' provisions too, and we've caught and hobbled a couple o' hundred horses." William says, "Will you take care of all o' that for us Sean mòr, me and Stephen have got to get away fast and see to the lassies, for I've no' got any more time to be wasting here." Sean mòr replies, "Ah'll do that for yie Wallace, you get yourself away now." William replies, "Tá Sean, I'll see yie back at the Wolf and wildcats later." Just then, William notices Adam and Richard Wallace resting nearby, he gets up and goes over to talk with them, as he walks through the bloody remains, he suddenly hears his name called out behind him, "WALLACE, LOOK OUT…"

Spinning on his heels, William is confronted by Lord Bormand. As William quickly reaches for his dirk, he notices that the Englishman simply gasps; then suddenly he falls to his knees and then onto his face. It's only then William sees Eddie óg standing behind Bormand… with a bloody dirk in his hand. William reaches down to Bormand and grabs his hair at the back of his head then pulls his head back, almost without thinking, William cuts his throat, straightens up, wipes his blade then looks at his nephew.

Eddie óg blurts out, "He was goin' to kill yie uncle, I had to do it…" William exclaims, "Eddie, what th'… where were you?" Eddie óg replies, "Ah'v been behind yie all the time uncle, ah'v been watching your back." It's only then does William realise that Eddie óg too is covered in the bloody grime of war. William looks at the body of Bormand and sees that he had held two daggers in each hand. He turns and says to Eddie óg, "Ah reckon that ah owe yie a life there Eddie óg, mine. Ah sure am glad that you didn't listen to me earlier when ah told yie to go home." William walks Eddie óg over to meet with his Ayrshire kith and kin where they spend some short time together, talking of what they will do next and where they will meet. William leaves Eddie óg with Adam and Richard, when Stephen and Faolán approaches, Stephen says, "We better git goin' soon Wallace, we don't have much time to waste here before us getting to Lanark and it gets dark. Eochaidh says she has our horses ready." As William and Stephen, make their way over to their horses, they notice that John Blair is wandering towards them looking very dazed, confused and covered in blood, he is also holding a sword in one hand and a dirk in the other.

"Blair?" exclaims William. John Blair simply gazes at William trance-like, there is no sign of him recognising his childhood friend, or even where he is. "Blair?" says William once more, "What's wrong with yie?" Blair replies, "Wallace, I need you…" William takes the weapons away from Blair and sits him gently on the ground; then he enquires, "What is it that you're needing?" Blair stares wide-eyed at William, "Uh… It's no' me, its just John and some of the other men, they're awfy badly cut up, they're calling out for you." Suddenly William remembers, "Where's just John?" Blair doesn't reply, William asks him again, "Blair, where is he?" Faolán nudges William, she says, "He's over there Wallace. I see him, there's Gormlaidh and Torrance with him too; they're all laying up against the signal rock over there."

They all rush over to where their companions lay in pools of blood. It's obvious that Just John is only moments from death, but when he sees William, he attempts to raise a bloody hand that William quickly grasps, then he kneels beside him. "Just John, we'll get yie tae true Tam, just you hold on…" says William. Just John shakes his head and tries to speak, but he can't find the strength, but William knows, he says, "I will see to your families needs just John, and when you meet my kinfolks…" William feels emotion returning as he looks into the eyes of his old friend. He sees his friend's hazy focus, a solitary tear rolls down his cheek, then his eyes fade a misty blue. William places his hand on just John's face and closes his eyes for the last time.

For a few moments, everyone remains silent, for they have lost a dear friend and a loyal brother.

Amidst the carnage, each and every survivor feels the same sadness and sorrow for someone lost, if not now, they will later, for none will leave this day untouched.

William looks at the bloody body of his friend, another who had saved his life this day, but at a great expense at a cost of his own sacrifice, tears at William's heart. Then he thinks of what has happened to Marion, Brannah… he begins to fret, not knowing what condition she may be in and all alone, and young Brian and his father… Brìghde too. He knows he must leave the Loudon now, not only to reach Marion, he also knows that shock, even for the victors after such a battle, will set in, and sleep or drink will be his only escape. But William can do neither till he knows that Marion is safe in his arms. Sean mòr says, "Wallace, get yer arse away from here, it's Marion who needs yie, and you too Stephen." William looks at Gormlaidh who is badly wounded and laying bloodied beside his severely wounded friend Torrance.

"I…" says William. Gormlaidh groans, "Away yiez go. Us two are as fine as it gets with all these feckn holes in us." Torrance says, "Don't you fret for us who are fallen this day Wallace; we'll get our own selves back to the Wolf and wildcats. You just get away from here and save as many o' our folk from English retribution, for there will be feckn hell to pay for this day's work." Sean mòr laughs, "Aye Torrance, but what a day it was." William hears the voice of Eochaidh nearby; "I've brought the horses for yiez, now yiez better get away from here and fast." William looks at Eochaidh, he says,

"You're wounded too." Eochaidh reacts, almost in embarrassment, "Are yie feckn blind Wallace... awe us folks here are fuckin' wounded?" Everyone laughs hearing Eochaidh's comment, even Faolán. In all the years they have shared with Eochaidh, the words she spoke this day are as many they have ever heard from her. William speaks with Sean mòr, "Will yie get the wounded to the Wolf and wildcats Sean; I'll send true Tam to help as soon as I get a message to him." William looks at just John, then to the road of the dead. He says, "And make sure that our folks now gone from us, are carried to the Wolf and wildcats to be with their families Sean, then I need yie to ring the forest with traps and guards." Sean mòr replies, "It'll be done."

Kerlie arrives breathless; he says, "Wallace, what about Fenwick." William exclaims, "Fuck, where is he?" Kerlie replies, "Boyd and Richie stripped him and bound him down by the auld oak tree where he flayed good Malcolm." William grips his dirk and storms off in the direction of the hanging oak, followed by Stephen, Sean mòr and Faolán. When William gets there, he sees that Fenwick is bound naked and sitting at the foot of the tree that was the execution place of his bond father Malcolm.

Fenwick cowers and cries great tears of remorse when he sees William storming towards him. William commands, "Get that cunt on his feet..." Fenwick is roughly hauled to his feet and immediately pleads with William.

"Have mercy my lord Wallace. These men accuse me of Sir Malcolm's demise, but it was not I who inflicted such barbarity upon him, it was Lord Cressingham and his squire, Marmaduke de Percy." William shows no sign of any reaction, but hearing the name Marmaduke de Percy is just one more time amongst the many times he has heard that name associated with the suffering, pain and death of his family.

"Marmaduke de Percy," says Stephen, "It's him again Wallace, that's the name so long sought after by Coinach. Wallace, he's the one…" William enquires, "Who's this?"

A young teenage boy covered in bloody cuts and bruises, is also bound naked at the feet of Fenwick. He is shaking uncontrollably with fear, but something about him reminds William of Brian Braidfuite, as an air of innocence and naivety emits from the frightened youth.

William raises his hand, suddenly the youth instantly shies away. William says, "No stranger to a beating then boy?" Fenwick speaks nervously, "Kill him Wallace, he is but a servant, why not vent your spleen on him, for he is of no consequence to me. My lord, I say to you that we should talk awhile, for I must inform you that you will most certainly gain a king's ransom when you return me to England, but I must be untouched and wholesome you see. And I shall certainly inform lord de Percy that you are indeed noble; and this day has been but a foolish misunderstanding between us." William exclaims, "A misunderstanding." He can scarcely believe what he is hearing. Bizarrely he is distracted when he hears Sean mòr speakin nearby. Sean mòr says, "Kill that wee fella too Kerlie, here, ahl do it…" The boy appears to be petrified in the extreme as Sean grips him securely by the hair of his head. Sean pulls a dirk from his belt and holds it against the throat of the youngster.

"Wait…" commands William. Sean mòr says. "Other than women and their wains Wallace, we've made sure that not one man nor any boy o' thinkin' age escaped from the back o' the train. This wee fella here might look cute the now, but some day he will be a man and will likely come back at us." Kerlie says, "Sean's right Wallace, we shouldn't let any escape, let him live and the wee bastard will be back some day wie an army." William says, "Untie him and get him some clothes to cover his nakedness." Kerlie glares at William; but he does as he is bid. Sean mòr says, "Yer makin' a big fuckin' mistake Wallace, but if this is what yie want?" William speaks to the youth, "How long have you been in the service of Fenwick?" The youth replies, "Since but a child my lord." William says to him, "Walk with me awhile."

The youth appears petrified. He glances at Fenwick as though seeking permission as he hastily puts on the clothes, William says, "Have no fear son, I only wish to speak with you." As they are about to walk away, William stops and enquires, "Tell me boy, what's yer name?" The youth replies, "Aylmer my lord." William smiles, "And what was it like learning the squires trade with lord Fenwick Aylmer."

The boy glares at Fenwick awhile; then he looks at William confidently. "He is a cruel man my lord." William grimaces, "No lord will I ever be boy, but see Fenwick there, he murdered my uncle on yonder tree, and that man he killed was like a father to me, and I as a son to him." The boy exclaims with obvious emotion, "That man was your father sir? I watched as Lord Fenwick…"

Suddenly the boy closes his mouth, as though he has said too much already. William feels a sharp pain wrenching at his heart and his mind, but now he has a witness, and he knows it. He says to the boy, "Then come Aylmer, walk with me now son and you can talk freely, for you have my word as a Wallace, and I swear to you, as one son to another, no harm will befall you. I'll make sure that the Brigand chief Sean mòr, nor any other man will go against my word. You should tell me the truth Aylmer, for I will know it, then I'll give you a horse, food, a pass, and then you'll be free to leave this forsaken place, protected and in peace." Everyone is surprised to hear such benevolent words, but none question William's motive. He walks a short distance away with Aylmer and talks to him out of earshot of everyone. After a few moments, William walks back to where Fenwick waits nervously. William glares at Fenwick with contempt, disdain and utter hatred. He says, "Faolán, will you take this young fella Aylmer here and give him a horse, then tell John Blair that I want him to escort this boy to Lanark. Get him some vittals too, for he is to go free from this place with my warrant, and make sure everyone heeds me, for any who tries to molest or does him harm, I will surely kill that rogue with my bare hands."

Aylmer looks at William then extends his hand.

Surprised, William looks down at the boy; then he puts a friendly hand on the boy's shoulder and takes him by his hand. Aylmer says, "I thank you for not killing me Lord Wallace..." William is taken aback at the very thought, "Aylmer, you should listen to me, go, I want you just to go home son, go back home to England and then you tell folks there what you have seen here this day. For our fight is not with you, nor is it with the common people of England, it's only against those who would come here to murder and enslave us..." William pauses and sees that Aylmer is barely hearing him, for he is shaking with fear as he watches Fenwick glaring at him. William nudges Aylmer. "That man will never beat you again Aylmer, I promise you this. Now listen to me boy, never you let any man ever lay a hand on you again."

The young boy looks up at William with hope in his eyes... then he smiles. William puts his arm around Aylmer's shoulders one more time; then he says, "Just you go home Aylmer, just go home son, you're free ..." Fiónlaidh canters up beside William and dismounts. "Wallace... we've searched the saddlebags of those English soldiers we dispatched down in the glen early in the morn." She takes a large satchel from the back of her horse and passes it to William, "What's this?" he enquires. Fiónlaidh replies, "There is a great deal of information in there, much of it telling of how many English troops are garrisoned here in Scotland. There's also full lists of all their commanders and office bearers, including the names of Scots that are feeding them information about those who didn't sign those Rageman's fuckin' rolls. Everything is in there that we need to lay out a plan and hit the English hard where it hurts them most." Sean mòr says, "It sounds like we might have our own death lists already prepared for us Wallace?" William smiles, "I reckon yer right there Sean. Will you make sure this information is sent as quickly as possible up to Ranald Craurford and to Bishop Wishart too, take it now and make sure that they receive every writ and document." Fiónlaidh says, "You should look at these too before we leave." She rummages in the satchel and pulls out two thick roles of velum parchment. William unrolls the parchments, reads them, then he grimaces.

"This is a comprehensive list of all those that are to be killed…" He looks at Fiónlaidh, "We've searched for this complete list for so long… Fiónlaidh, will you make sure that Wishart sees these too and get them scribed twice, keep and copy one, then I need yie to send the other copy to Andrew Moray up in Avoch, for many of his kinfolk are also mentioned on this fresh list too, go now… and stay safe." Fiónlaidh calls out to her Ceitherne Sparr, "Go get food and vittals packed now, hurry, for we're leaving for Glasgow town right away." As Fiónlaidh mounts her horse, William calls out to her, "Fiónlaidh wait… I want you to come with me, will yie send one of your trusted Ceannards instead with an escort. I reckon I need both you Eochaidh and Faolán to come with me to Lanark." Fiónlaidh turns her horse and walks back, she says, "I'll send a Ceannard Aicé, for there's no other that I trust more than those of rank that would be sure to deliver these dispatches." William replies, "Then find her and get her to leave now with her guard." Fiónlaidh replies, "It will be done." As Fiónlaidh canters off, William hears his name being spoken behind him. "Lord Wallace, I must have words with you, words that shall be of a great benefit to both of us good sir." William turns and sees Fenwick nervously looking at him. "My ransom good sir?" queries Fenwick, "shall we discuss my worth lord Wallace?" But William has no thought or a care for ransoms, seething; he pulls out his dirk and walks towards Fenwick, glaring at the English lord with a rising hatred in his eyes. "Wallace..." says a voice nearby. William turns to see who else speaks his name, nearby, a wounded Scot steps forward. William enquires, "What's your name ma friend?" The wounded man replies, "Fairbairn..." William says, "Don't I recognise you from somewhere?" Fairbairn replies, "Aye, and I you, for I'm the former keeper of Lady Marjorie's hunter hawks." William enquires, "What do yie want from me Fairbairn, for I must soon be leaving this place with much haste."

Fairbairn points at Fenwick, then he replies, "It was him..."

"What do yie mean, it was him?" enquires William, he is momentarily confused. Fairbairn continues, "Me and ma friend who was killed here earlier this day, we were out hawkin' nearby for lady Marjorie... the day that Malcolm Wallace was murdered, we saw everything, but we couldn't do anything to save him. We was deep in the woods up there when we heard a big commotion, so we got as close to the English camp as we could without being seen, near to this auld oak if the truth be told, that's when we saw that English lord and another, Cressingham I think his name was, and there was one other wee dirty bastard there too, he was wearing the mark o' the De Percy's on his tabard... Wallace, we watched as they slaughtered Malcolm before our very eyes, but there was nothing we could do to save him, it was this fuck here, he took particular delight in stripping the flesh from Malcolm's body with a bull-whip." William says, "You've just confirmed everything young Aylmer confided in me." Fenwick pleads desperately, "No sir, it was not I… That man is a filthy liar. My lord Wallace, don't you listen to him, he's but a common peasant, and the boy…"

William glares at Fenwick, who raises his hands to plead.

"My lord Wallace, please, I'm worth…" Suddenly William lunges forward and viciously slashes Fenwick across his lower stomach and abruptly cuts through his bonds, then he steps back, threatening to plunge the blade deep into Fenwick's heart, but he halts, visibly shaking with anger. William then watches Fenwick, who screams and looks down at his stomach, then he looks back up into William's eyes, for a moment, nothing apparent happens, then very slowly, a long slash begins to open up all along Fenwick's stomach, followed by his entrails beginning to ooze and tumble out from his body in a mesmerising slow motion. Fenwick screams again as he tries to cup his unfolding gut in his hands. William speaks to him with utter contempt...

"Now you may go free Englishman."

Fenwick stares back in disbelief. Turning away from Fenwick, William speaks with Fairbairn. "I'm sorry for the loss o' yer friend Fairbairn, but ah do thank yie for the recall o' your witness, and for your presence here this day. You go get your wounds tended, then if yie choose to do so, ah would be honoured if yie were to join our folks deep in the Wolf and wildcats, take your family there too if you have one; for there's nowhere else in Scotland that will be safe after this day becomes known." Fairbairn nods his head as both shake hands. "C'mon Stephen," says William, "No more time will we be dwelling in this place, we must be getting' back to Lanark before nightfall." Stephen, sitting on the ground tending to his various wounds, smiles and reaches up. William clasps Stephen by the wrist and pulls him to his feet. Faolán goes to Stephen's side to help; then they walk together towards their horses just as Fiónlaidh arrives. She dismounts and says, "The dispatches are already on their way to Glasgow Wallace." William replies, "Good, now let's get movin', for we cannae be wastin' time here." As they walk away, William says to Faolán, "If anything's happened to Marion..." Just then, Sean mòr calls out, "Wallace, what will we do with all o' this equipment the English have generously gifted us?" William replies, "Sean mòr, if there's anyone that knows the value of chattel and siller, especially the latter, it's you, deal with it all as yie see fit."

Happily, Sean mòr smiles and slaps his son Seven fingers, boisterously on the back of the head, "There yie go ma bonnie boy, didn't ah no' tell yie that Wallace there would make us a fine Warlord?" Suddenly Robert Boyd appears and fronts William in a rage, "What about this bastard Fenwick Wallace, why the fuck did you let him go free, that bastard murdered my wife and children... and your uncle too, and you've set for the fucker to go free?" William glances at Fenwick, who is staggering along the Ayr road in his own little world, desperately nestling his intestines in his arms and trying to push them back into his body. William replies, "I did set him free Boyd, now you may do with him what you will."

Boyd grins, pulls a keen-edged skinning knife from his belt, then he walks menacingly towards Fenwick.

Faolán says, "Let's get goin' Wallace, it'll no' be long before dark, and rain is now beginning to fall." Faolán hands William and Stephen the reigns of Warrior and Fleetfoot. They mount quickly, then they ride away fast in the direction of Lanark town. As they reach the highest rump on the southern brae of the Loudoun, they stop and look back down at the Winny

Wizzen gully at the centre of the great woodland, all that can be seen is a thick bloody patchwork of crimson reds, akin to a butchered open wound in the green flesh of Magda mòr, soaking the entirety of the ground for half a mile; no-one says anything, all knowing it is the scene of the first, but with certainty, it is not the last bloody battle against the English. They turn and spur the horses to a fast gallop, they know they must get to Marion, Brannah and Brìghde with much haste…

Lanark Stragglers

mperial Lanark Castle, is unusually quiet as a blood red sun lazily sets in the west. Hazelrigg, the new sheriff of Lanark, is hosting an important private meeting in the Lord of law's compartments, situated above the ancient parliamentary halls of the royal castle. He glances out the window to see his guards at the North port gate, all gathered around rump braziers warming themselves and lazily drinking ale. He mutters contentedly; "All quiet in this godforsaken place, as it should be..."

The only disquiet in the empty castle yards occurs when the hens and chickens skitter past the gate guards to rush back to their coops, shortly before the night foxes commence their hunter's prowl. The imminent Lord, Sir Henry de Percy; is supping fine French wine as he sits gazing at the flames rolling around logs in the majestic fireplace. He enquires, "Is there any sign of him yet?" Hazelrigg replies, "No, not yet m'lord, but he can't be that far away now, I'm sure." De Percy appears uncomfortable, he moves awkwardly in his seat. "I should have left with my wagon train for Ayr castle earlier this morn; I tell you Hazelrigg, this is most unsatisfactory to be sitting here in this bloody cold castle, especially when I'm due to be in Glasgow for an important statute meeting by mid-day on the morn. I should be preparing everything meticulously that I require for this meeting, bah... I just don't have the time to be wasting here, not when there is so much work still to be done to tame these bloody Scotchmen." Hazelrigg replies, "Well my lord, I'm sure that Lord de Valence will be hereabouts very shortly, reputedly he is very punctual, and nightfall will be upon us very soon." he continues, "Perhaps, if I may my lord, I could arrange for someone to ride out to see if…" Loud knocking on the door interrupts their conversation. Hazelrigg calls out, "Do enter." The door opens and a guard appears.

"Excuse me my Lord, I don't mean to disturb you, but there's an old Scotchman waiting outside, he says that he wishes to speak personally with lord de Percy. He tells me that his name is Sir Ranald Crauford of Crosbie and Ayr." Hazelrigg replies, "Yes, yes… do bid him enter."

As Ranald enters the chamber, De Percy raises his hand then says, "Ah, I bid you a warm welcome my lord Crauford, I do trust that you have had a very pleasant journey from Rosbroch castle?" Ranald replies as he casually wanders over and hangs his brat over a nearby chair. "I did my lord, though I almost missed the council meeting having to travel from Glashow at such short notice, but I must admit, the journey was very rewarding …" he then takes a seat to sit by the fire as De Percy continues, "And your meeting, it was worth your while attending I'll wager?" Ranald replies, "Aye, it was a very fruitful meeting indeed my lord, though I must be tellin' yie, it was sure an unexpected surprise when I received the message of reference from you, supporting my reinstatement as the Sherriff of Ayr… and sanctioned by King Edward himself. I'm very grateful to yie for your kind words o' support."

"Oh, not a bother at all my dear Crauford, it was nothing, I can assure you…" Taking a sup of wine, De Percy then enquires, "I say Crauford, do you know the whereabouts of my good friend, Sir Aymer de Valence, he should have been here by now and it's getting rather late in the eve; did you not travel with him in his train coming up from Rosbroch? I've been waiting here all eve for him and I'm getting rather impatient for his company; and his presence is urgently required at the meeting of the Lords Temporal in Glasgow on the morn. This is most unpleasant; we should have already reached castle Gray rock by late this eve don't you know."

"I believe he shouldn't be so very long now my lord." replies Ranald. De Percy sups more wine then continues, "Do tell me then Crauford, would you know if he is yet far from Lanark?" Ranald replies, "Not so far m'lord. I reckon he may only be a sand-hour away from arrival, if that. I tell yie this though lord Percy, I found Lord de Valence to be a very entertaining and world-learned host on our journey. When we reached the village of Biggar, he stopped the train so that we may have a timely rest and some vittals. We ate heartily there and refreshed ourselves with some of his very own fine wine. After our meal and conversation, he wanted to stay just a little awhile longer to learn about the locality, it was then that I took the opportunity to ride on ahead to visit with Lord Braidfuite, curiously though, I found that he wasn't in his residence, nor was he at the Bruin hoose, which I thought to be very unusual, for I had prior arranged to meet with him upon my return from the Sherriff's council..."

De Percy glances at Hazelrigg; he shakes his head then looks away again. Ranald sees the glance and is curious, for it intimates to him that something not good may be at play regarding Sir Hugh's welfare, "Tell me my lord, has something happened to him?" Hazelrigg exclaims, "Ah well, my lord Braidfuite..." He walks over from the window and sits himself down at the fireside near Lord Percy and Ranald, then says, "Unfortunately Crauford, I'm afraid I have to tell you there was rather a nasty incident that occurred betwixt lord Braidfuite and I the other morn, and as I say, it was a tad tedious and most unfortunate, for I must admit to you, I had to verily chastise the seditious lord most severely for his insolence and treacherous behaviour, yes, it was both he and that rebellious son of his that did speak candidly before my very ears of treason, my God, it was quite disturbing indeed."

Appearing somewhat confused, Ranald exclaims, "Treason, sedition… what, naw never, not from the mouth of Lord Braidfuite? Naw Hazelrigg, you're surely much mistaken. Sir Hugh has the well-being of everyone at heart, regardless of their rank, station or where they may come from, he has no interest in politic by his very nature." Hazelrigg replies, "I'm afraid it is so Crauford, for it was before my very eyes he did demonstrate his treachery thus." Ranald enquires, "So what happened, I mean, where is Sir Hugh now, what have you done with him?" Smirking, Hazelrigg replies, "Unfortunately, Lord Braidfuite now lies betwixt a dullard's life and the will of God." Now seriously concerned for the wellbeing of his old friend. Ranald enquires, "Tell me Hazelrigg, where is lord Hugh at this very moment?" Hazelrigg replies, "Well, I believe the matrons at saint Kentigerns infirmary are now tending his needs." Ranald enquires, "But why, what's happened to him?" Hazelrigg laughs, then says, "Alas, it would appear he suffered minor injurious pains when he made to attack my very person, indeed he did. We had to restrain him somewhat don't you know." Ranald exclaims, "Ach naw, I'm hearing your words fine enough Hazelrigg, but ma senses are telling me o' a much different story, for Lord Braidfuite is a very peaceable and a soul-gentle man, everyone knows this to be the truth of it." Seemingly unconcerned, De Percy shrugs his shoulders as he sups some more wine. Curious, Ranald says, "There's something amiss here Hazelrigg," he then enquires, "and you also say to me that his son Brian was involved somehow too, so where is he now, and where are the maids, both Marion and Brannah?" Hazelrigg replies, "Oh deary me Crauford, you are beginning to appear as though you may have more than just Braidfuite's welfare at heart, perhaps you may harbour thoughts of dissention too? Anyhoo, one should not concern oneself with the rebuke of traitors." Before Ranald can question Hazelrigg any further regarding the fate of the Braidfuite's, Hazelrigg swiftly changes the subject. "May I be so bold my lord Percy, but I must say to you in all sincerity, I am more than just a tad surprised regarding our king's decision in the case of Crauford here. It's a most disconcerting and troubling appointment it would seem to me, ah yes, especially considering the unsettled climes hereabouts, and also with the behaviour of that rapscallion nephew of his breaking his bonds once again."

"Should you be concerned?" enquires De Percy casually.

"Well, eh, yes my lord?" replies Hazelrigg, appearing somewhat embarrassed and taken aback by this curt comment from lord Percy. He turns smartly to Ranald. "Crauford, if you please, what do you think the reasons may have been to inspire our good lord King Edward to reinstate you as the sheriff of Ayr County at the Rosbroch council, I mean, it is a most puzzling and eh… a very peculiar choice too I may add? Though I cannot begin to wonder what our gracious king was ever thinking to allow you to rise to such an important appointment, a foolish mistake in my opinion."

Still pondering over the fate of Sir Hugh and his family, Ranald replies, "I wouldn't try and guess what's in the mind of King Edward Hazelrigg, perhaps you should ask lord Percy, for I believe I owe his majesty's final decision to him.

Though I must say this plainly, to hear you as an English Sherriff, having the temerity, even the audacity to question the validity and decisions of King Edward and perhaps even the judgment of your superior here, Lord Percy, I'll ask you this question Hazelrigg, if you would be so kind, would it not indicate to myself and Lord Percy and any other upon hearing these dubious words from you, as an expression of your rank disloyalty, perhaps sedition, maybe even your careless words could as easily be interpreted as treasonous talk regarding the decision making of King Edward?"

De Percy laughs out loud, "My, you certainly are verily a wise one dear Crauford, your sharp wit surely confirms to me it was the correct decision to have supported your reinstatement as the sheriff of Ayr, of that I have no doubts whatsoever. What say you Hazelrigg, do you dare to be so bold and reckless as to question the thinking and decisions of our King, then express these doubts about his wisdom publicly?"

Extremely flustered, Hazelrigg stammers, "Why eh, no, of course not my lord, I just thought…" De Percy sneers, "You just thought, fool. Fill my goblet with more wine Hazelrigg and see to the fare of my good sheriff of Ayr here too." Ranald says, "Aye, and ah must be thankin' yie once again Lord Percy for your faith in me, for unlike Hazelrigg here, I wouldn't question, nor ever presume to doubt King Edward's judgment, though I have to admit, I'm still a little surprised that I'll be resuming in my post as sheriff, and by his approval."

"There are many reasons for this decision dear Crauford," replies De Percy, "mainly though, for any who doest knowest you for the briefest of times, would quickly come to assess that you are a godly man, a man who does hold the respect and love of the people of your Sheriffdom, Yes, it was absolutely the correct decision." De Percy glares at Hazelrigg then he continues, "Not like this bloody jumped-up fool's butter-maid Hazelrigg, who stands before us with his mouth open all agape." De Percy shakes his head completely exasperated, then he exclaims, "My god man, what on earth was in that peasant head of yours when you thought to hang lord Braidfuite's son, I mean, of all the people… surely you could have chastised the boy first and still made yourself a public spectacle of his humiliation, but I ask you Hazelrigg, why did you torture then hang the boy?"

Hearing De Percy's remarks shakes Ranald to the core, but he remains outwardly unmoved in appearance. Hazelrigg meanwhile, is infuriated. He barely conceals his embarrassment at being chastised, in particular in the presence of a lowborn Scot, in his opinion. De Percy continues, "Have you forgotten your own stain so soon Hazelrigg? Though your elevation was well earned, I grant you that, but you must never forget that you were once but a mere simpleton and lowly servant on my household estates in Yorkshire, and as such, you can just as easily be returned to those duties should I wish it so." De Percy sighs, "By m'lady, why ever did I bother?" He shakes his head again and looks to the fire once more. Hazelrigg enquires nervously, "But… I'm not quite sure what you mean my lord?" De Percy replies angrily, "Refresh our fare you blundering fool… and be quick about it, if you don't realise what you have done, then I may have to reconsider your continuing elevation through merit. Perhaps the heady heights of political power are now well beyond your peasant wit of any understanding or comprehension."

Scrutinising Hazelrigg as he nervously pours wine into the goblets, De Percy continues, "Tell me Hazelrigg, allow me to understand, do you really think that your actions against the Braidfuite family will actually enamour his daughter to wed your son, do you really believe the execution of master Braidfuite is the most persuasive of arguments to be winning over the hand of the maid?" Ranald is completely taken aback hearing Percy's comments; he is also becoming extremely uncomfortable in the vitriolic company of these two Englishmen.

"Yes my lord, of course my lord," replies Hazelrigg, "I do understand what you say, but the punishment meted out was just and necessary, for the young fool knave left me no other choice." De Percy exclaims; "No other choice? Damn you man for your incompetence and gross stupidity, don't you know that you will always have important choices to make when in governance of a new territory, that is your remit you fool, you're supposed to have the judgment of Solomon when you make these types of decisions over those to whom we govern, especially with our King preparing an expedition against Philip of France, we cannot afford any cause for grievances that may lead to insurrection or a rebellion in our new territories." De Percy glances at Ranald, as though perhaps he may have said too much in front of him.

"My Lord," says Hazelrigg, "I deemed the punishments to be necessary under the circumstances, since Braidfuite and his seditious son publicly insulted me and besmirched my good name, in regard to my position as a representative of our noble king in this shire. But even then by God, the son virulently questioned my authority on more than just the one occasion, in fact, so bold was he, that he even challenged me thus in front of my men as my witness. But my lord, even in the face of such vitriolic provocation, I still plied a great restraint upon the youth, not just the once nor twice, but thrice more. When young Braidfuite, though he be warned many times, continued his insolent tirade against me and was actively encouraged by his seditious father, but for the greater good, I plied great restraint by bidding him to leave our company immediately. But my lord, t'was not long before the young cad returned with malice of intent in his heart, it was then I saw he had armed himself with a weapon to obviously do me harm; but trying to cool his spurs was going to be of no avail. Without just cause, he viciously attacked me. It is for these reasons I do believe; he left me no other choice nor any other recourse of action. And I say this to you in all sincerity my lord, it is much to my personal regret the final outcome."

"You see Crauford?" says De Percy. He shakes his head in apparent dismay, "This is the type of idiot I have to deal with, now do you understand my friend, he has a twisted tongue in his head, I believe that he actually thinks that it is simply for licking arse or barefaced lying, this man here is just another example as to why it is vital to keep one as respected as you are in a position of authority. I tell this to you Crauford, because we English have no intention to be quarreling with you Scotch, nor do we wish to give cause for any native fool to be raising up arms against us in rebellion." Ranald enquires, "I would beg an answer from you my lord Percy, but to which Braidfuite daughter do you refer, is it to the maid Brannah or is it the maid Marion that is being sought for wedlock?" De Percy replies, "I do believe it to be the elder sister who has been selected that does merit this union, is this not so Hazelrigg?"

"Yes, the maid Marion my Lord." replies Hazelrigg.

"Marion?" gasps Ranald. De Percy says, "It would seem to be so my dear Crauford. Is it of a concern to you, as it would appear to be so by your pallor?"

Shaken, Ranald replies, "No, why eh, no my lord, it's just that I've known the maid since she was but a child, she's a kindly, intelligent and a very refined young maid, but your earlier description of sheriff Hazelrigg here, as a fool wearing bent spur's, surprises me at this apparent mismatch?"

De Percy replies, "A simple union of expediency my dear Crauford, nothing to concern yourself with." He turns to Hazelrigg then says. "Listen well to me Hazelrigg, unless you want to be going back to picking weevils from grain heads on my Yorkshire estates, then you had better believe this of me and be making certain that bloody son of yours does soon woo the Maid's hand, or I shall quickly find another who will." Ranald's mind is in a turmoil; he knows William and Marion are already wed, blessed by the faith keepers of the Breitheamh Rígh, he also knows this proposed wooing of Marion by Hazelrigg's son, is a complete disaster in the making. He enquires, "Then my lords, may I go see to Lord Braidfuite, for this news that you tell to me, it's quite out of character and so unseemly when it's aligned with the personage of Sir Hugh, I mean, how could this tragedy have happened?" Hazelrigg replies, "I am afraid it was as I said Crauford, it would appear that the situation, though very grave indeed, upon reflection was perhaps simply just an unfortunate little contretemps that got out of hand."

"Then where is Sir Hugh now?" enquires Ranald. Hazelrigg replies, "Like I said to you before Crauford, I believe that he will be in the infirmary of Saint Kentigerns."

"He's still in the Infirmary," exclaims Ranald, "I don't understand, is he badly injured, what did you do, what have you done to him?" Hazelrigg replies, "I'm afraid I had to chastise lord Braidfuite rather severely, for regardless of his rank and station, it surely cannot be tolerated that any of your Scotch simples, be he high-born or low-born, may ever think to slight a representative of the English Crown in our new province, that is one command from our glorious King that I surely intend to enforce with great rigour, vim and with the use of a firm fist and boot. Your Scotch brethren Crauford, they are all like pagan children, therefore, they need to be treated and chastised as such. You mark my words Crauford, mark them well, I do urge you to be making no mistake on the solemnity of my countenance, there will be no sedition nor any peasant uprisings in this shire, no sirrah, not as long as I am the sheriff here."

Ranald is both enraged and extremely disturbed upon hearing this information.

After sitting for a few moments in silence, De Percy enquires curiously, "So then Crauford, to take my mind off this fool's diatribe, tell me about this rapscallion nephew of yours as Hazelrigg calls him, this eh, William Wallace I do believe his name is?" Ranald exclaims, "William?" De Percy displays a wry smile as he sups more wine, then he continues, "I say to you Crauford m'dear, that boy has had a charmed life so far, yes, very charmed indeed since you last posted his bond. And I must also say this to you; I do appreciate that the disturbance we had in Ayr town a few months ago, as I am well informed, was truly not of his making. But I have also noted that since his apparent disappearance, which was most unusual in itself, rumour has it that he did not die as was first thought, but that he doest now dwell in that hellish Wolf and wildcat forest with Brigands, outlaws, dispossessed men and ne'er-do-wells… is this true?" Aware that De Percy is a most clever and extremely shrewd man, Ranald knows that any denial of William's fate would not serve him best. He also realises, De Percy has not yet heard of his nephew's recent exploits only a week since, when he raided Ayr castle. Ranald replies, "It's true what you say as far as I have heard it so my lord, though I have not yet met him in person, nor have I received any communiqué from him. It has also been confirmed to me from other reliable sources that yes, he still lives, but that he's in a perilous condition as a result of his internment and treatment in the Ayr castle dungeons."

"Quite so Crauford," says De Percy. He says, "that is the same accurate account that has been brought to me very recently by my spies in his camp."

"Spies?" exclaims Ranald.

De Percy smiles, then he says, "Why yes, of course my dear Crauford, informants, spies… call them what you will, but these are men who have Scotlands best interests at heart, for though you may be a very amiable and personable fellow yourself, most of the vulgar's in this realm and hereabouts do not share any enthusiastic conformity to the new order." Ranald can barely hold back the anger rising in his breast as De Percy continues, "So do tell me Crauford, do you think with these quite extraordinary blessings of luck your nephew apparently has, we should give this young relation of yours one last opportunity to be welcomed into the arms of the King's peace, would you once again stand surety if it were to be so? But I must also warn you Crauford, any further transgressions from that whelp, will most certainly mean the forfeiture of your entire estates, and possibly the dungeons for you and your family?" Ranald replies, "I hear you my lord, but I do believe that he would earnestly seek the Kings peace given the opportunity, for he is desperate to…" Ranald pauses abruptly when realising he was about to say that William's true desire is only to raise a family with Marion. De Percy notices the pause, he enquires, "He is desperate to do what Crauford, why such hesitation?"

Ranald confidently replies, "Naw, no hesitation my lord, I believe that he is desperate to be living at peace under the new governance, that is what I hear my lord, I…."

Hazelrigg interrupts, "Have no fear about that filthy outlaw my lord, for I shall bring this miscreant Wallace to justice on the end of a rope, I still intend to rule this shire with a rod of iron." De Percy simply glares at Hazelrigg; then he enquires,

"So tell me this Hazelrigg, do you think that this iron rod and boots of yours will be enough to quell this Sherrifdom where no trouble nor dissention exists at the moment?"

"Yes, I certainly do my Lord," replies Hazelrigg, "I shall be letting these Scotch beggars hereabouts know by undeniable examples and without any shadow of a doubt, who their new masters are. By m'lady, there shall be not one silver penny clipped nor one single drop of English blood shed in the governance of this miserable shire…" There is a knock on the door once again, Hazelrigg calls out, "Enter…" A gate guard officer appears in earnest and beckons to speak with Hazelrigg urgently and in private. After a few brief moments, Hazelrigg appears to grow very pale. Curious, De Percy enquires, "What's to do Hazelrigg, what is it that so causes your features to appear so calamitous?" Hazelrigg dismisses the guard; then he turns to look out the window. "Speak up man," commands De Percy, "what ails you so?"

"My lord, it's…" replies Hazelrigg, he hesitates, then he says, "it's about your baggage train, it's been eh…" Hazelrigg mumbles and stammers incoherently.

Lord Percy, now getting extremely irritated, enquires brusquely, "Speak up damn you, have you lost your bloody tongue, what's this news that fellow brought to you regarding my baggage train?" Hazelrigg exclaims, "My lord, your train, apparently it was ambushed and… and it's been utterly destroyed. The fate of Lord Mableton, lord Bormand and your household guard my lord; it would appear that they're all dead…" De Percy and Ranald are completely stunned to hear this news. Hazelrigg continues, "There seems to have been an insurrection roused by cutthroats and waylayers, they have caused a great massacre to be put upon the train, with very few survivors." Beside himself with rage, De Percy raises himself from the chair, smashes his cup against the wall and demands an explanation, "How can this be? This is impossible, you say that Mableton and Bormand are dead, my train destroyed and household guards dead too, this surely cannot be true, those are many of my finest knights and nobles attending upon that train, and what news is there of Fenwick?" Hazelrigg stammers nervously, "My lord, the gate keeper said to me that all of my men who were en route to assist your wagon train, they've been sorely massacred too."

"Destroyed, killed, massacred..." exclaims De Percy, "You've surely misunderstood what that man said to you. Again, tell me, what did he say?" Hazelrigg replies, "My lord, he said that a large army of brigands has attacked both your baggage train and my men at a place not far from here, I think he called it, yes, he called it Loudoun hill... It appears to him there are very few survivors, if any, who escaped."

"Survivors?" exclaims De Percy, "What do you mean survivors, this cannot be possible, there would be nigh over five hundred of my finest household attending that train, most of them experienced men of war, including a squadron of my heavy Destriers? Nae Hazelrigg, this cannot be true, it's not possible. Bring that man back here that he may give us a full account? If I find this is a drunken hoax by some of your slovenly men, I will have them hung from the gibbets outside this castle."

"Yes my lord." replies Hazelrigg. He quickly leaves to bring back the guard officer. De Percy appears extremely shaken, he looks at Ranald, "If this be true Crauford, who could have done such a thing, who do you know that could raise such a band? No, this must be wrong, I cannot believe that nigh five hundred of my men... it would take at least two thousand or more of you Scots to contemplate such impudence." Ranald says, "I don't know what to say my lord, for all of Scotlands martial men have been stood down, imprisoned or are on their way to France in king Edward's service." De Percy snarls, "I warn you Crauford, if this be true, then you had better find out who's to blame for this calamity, for I shall hold both you and Hazelrigg responsible." De Percy sits down again at the fire beside Ranald, he exclaims, "I still cannot believe this, I won't." Before Ranald can make any comment, the door opens and a tall English knight walks in. De Percy immediately stands up to greet him. He exclaims. "Aymer." the knight replies, "Lord Henry..." Ranald also makes welcome. "Lord de Valence." Aylmer replies, "Crauford." Percy enquires anxiously, "Have you heard the news?"

Appearing somewhat puzzled, Aymer enquires, "What's the news?" De Percy replies, "There seems to have been a skirmish nearby, with Scotch brigands or bandits apparently attacking my baggage train." Removing his gauntlets, Aymer says, "I have heard nothing of such a thing. How come you by this report, what details or facts have you got that this mischief is to be believed?" De Percy, appearing somewhat bewildered, replies, "I know not yet the detail of it all, or if it is entirely true, for it was one of Hazelriggs men who but moments ago just delivered this news to us."

"No," says Aymer, "there is naught that I have heard upon my journey to this place my lord. I had stopped at the short while ago at the little hamlet of Biggar just a few miles from here, for rest and refreshments; that is the cause of my late arrival. Whilst I was there, I encouraged then I listened to all the usual native gossip and trivia in and about that wretched place, but there was nothing untoward, nor was there anything remotely spoken about any brigands or waylayers being nearby, far less any mention of an attack?" At that moment, Hazelrigg returns to the chamber with the castle keeper. Hazelrigg welcomes de Valence, then he introduces the keeper, "My lords, this is Sir Robert Thorn, he will reveal to us all that he knows from his men at the moment." As they all gather around the fireplace, Thorn proceeds. "My lords, there has been a report of a terrible event to which I'm yet awaiting actual confirmation, but if it's true all that I've heard, then my lords, it would appear that a great disaster befalls us."

De Percy enquires, "What have you heard man, speak up?"

"All that I know my lord," continues Thorn, "when I first heard the rumours, I immediately sent some of my men out on patrol, it was not long before they came across scattered sundries of wretched and bloodied Englishmen, many they say had obviously been set upon and suffered severe injuries by gangs of way-laying brigands, all hailing from that accursed woodland they call the Wolf and wildcat forest. Apparently, the survivors said they were the wagon drivers or drovers from your baggage train lord Percy. When interviewed further by my men, the survivors said that there had been a terrible attack upon the entire train, only they managed to escape a great slaughter themselves, but none of them knew of the whereabouts or the fate that may have beheld the Lords Mableton, Bormand and that of Lord Fenwick."

"A great slaughter..." exclaims Percy, "no, I still won't believe it; this just doesn't make sense? I know that Lord Fenwick is somewhat of a blowhard regarding his self-worth and esteem in battle, but even he is experienced enough to thwart any uncouth banditry incursions, and there was nigh five hundred capable and worthy men in attendance upon my train, with many squires and heavy knights in the entourage too? Fenwick also has my personal guard troop with him, led by the very capable and trusted lord Bormand, he is there to advise him should there ever be any trouble, but even at that, and though no trouble was expected or anticipated, I say again to you all, nay, there are none so bold in this broken realm to attempt such a dastardly thing." For a few moments, there is an absolute and shocked silence, then Aylmer exclaims, "My nephew Lord Percy, he is a squire with Lord Fenwick…" De Percy is grimly focussed on the fire, still refusing to believe such an event could be possible. He mutters quietly, "I too have many family members who are with that wagon train." De Percy demands, "How come you by this ludicrous story Thorn? Surely there are none yet who are here in this precinct that is an actual witness to this supposed massacre of my men?" Thorn replies, "Lord Percy, my troop captain has already sent relay riders back to inform us of what they have found, and as far as I know, he intends to ride on to the vicinity of the Loudoun Hill to find out what the actual facts are. My lord, I believe that we will know the truth of it all very soon."

Once more, all present in the compartment go extremely silent as they consider the grave ramifications of this news.

Aymer enquires urgently, "M' lord Percy, how many men do you have here in this castle?" De Percy replies, "Not many, twenty or so perhaps of my own personal guard? Most of my men were with the train, which are many of the boldest, finest men from my estates and personal household." Aylmer continues, "And in your company here Hazelrigg?" Hazelrigg replies, "There were one hundred and fifty knights and men of this castles contingent a little while ago, but I'm afraid one hundred of them left to join with the baggage train." Thorn says. "We have nigh on twenty men here who are at arms my lord, the rest are servants. But I have ordered everyone to be on their guard and to be on high alert all around the castle precincts, perchance that these foul rumours have any truth." Aymer says, "There is twenty in my small train, that's not many I grant you, but they are all good and stout fellows." De Percy is still visibly shaken, he says, "No, I still cannot begin to think or even consider that this malicious story can be true, it is not acceptable." Aymer enquires, "If it actually were possible my lord, then who here in this land could be responsible for such a bold strike against our men?" Everyone turns and looks to Ranald. "Crauford…" says Percy, "If I hear that your nephew has had a hand in this, by the God's in heaven and hell, I swear to you Crauford, I shall have you and all of your familie's necks stretched and your lands forfeit by the morn's sunrise."

"My lords," replies Ranald, "lies do spread much quicker hereabouts than any truth…" Suddenly, all goes quiet when they hear the castle tower bell begin to peel and alarm bars are beat. Hazelrigg rushes over to the window then looks outside, he exclaims, "My lords…" De Percy urgently enquires as he too rushes over to the window, "What is it, why are the alarms ringing?" Hazelrigg appears shaken, "My lords, look to those wretches out there, it appears the report may have validity." As they all gather around to peer out the apartment windows, they see streams of extremely bedraggled women and children, accompanied by a few seriously wounded men, all rushing through the outer north port barbican gates of Lanark Castle. Both concerned locals and soldiers alike, quickly rush to gather and gaze on in disbelief, as the wounded, destitute and desperate, rush to seek the safety of the Castle.

Not very far outside the castle precincts, well secreted and sheltering in the dense woodland and gorse scrub upon the old smithy hillside, William Stephen, Faolán Eochaidh and Fiónlaidh watch closely as the destitute stragglers from Percy's baggage train rush to gain safety and shelter. Stephen says, "What do yie want to be doin' then Wallace, for oi' sure have a need to be gettin' into that place, like bleedin' fast?" William replies anxiously, "Ah know Stephen, fuck me ah know. And if everything we've heard about Marion, the lassies and lord Braidfuite is true, then I'll fuckin' kill every one of those bastards in there." Stephen says, "Oi'm wit ya Wallace, we've got to get into the Castle town, but how do we do it? Jaezuz me feckn brains are boilin' hot wit' me over-tinkin'?" Faolán nudges William, "Wallace, why don't we join those stragglers from the train to gain entry into the town, that should be easy enough?" William glances at Faolán, Eochaidh and Fiónlaidh, "You three can't be goin in there, but me and Stephen could. And before yiez ask why, look at yiez... yiez are dressed as pure Gallóbhan, there's never a chance that yiez would get in there." William scrutinises the three women, "And look at those wounds about yiez, they might be covered fine, but they bleed bad, yiez would be best tendin' to them out here."

"Wallace is right Faolán," says Stephen, "we might get in, for we're as bloodied and bruised like so many o' the train masters and drovers down there, but you three Faolán... naw, uze would be getting' huckled straight away, for I reckon there are no any women in that there fair town o' Lanark that looks like any Gallóbhan I know, not wit' uze three havin' such bruisin' and battle scars as yiez both have this day." Faolán curses under her breath; then she enquires, "So what do you want us to do then Wallace?" William scans the broken lines of stragglers, then he replies, "I reckon that most of de Percy's train and the castle guard o' the sheriff were in that train, so there cannae be that many of the English soldiery left in there..."

"Less than a hundred maybe," says Stephen, "ah' tink though that would still be a stretch for us, even for the five o' us." William resumes his scanning of the stragglers, then he points and exclaims, "There's John Blair over there, he's wit' that wee English fella we let go back at the Loudoun hill;

maybe we could get in there with them?" Everyone looks to see John Blair leading the young Englishman on horseback over the olde mouse bridge.

"I don't think that's such a good idea," says Faolán, "that wee English fella will surely call you out to the castle guard as soon as yiez are through those gates." Stephen says, "Faoláns sure enough right there Wallace, we couldn't never ever be trustin' the wee English fucker. If oi was him, oi would make bleedin' sure we were both caught and fucked up for what we just did to his master." William replies, "We have to do somethin', for the longer we wait…"

A familiar signal whistle is heard coming from not far away behind them, like the song of a startled lapwing, it interrupts William and causes them all to turn away from the scene. They wait for a few moments, then they see Boyd and Kerlie with about a dozen Wolf and wildcat Gallóglaigh approaching them. As the two groups meet, William exclaims, "What are uze all doin' here?" Kerlie replies, "Big Sean mòr sent us, he sez to look out for yiez and to be watchin' yer backs." For a moment, William simply gazes at Kerlie, as though he is in a daze, while Stephen welcomes Boyd and the Gallóglaigh. Stephen enquires, "What's wit ya Wallace, we could do with some help to get into Lanark?" William shakes his head, "Ah'm sorry Kerlie, but ah was just thinkin' there… Boyd, your auld fella has a bothy stall in there for the fair market days hasn't he?"

"Aye," replies Boyd, "and he has a fine wee townhouse up there near to lord Braidfuite's house too, it's away up the third vennal just after the gatehouse… why do yie ask?" William replies, "We could sure be usin' yer auld Dá's house once we get in there, at least we could stay there untill we can work out what we're goin' to do." Boyd replies, "Aye yer right, it's a safe place ah reckon." William says, "Listen Boyd, if yie think it's too big a risk for you and your family, we could likely hide somewhere else, maybe up at the auld Kirk grounds or in the Kentigern orchard would be safer?" Boyd replies, "Naw, yer fine in the hoose Wallace, the auld fella is away down in Galloway, if we break the door-bars like it's been done in by ne'er-do-wells or drunkards, then ah don't reckon it would be much o' a problem, that way if things really get fucked up, it will look as though we smashed our way into the place." Stephen says, "What would yie have bars on yer bleedin doors for?" Boyd laughs, "To try and stop folk like us from breakin in while me auld fella is no' thereabouts."

Everyone laughs, then they begin to scan the stragglers.

"Faolán..." says William, "How long would it take you and your lassies to get to our camp in the Wolf and wildcats with a message, then get back here?" Faolán replies, "About a day... why?" William continues, "Get there as fast as yiez can, I need yie to find out if Marion, and Brìghde are safe back there with the wains, then get back here as quick as yiez can to let us know. We don't know what's goin' on in Lanark town at the moment, but they will sure soon enough be in a ragin' panic when they find out about what happened at the Loudoun hill. Once we get in there, if we find out that our lassies are no' there, you try and get word to us if they're back at our camp." Faolán enquires, "Ah'll do that Wallace. So, what's the message about that yie have for me?" William replies, "Gather as many o' the Gallóbhet' as yie can, then set them to work as fast as possible, yie know what to do." Faolán smiles wryly, then she replies, "We'll leave now, will yiez be basin' yerselves in Boyd's hoose?" Boyd replies, "Aye, ah'll make sure someone is there, and ah'll send a wain out here regular too, startin' from early morn, they'll be meetin' with yiez right here when yiez get back." Faolán nods in understanding; she says, "Wallace, why don't we get all the other Gallóglaigh to scout for any loose English patrols on the fringes o' the forest between here and Ayr, we could maybe even get some o' Sean mòr's Dregern to hunt them down east o' Lanark and as far south as the Ettrick too?" William replies, "Faolán, yie are ahead o' me already, aye do it, that should keep the bastards right busy awhile…"

Smiling, Faolán, Eochaidh and Fiónlaidh make for their horses. Stephen enquires, "What was she talkin' about there wit the message Wallace, what's that bein' all about, for you two sure have got some communications goin' on there that doesn't waste time on many words big fella?"

"True," replies William, "She's goin' to cause as much murderous chaos as she can within thirty miles all around about Lanark town, any English soldiery in there worth their salt, they'll have to send patrols out to be helping their distraught friends."

"Ah…" sighs Stephen, he smiles then says, "She's sure a very foin' and deadly lady that Faolán is." William says, "Kerlie…" Kerlie enquires, "Aye, what is it?" William replies, "I need you to keep a good watch out here for us, for there's only me Stephen and Boyd goin' in there." Kerlie replies, "I'll tell our bowers to get the best flights sighted on the gates." William says, "Another thing, Stephen, and you too Boyd… we're no' taking' weapons in there with us, none; leave them all out here wie' Kerlie." Stephen and Boyd are flummoxed. Stephen exclaims, "No fuckin' weapons, Wallace, are yee feckn mad?" William continues, "Naw Stephen, no weapons, no dirks, no blades, no nuthin'. If we get stopped goin' in there and those bastards find anything on us, then we're fucked." Boyd says, "He's right Stephen, but ah'll tell yiez, once we are, up at me Dá's hoose, he has a stockpile o' old weapons that he keeps for barterin' at the smithy market?" Stephen curses, "Fuck, I'm no' bleedin' happy about this Wallace, oi tink it's a feckn bad idea, but ah trust yie…" William says, "Then let's do it, for we've not got the time to be wastin' out here." Boyd enquires, "Wallace, what's the plan?" William replies, "We should be strippin' off not just our weapons, but all o' our Gallóglaigh armour too, we'll join in by lookin' like the stragglers, I reckon it's the only sure way that we've got any chance o' getting' in there."

"That's it?" exclaims Boyd, "Yie mean, that's yer plan?"

"Aye," replies William, "ah reckon so." Stephen and Boyd glance at each other bemused as William continues, "Look there, see, many of those stragglers are bloodied and wounded, they don't look se' very much different from us, ah reckon the English guards will be too busy helpin' those wounded straggler fella's to be givin' us much notice. And if the English commanders have any fuckin' sense at all, they'll be using all their spare men to make sure the castle is no' going to be attacked on all sides, so, I think goin' in se' bold as yie like and straight through that port gate, is the best chance we have." Stephen says, "Wallace, ah'm still no' se' sure about this, why don't we split up as soon as we're through those gates, then we can meet at Boyd's hoose, if we miss that, then make the meet up at the Bruin hoose?"

"Aye, that makes sense," replies William, "but no' at the Bruin hoose, ah don't want Marion and Brìghde brought into this if we get caught. We should make the meet for the back-orchard o' Saint Kentigerns." Stephen and Boyd nod their heads in agreement. William continues, "Right, so let's get all our fightin' kit off right now, then get to be joinin' in with those stragglers down there before it's too late." Boyd says, "Listen Wallace, why don't we help to carry you in between us, as though yer wounded, for you're such a big fit an' healthy lookin' bastard, ah reckon any way that we can dumb yie down so no' to be noticed is gonnae help."

Everybody laughs, then Stephen says, "That's a good idea Wallace, for it looks as though yie've used yer face as a last line o' defence in that we scuffle we just had up at the Loudoun, so usin' Boyd's way, yee will sure be passin' off easy enough as a right big dumb-fuck mute that really does need help." Once again everyone laughs as William, Stephen and Boyd quickly disrobe their Gallóglaigh battledress and all obvious warlike equipment. "Lets git goin' now Wallace," exclaims Stephen, "ah need to be seein' me bonnie darlin' Brìghde, for a sure ahm hatin' the way ahm feelin' in ma bleedin' gut right now, for the last time that ah had this type o' feelin' in me gut, was when…" William looks intently at his friend, then he puts his arm around Stephen's shoulder and pulls him close, the keen understanding of what happened at the Glen Afton massacre, is still raw between the two friends. William says, "C'mon, let's go…"

Kerlie says "Go safe, we'll keep yiez covered as best we can."

The three friends surreptitiously slide down the embankment; then they casually sit at the side of the road as though resting. After a few tense moments, they are thankful when they see that no one really notices them amongst the desperate refugees fleeing from the slaughter of the Loudoun hill, all of whom are too busy rushing and panicking to get into the safety of Lanark castle and town precincts.

Stephen says, "Would yee just be lookin' at the state o' them all Wallace, they're really all fucked up, and not one o' them in that group o' stragglers is giving us a second glance, let's go for it right now. C'mon, lets move…" Boyd agrees, "Aye Wallace, let's get in there now, mirth aside, ah reckon you should get yerself' in between me and Stephen and we'll kinda co-carry yie in there, just you keep yer big fuckin' head down till we're well inside and sorted." William says, "Wait…" Stephen enquires, "Wait? Wait for bleedin' what? We need to get into that town Wallace, before we're left out here all on our own." Standing upright, William points to a small group of wailing women, who are screaming desperately at their frightened, exhausted children to hurry them up, but it is obvious that the children are completely bereft.

"Quick," says William, "let's go get those wains and put them on our backs to help those women," Boyd exclaims, "What the fuck Wallace, you want to help them… for what, they're fuckin' English and have no cares about our plight?" William replies, "Naw, they could just as easy be our women and wains standing there Boyd, and besides, I reckon it'll be a better ploy to get us into the town. With those women and wains there, we might even be lookin' like we're just more families seekin' shelter." Stephen immediately goes over to the closest child and lifts her up in his arms, everyone watches, then, as Stephen looks into the tearful eyes of the young girl, a broad Irish smile sweeps across his face as the young girl puts her arms around his neck. "Oh, thank you kind sir," says the mother. William and Boyd quickly seek out more of the most distressed children and lift some of them onto their backs while holding the hands of others. The mothers of the children are grateful and quickly seek the sanctuary of these burly men, who have taken to help them in their time of need.

At that moment, a troop of English horsemen thunder around the bend on the road, knocking stragglers asunder mercilessly, as they gallop on up the old road towards the gatehouse at speed. "That's him," exclaims Stephen. "That's fuckin' him…" Boyd enquires, "That's who?" Stephen points and looks at William, "That's him Wallace, that's that fuckin' de Percy bastard we've been lookin' for, I'm sure of it." William is stunned to hear Stephens words, he enquires, "Are yie sure?" Stephen replies, "Sure oi'm fuckin' sure. I swear that's him."

William enquires, "But you've no' really met him, how could yie tell it was him." Stephen replies, "That coat of arms that's on his horse-coats and shield. I might never yet had a right good look at the bastard, but I've memorised every detailed description of his coat o' arms into me brain, every fuckin' day I see it, I'm certain that's him Wallace." William says, "I'll know for certain when we go in there, and if it is him…" Boyd interrupts, "Whoever the fuck it is, we had better get in there now before this column o' stragglers dies right down and we're the last to be getting' in, then we'll be noticed for sure." William nods his head to move on, when he realises the mothers are all staring at him. He says, "Don't uze worry mother's, we'll be getting' yiez in there safe and sound."

One of the mothers puts her arms around her child, points at William and says in a fearful panicky voice. "But… but you're one of those evil Scotchmen, and they're the one's who attacked us on the road this morn?" Concerned that the woman may begin screaming for help, William quickly moves in close to her, then he looks down and smiles sympathetically, he says to her, "Now don't you be frettin' or worryin' yourself there mother, for just like you English folks, we Scots are not all the same. We'll make sure to be lookin' after yiez all till we get into Lanark town, for it's certain that no one will cause yie any ill nor harm while we are by your side." William's demeanor and his words appear to placate the concerned mother. They all gather quickly and move towards the sanctuary of the castle Gatehouse.

As they finally walk through the main gates, Stephen says, "It's like Boyd said earlier Wallace, there aren't too many guards about the gates, those mesnie that are here are in utter confusion tryin' to tend to all the wounded and sortin' out petrified stragglers." Boyd says, "Just keep goin' and try tae look as if we're petrified too for fucks sake." Within a few moments, they are soon walking under the barbican and into the main town. "We're in Wallace." says a jubilant Stephen.

"Aye," replies William, "but we have to get to Boyd's house quick before we get challenged."

As they finally clear the outer gates and walk into the inner sanctum of Lanark town, the little group consolidate and let the children down to be with their mothers, just then, William looks across the barbican square and sees his uncle Ranald standing with de Valence, Hazelrigg and Lord de Percy. Boyd exclaims, "Fuck me Wallace, there's Ranald Crauford up there with those English knights, what's he doin' here?" William replies, "Ah don't know, but we'll likely find out soon enough." Suddenly he notices that Marmaduke de Percy and some of his men are walking from the stable barracks, directly towards them.

For just a brief moment, even at quite a distance, their eyes meet and make contact. Marmaduke is halted immediately by this sudden glance, he says to his man-at-arms, "You, Thorpe, I say, do you recognise that large dalcop that's standing away down there by the barbican gatehouse?"

Thorpe looks towards the little group, after a moment he replies, "I don't think so my lord, is he important?" Suddenly Marmaduke gasps, "It's him, I'm certain of it..." Thorpe enquires, "It's who my lord?" Marmaduke replies, "Hurry Thorpe, send some of the men to warn those mesnie at the gatehouse to drop the outer portcullis immediately, lock the barbican doors and then quickly close off all exits for that man. I want him taken alive. Now move, get some of the other men to surround those Scotchies now, I don't want any of them escaping through your stupidity." Thorpe replies, "Yes my Lord. He must be of great importance to you?" Marmaduke replies, "He certainly is Thorpe. I believe that man down there is a vulgar felon I've been searching for since I first came to this wretched land, I'm damned sure that it's him, yes, Wallace, that man's a brigand chief that's wanted for many murders…"

"Stay easy…" says William. Stephen and Boyd have also noticed Marmaduke approaching. All three of them instinctively use the children to cover their obvious characteristics in comparison to everyone else nearby. When the mothers attempt to take the children away, they too see the soldiers coming towards them. Suddenly the children start crying and screaming while clinging desperately to William, Stephen and Boyd for safety, "It's the soldiers…" says one of the mothers, "the children, they are feared of any armed men they see after such evil they've witnessed this day."

The three friends try desperately to calm the children down as de Percy and his men gain ever closer, but to no avail, the disturbance at the gatehouse causes other soldiers close-by to quickly look around, then they too begin approaching to investigate the situation. The noises being made from the Portcullis dropping, attracts everyone else's attention. Distracted too by the disturbances, Sir Henry enquires, "What goes on down yonder at the gatehouse?" Hazelrigg replies, "I'm not sure my lord?" They all look over to see what the disturbance is all about. Ranald too peers down towards the gatehouse, he is taken aback when he realises that it is William and Stephen who are standing inside the port archway to the gatehouse, and seemingly the immediate focus of everyone's attention, but he says nothing in the fervent hope the apparent disturbance will quickly quieten down before William is recognised; and that the three friends may then disappear safely into the gathering crowds.

As Marmaduke gains much closer to William, he stops, points, then he calls out, "You there, I know you don't I, your name is William Wallace, isn't it?" but there is no reply from

William as he tries to shy away. Marmaduke calls out once more, "I say, you there; I mean you, the large sard down at the barbican…" William looks directly at de Percy. Suddenly the absolute and undeniable spark of recognition between the two adversaries is dramatic. Marmaduke immediately waves to the Gatehouse guards then points manically at William. The Portcullis slams down to a rest and the gatehouse doors are firmly shut and barred, completely blocking off any escape route back out through the town gates. The guards then lower their keen halberds and move menacingly towards the three friends. Marmaduke hastily orders his men of the crossbow to move quickly to intimidate and force William, Stephen and Boyd, hard up against the bailey wall.

"Looks like we're sure fucked now," says Stephen. "I'll strangle these English wains wit' me bare hands if I must, for us to be gettin' away." Boyd curses, "Jaezuz' bones, what are we gonnae do now Wallace, we've no got any weapons on us; and those bastards have got us real cornered."

It's not long before Marmaduke and a large group of English soldiers have the three friends, along with the mothers and the children, all hemmed in and surrounded with their backs pressed against the bailey wall. For a few moments, nothing is said during this stalemate, while other English soldiers move in to complete the encirclement.

"Take your wains away now mother," says William as he passes the children in his care over to her. "I said earlier you would be safe by my side, ah'm sorry, but now that's no longer true. So take your children away now and leave us… go, go quickly." Frustrated, Stephen and Boyd glare at William, then very reluctantly, they too discharge the children to the mothers who had entered Lanark town in their care. As the mothers and children escape the deadly encirclement and rush to safety, William, Stephen and Boyd can only wait…

and watch. "Wallace," says Marmaduke, with a smug expression of satisfaction evident on his face, continues, "At long last Wallace, I have you now. I can honestly say that it's good to see you here this day, finally by God. You have no idea how long it's been in my mind to have you caught like a little mouse in a trap, and now... you most certainly are." William says nothing by reply, but both he and Stephen are seething inside, contemplating any way they may end the bastard de Percy's life, no matter what cost to themselves. Looking at the ground in front of them, they reach down and grab long manacle chains, used earlier to shackle traders that had been arrested and imprisoned. They wrap the chains tight round their fists and prepare to fight.

"Seize those men..." orders Marmaduke. "I want them taken alive, if any of you kill them, you will take their place on the gallows, now beat them down with staves." De Percy's men prepare to move in on the three companions, but they hesitate. Thorpe says, "My Lord, it would be easier to kill them with bolts and flights?" Marmaduke turns on Thorpe and slaps his face hard. "Do as I say Thorpe, or you'll be the first to dance on a rope-end." Thorpe, Angered and infuriated by the degrading slap from de Percy, brutally manhandles his men forward; shouting at them, "Take them..."

Boyd suddenly reaches out and tries to grab the nearest halberd held by an English soldier, instantly he is struck by a crossbow bolt that penetrates deep into his shoulder, felling him to the ground. Some of the other English soldiers begin to pelt the three friends with stones, causing them to cower down against the gatehouse bailey wall; Thorpe's men quickly rush forward with their heavy cudgels and start beating the three friends, still cowering from the stoning onslaught. William and Stephen attempt to raise themselves, but they are quickly overwhelmed as more soldiers appear and rush in with their staves and cudgels to beat the three friends most severely.

"Enough." commands Marmaduke de Percy.

The soldiers immediately back away from the three friends, who are now prostrate on the ground, heavily battered, bruised and bleeding. William and Stephen help Boyd to his feet, then they painfully push themselves up the wall to stand defiant. Stephen wipes blood from his head, he says, "Oi reckon we could still take these durty fuckers right out now Wallace." William looks at Stephen, almost laughing at the surreal yet genuine intent of Stephen's comment, just then, Marmaduke calls out for the mothers and children who had entered with the three friends, to be brought to stand before him. He speaks quietly with Thorpe, who then turns to speak to some of de Percy's soldiers, suddenly, the mothers and children are subdued and forced to their knees facing William; daggers are then held menacingly across their throats.

"What's it going to be Wallace?" says Marmaduke. "Is this going to be some noble struggle where you try to escape, but you end up dead, or will you force me to cut the throats of these baggage train whores and their tit-rats, and you will still end up dead regardless? Or Wallace, you can surrender peaceably, and we may talk awhile, then we will hang you for the murder of my good friend Selby in Dundee, and many others no doubt. So, what's it to be Scotchman?" Stephen mutters, "Wallace, oi'm going to kill that bastard…"

Sir Henry De Percy approaches and demands an answer, "What goes on here, what's this fracas about?" Marmaduke glances round to see his father standing behind him. "Father I, I…" Sir Henry growls, "Don't bloody stutter you idiot; what's going on here boy? You have got three local ne'er-do-wells hard pressed up against this wall and you're taking up the valuable time of these soldiers, what are you thinking when we have to gather all the men to man the ramparts in the event we are attacked... and what are you doing with those poor bloody women and their children on their knees there, release them now, at once, do you hear me?"

"But father," exclaims Marmaduke, "this man here, this is William Wallace, he's the infamous outlaw and the cruel murderer of many innocent Englishmen, a brigand chief and warlord by all accounts." Sir Henry is quite dumbfounded by his bastard son's revelation. "Where is Crauford?" demands Sir Henry. "Fetch sheriff Crauford to me now. We shall soon confirm who this wretched fellow is." Sir Henry rubs his chin, then he smiles and enquires, "So you are William Wallace, are you?" At that moment, Ranald, who had been trying to stay out of sight, walks through the gathering crowd and stands beside Sir Henry, knowing only too well that Sir Henry will not be fooled. Aware that he must speak the truth, Ranald exclaims, "William, it's really you?"

Hazelrigg also pushes his way through the crowd. When he reaches the position where Sir Henry, Ranald and Marmaduke are standing, he see's William and immediately exclaims, "By God sir, I do know that knave's face, I had him on the end of a rope last year, just after I caught him stealing horses near a small town called, eh, what was it now? Ah yes, Paisley, but he was, ah, not that he 'Was' but he 'Is' a servant of Bishop Wishart. I knew it, I knew that Wishart fellow would have links to outlawry and felons, now I have got the evidence to prove it." For a few brief moments, there is an unusual silence at the corner of the Lanark town's gatehouse. William, with his back hard pressed against the bailey wall, looks away up the steep hill towards the main castle proper, there he sees what appears to be hundreds of local people beginning to gather, watching this unusual spectacle unfold from their almost theatrical vantage point, a fact that is also noticed and observed by Sir Henry. "Wallace?" says Marmaduke. "I shall make this plain for even your tiny Scotch brain to understand, I want you and your fellow dogs to surrender to me now, then we shall take you up to the castle without any further ado. Or we shall simply hang lord Crauford here first, for you have breached his bond with us over surety for you, what is your will?" Crauford looks to Sir Henry, but there is no response.

"Take him." Orders Marmaduke. Soldiers immediately seize Ranald. "No, wait…" says a voice nearby. Sir Aymer de Valence approaches Sir Henry and speaks a few discreet words to him in private. Sir Henry looks at William while he scratches his chin thoughtfully, then he steps forward a pace and call's out, "Wallace, I do not have the time for this foolishness so I shall put this to you, that although we thought you dead, it would appear so that you are not. Now this may be some type of witchcraft, or perhaps even you are some revenant from those evil woodlands that's come to cast spells over us, and as such, you should be burned at the stake along with your associates, but I think not, rather it is just simply good fortune intervening on your behalf, that allows you to stand here before us this day." William states brusquely. "So, what's your fuckin' point Englishman?" Sir Henry replies, "Ah, you should be guarding your tongue somewhat Wallace, don't you know that arrogance and ignorance are shadow bedfellows that may eventually cost you most dearly…"

"But Father," exclaims Marmaduke. "Wallace …" Sir Henry turns immediately on his bastard son, "Boy, do not ever call me father; you will address me as Sir Henry or my lord." Upon hearing these public comments of chastisement, a great sigh of consternation begins to ripple through the gathering crowd of onlookers.

"I shall say this to you master Wallace," continues Sir Henry, "there's neither the need nor the time to be debating the why's or wherefore's, for I previously gave the good Sherriff Crauford here my pardon for you, and that pardon is also my word, therefore, it still stands." Sir Henry turns his back on William to face the gathering crowds and soldiers, who all appear with expressions of complete confusion or bewilderment. He says, "I say to you all, that his man who now stands before us, William Wallace, has been very much wronged and slighted in the eyes of the law keepers of this, our new province. He has been much maligned by some, that I do believe have with the heinous intentions, made a bid to discredit my good judgement, therefore, I shall seek out and punish those responsible. In the meantime however, I shall endeavor to rectify this miscarriage. Now all of you, go about your business, there is nothing more to see here."

The expressions of absolute horror and disbelief on the faces of Marmaduke and Hazelrigg are obvious to all. Sir Henry turns to face William, Stephen and Boyd, who also have expressions of disbelief etched all over their faces. Sir Henry steps forward slightly, then he says to William, "May I talk with you in private?" William is astounded, confused, but extremely wary. He sees Sir Henry taking another few paces forward towards him; William reciprocates as he too steps forward, to the point where they may both talk discreetly... and in private.

"What's this play about Englishman?" enquires William. Sir Henry replies, "Walk with me Wallace, I do insist. And please, do call me Henry, there's absolutely no need for any formalities between you and I when we talk in private." But William does not reply, such is his confusion and acute wariness in this most unusual situation. Sir Henry continues, "If you talk with me Wallace, you may find it to your vantage, and that of your associates too. And pending the conclusion of any agreement we may reach, as a gesture to you of my good will, you may send your Irishman and that other Scotchie friend of yours up to the Saint Kentigern's infirmary right away, for I do believe the wounded fellow there should have his wound treated properly. Or, you may let that bastard son of mine shoot you all down with flights and bolts, but only after you witness the good sheriff Crauford being hung from the ramparts by the neck till dead, for giving succour and aid to wanted felons. It is your choice to make Wallace, for I want this matter concluded, indeed, I insist that we end this matter now, for I have better things to be doing that requires my urgent attention?"

Quite taken aback at this unusual turn of events, William looks deep into the eyes of Sir Henry, looking for any signs of treachery, but in his own brief rationale of the situation, why would there be. "Aye, ah'll walk with yie Englishman." he says with a hint of caution in his voice.

"Wonderful." replies Sir Henry. "I knew you would see it my way." Sir Henry turns towards the ensemble before him, who are eagerly awaiting the outcome of the private conversation between himself and William, though it is clear to all by the expression on the faces of Hazelrigg and the bastard son Marmaduke, they are far from amused. William says, "Stephen, take Boyd up to Saint Kentigerns infirmary, I'll be stayin' here awhile with Lord Percy. I'll catch up with yiez later." Stephen exclaims, much to the amusement of Sir Henry, "What the fuck are yee doin' wit' him Wallace, it must be some kind o' trick, don't you be trustin' that bastard?" William replies, "It's like this English fella has just said Stephen, I have to make a choice, but it's sure no' a choice that I thought I had a wee while ago, to walk and talk, this would seem to me like the better choice to make."

Sir Henry says, "He's a very lively fellow your Irish servant, rather astute too I would warrant." William says, "He's not ma servant Englishman, he's ma friend." Sir Henry replies, "A friend, really? Sadly, that is a luxury I cannot afford myself these days, and please, do call me Henry." Suddenly Marmaduke inexplicably calls out…. "Hang them now. They are murderers of English soldiers." Immediately there is tumultuous disquiet arousing amongst the English soldiers of Marmaduke and Hazelrigg.

"Thorpe," continues Marmaduke, "secure those felonious villains now and have them prepared for the gallows…"

As both Marmaduke and Hazelrigg's men move forward, Sir Henry moves quickly in defence of William and pulls on his sword, at that same moment, Sir Aymer walks briskly over to stand beside Sir Henry, both their personal bodyguards of battle-hardened veterans also pull on their swords. Sir Henry raises his hand firmly and speaks with authority…

"You will halt where you are, all of you; there will be no killing here this eve. These men you wish to hang have previously gained my pardon, and as such, they are under my protection. To my knowledge, they've not acted out of self interest, but I warrant that it was more to the contrary, for they have acted out of self-preservation from attacks committed by less reputable personages, who doest bring shame upon the name of our King. Therefore, any man who would dare move to harm them, also moves to harm my very person, and by proxy, that of our gracious king; and that same man or those who sanction him to do so, shall surely suffer the most extreme consequences from such an action."

"My lord," protests Marmaduke. "But this is preposterous, you cannot do this…"

"I said, any man…" concludes Sir Henry forcefully. He continues, "Hazelrigg, get your men to man the ramparts,

I want them all watching for hostile movements and then reported to me immediately, is that clear, do you understand?" Hazelrigg appears shaken, "Yes my lord, at once my lord."

As Hazelrigg commences to enact his duties, Sir Henry then turns on Marmaduke, "And you boy, go to my chambers and wait there for me to attend you, once you have detailed exactly why you are here, you are to leave directly for Glasgow and wait for me in my chambers there, now move." Marmaduke throws a vile grazing look towards William, not un-noticed by Sir Henry; then he replies, "Yes my lord."

Sir Henry turns and notices that William is also seething; he glances back at Marmaduke and his men walking away, then back at William. He says, "I can see that you have a desperate yearning to kill the bastard Wallace, I can see it written all over you, yet you stand here and let him simply walk away, how is it so?" William replies, "I have so much more than a yearning Percy," Sir Henry replies, "I can understand that." William can barely break his focus on Marmaduke, but the strange unexpected, almost bizarre behaviour of this English knight perplexes him. He looks at Sir Henry then says, "I will kill him Percy, mark my words, I will surely kill that man for what he has done to me."

"That may be so," says Sir Henry, "but not this day I'm sure, for should you break good Ranalds bond, then I would certainly have to hang you, and believe me, I have no wish to do so, besides, then what would the point of our little chat be? Out of sight is out of mind my dear fellow, you must always remember that." William looks Sir Henry square in the eye. "Why this Percy, why, I mean, for what purpose is this charade that you are playing out here in front of everyone, you could easily have killed us in the blink of an eye, like so many others who have fallen to you English, then there would be no more problems from us, but you... I don't understand?" Sir Henry replies, "Wallace, I'm aware what that runt, who unfortunately carries my good name, has done. I cannot change that, but I'm pragmatic, and as such, before we discuss matters, shouldn't you be getting your man sent up to the infirmary before he bleeds out?" Suddenly William realises Boyd is urgently in need of help, and fast.

"Wallace," says Sir Henry, "You really should get that man up to the infirmary with your Irish friend, I'll arrange for him to see my personal chirurgeon up there to tend him, for I do so wish to talk with you, if you would be so kind?" William again looks deep into the eyes of Sir Henry; there is something, just something that is profoundly honest in this Englishman's words, and in his eyes, yet… William replies, "Aye Percy, I'll walk and I'll talk with yie."

While William goes over to Stephen and Boyd, Sir Aymer talks with Sir Henry. "M'lord Percy, that was extremely interesting and very entertaining the way that you handled the situation, I think that if you had made a martyr out of that large chap Wallace, not only are there apparently a host of Scotch villain's out there, who we must assume would wish to get in here and cut all our throats, I do believe that the local population within these town walls, may have been incited to insurrection as a result, now you appear to be their local hero for sparing their man, to which, I compliment you and do totally agree with your actions?"

"Why thank you Aymer." replies Sir Henry, "But you know; there's something about that Wallace fellow that is very likeable. For some reason, he's escaped the gallows or the headsman's axe on a number of occasions in his short life, curiously, many of those occasions were as a result of my inadvertent pardons granted to him through his uncle. And the fact according to your nephew young Aylmer, that Wallace saved his life by fighting off some brigand warlord who had supposedly slain the entire entourage of my baggage train, that has me extremely curious indeed, intrigued even. T'is a pity he was not an Englishman, I could really use his kind, instead, I must put up with sloth-patted fools and craven fazart's of our own to rule here."

"A life for a life…" says Aymer, "a very honourable gesture, to which I do thank you m'lord." Sir Henry says, "I don't think my bastard nor Hazelrigg see it that way though my friend." Aymer replies, "Nevertheless, I do concur with everything you have made possible this day. And once again, I do thank you on behalf of my nephew for sparing the life of Wallace." Sir Henry replies, "We shall talk more on this later."

Aymer nods his head in agreement., "I shall take my leave of you good sir, for Sir Thomas de Gray has arrived, safely thank God. He now awaits in my castle chambers; I shall speak with you later." Sir Henry calls out, "Just a moment Aymer, I rather fancy we should leave for Glasgow before sunrise, I believe that with the escort of Sherriff Ranald and his men, and possibly with the attendance of Wallace too, then I do not fear for any mishaps with bandits or ne'er-do-wells on route. Besides, we should already have been in Glasgow this day; how say you?" Aymer replies, "I think I should feel a lot safer travelling with you and Wallace, than staying here any longer in this place, quaintly romantic though it may be." Sir Henry laughs aloud, "So be it my friend. I shall spend some time with my new-found Scotch associate, then I shall meet with you at the stable yards before the daybreak bells." Turning to see where William is located, Sir Henry is immediately startled by the fierce glour emitting from his 'newfound Scotch associate.' who is watching him intensely.

As the night criers light up the town's torches and braziers, Sir Henry says, "Come Wallace, shall we go over to yonder inn and share fine bread and ale together? There we may find out what we do have and what we do not have in common, then we can establish the common ground we may both place our feet upon, without thoughts of killing one another? Is that an agreeable suggestion for you to consider?"

William is finding it extremely difficult to accept such kind and benevolent platitudes coming from this Englishman, but there is also something very appealing in his nature too. William replies, "Aye, ah reckon so, I'll listen to yie awhile Englishman, and you have ma word that I'll not try and kill yie too." Sir Henry replies, "Splendid, splendid, there's a good fellow." The candor of Sir Henry is disturbing and unsettling William as they walk over to the Inn, there they sit down outside at a large oak bench. Refreshments are soon brought to them as the conversation continues.

Throughout their unusual meeting, Marion is constant at the back of William's mind, nagging and burning away at his thoughts of where she might be, what's happened to her, he knows he must get away to try and find her…

"May I?" requests Sir Henry. William's thoughts are disturbed by this vague question. William enquires, "May you what?" Sir Henry replies, "That talisman around your neck." William is curious, "This?" He hadn't realised he has been toying with the Aicé talisman all the way through their conversation. He continues in a slight fluster, "Why this is nothing, well, it's something that's passed down the generations of my people, then to me."

"Wonderful," replies Sir Henry, "though I'm sure I have seen one similar before, and only recently I may add." Cautiously, William enquires, "Where could you have seen another such as this?" Sir Henry replies, "T'was of a different precious metal I believe, now where was it that I saw it? Ah, now I remember, t'was around the neck of a fair maid." There is no concealing the immediate concern that becomes apparent on William's face. Sir Henry continues, "Yes, it was adorning the maid as I say, or should I say, it was adorning your wife Marion when last I saw her. Yes, very pretty indeed." Thumping his fists down on the table, William erupts in anger, then he demands an answer, "Stop playing me for a fool Percy, what is it you really want from me?" Sir Henry replies, almost casually, "I will tell you what I want from you Wallace, I want your service, I want your loyalty, and most of all, I want you by my side."

William is mortified by this request as Sir Henry continues.

"For reasons beyond both our understanding Wallace, I have known about you ever since I set foot in this realm, indeed, on many occasions I have signed my own reputation upon your uncle's bond to grant you a pardon. Even on the morrow, when I shall be attending the Glasgow guilds council, don't you know, even those men wish you dead, for your reputation is damaging their traders profits to such an extent, you are highest on their list of grievances." William is completely taken aback by these revelations.

Sir Henry continues, "Wallace, even at Invergarvane, where you or your men did kill my most favoured horse from underneath me, and you very nearly killed me too, are you not aware that my presence there was as your own, to stop more bloodshed, not be party to more of it being spilled? Yet, here I am, once more pondering over why I have gifted you life, when any other man would now be food for worms. Even when you were presumed killed by the guards at Ayr Castle, yet here we both are, sitting across from each other at the same table, sharing fine ale and bread together, does it not make you want to stop and wonder too?" William is tired, fatigued, desperate to see Marion and cannot make sense of the situation. He says, "It... I don't know what's going on, but I cannot do what you ask of me my lord Percy."

Sir Henry says. "Do call me Henry, there's a good chap. I must tell you Wallace, I know so much about you. I know what has been done to your family and I do offer you my sincerest apologies for what's happened, both to you and to your people, it is unconscionable. Yet, I also know from my own experience, that these words will probably mean nothing to you, perhaps they may even make you more enflamed with a grievous hatred for the English. But I say this to you in all sincerity, you must always look to your own back first before you try and strike me down Wallace, for we English would not be here, but for your own fellow Scots inviting us through an open door. Your familie's own demise, savage and despicable as it was, had been initially instigated by one of your own fellow Scots. I like you Wallace, I like everything that I've heard about you, and it is confirmed now that I have met you. If you really want to affect what's happening within this realm, then I need people such as you to help me make these changes, that is why I want you by my side, but should you choose to be outwith the law, then I'm afraid, so be it."

"What you ask of me is nigh impossible Percy. Too much cruelty and hatred has been inflicted upon me and my people; the cruel torture and murders that your soldiers have thrust upon a peaceful loving people, I could never have dreamt o' in my wildest nightmares. But now, now I live in breathe the reality that you and your king has placed upon me." Sir Henry says, "Think of Marion and your child then Wallace, do they not need protection, what has already been put upon her could have been prevented..." William is incensed, "Shut yer dirty fuckin' mouth Percy, or..."

"Or what Wallace, or you will do what?" William is fatigued, fretting and does not reply, Sir Henry continues, "I thought so, do not place your guilt upon another in regard to her protection, you are her husband, but when those men, and it is as much to my own shame as it is yours, but when they plied rapine upon that household, I ask you, where were you?" William is suddenly overtaken by guilt, stress and in particular, the slow-burning fatigue from the exertions placed on his body from the battle of Loudoun hill. His head spins and he feels nauseas. Sir Henry says, "Here, drink some ale Wallace, it would seem the beating you received upon entry to this place, is but a part of those other injuries you carry from this day, here, drink…"

William accepts the ale from his sometime host.

Sir Henry continues, "I want you to come into my service Wallace, do this for me and I shall protect Marion as though she were as my very own daughter, and you shall both have the land to raise a family in peace and be free of all the misery and mistrust that is now the currency of this realm. But alas, should you reject my offer, I shall still honour my word to you and will ensure that my pardon still stands, but for how long I wager, and what then of Marion and your child without my protection, what say you now?"

"Why Percy," enquires William. "I ask you again, why would you offer this to me?"

"Apparently," says Sir Henry, "there was some sort of insurrection, of which I know not yet the full details, but there will be extremely punitive repercussions because of it, believe me. But since there has not been any further incidents, such as an attack on this town and castle, I must assume what happened may simply be an isolated incident, and as such, must be played down." William enquires, "What do you mean? There were many Englishmen killed, and mostly from your own household… eh, so I've been told?" Sir Henry grins: then he continues, "Ah, but those killed can easily be replaced, as there are many hungry fools who are anxious to fill dead men's boots, though it is a tad distracting.

What is of greater importance to me and my King, is the serious implications and example this may set to the rest of the population in Scotland, and that my friend, we cannot have. So, whomever was the leader of that little 'incident' shall we call it, eh, at Loudoun hill, was it?" William nods his head as Sir Henry continues, "This incident has but served to ensure that there will be even greater punitive control over this realm, and as a result, will most certainly be the cause of many more deaths of your fellow countrymen, for though what happened will not be widely reported, King Edward will have his blood for blood, I do believe that you people here call it, 'paying the blood tax,' am I correct?"

"Wallace?" enquires a young voice nearby. William immediately turns his head and is totally surprised to see Aylmer standing beside John Blair.

"Aylmer," exclaims William, "I'm sure glad to be seeing you here young fella, and you too Blair." William is genuinely pleased to see Aylmer, but he is also concerned as to what he has said or what he might say about the Loudoun hill. Sir Henry says, "Aylmer here, and also this priest, has told us all about what you did to save him from the Warlord who massacred my men, ah, what was his name again Aylmer?" The boy looks at William directly. Without taking away is gaze, he replies, "The warlord's name, it is… it's John Moor my lord."

William's eyes light up, he exclaims, "John Moor?"

Aylmer looks at Sir Henry and says, "Yes my lord, his name was John Moor, I shall never forget it. He was going to chop my head off, but Sir Wallace here, he fought him off, then saved me and John the priest, who then protected me all the way here." Blair says, "By all that is holy my lord, and upon the blessed scriptures, this boy Aylmer speaks the truth to you." Sir Henry, still smiling, says, "Yes, that may be so."

He continues, "This brave deed Wallace, this is what really tipped the balance and saved you from the gallows this night, but isn't life so strange on occasion, for we could have been enemies you and I, yet this situation has given us the opportunity to finally meet and break bread together. We may never be friend's Wallace, for I am too old for that nonsense, but what I have seen in my life, well, let's just say that I do wish the world was a much better and kindlier place than it is. I do believe that it still could be, but then, nothing stops progress Wallace, that is why you must now sincerely consider my offer to you." Sir Henry then prepares to leave. He says "Come Aylmer, we must go to meet with your uncle, for we leave very early on the morn. And you Wallace; do think of all that I have said. For when I leave here before sunrise, I would dearly wish it so that you were by my side upon our trip to Glasgow."

"I will think on it Percy," replies William, "my answer will be in your company by morn, or not, either way, you will have ma reply." Sir Henry simply nods; then he says, "Come Aylmer." He turns and begins to walk away.

"Henry..." says William.

Sir Henry turns and sees Wallace grinning, he too grins, then he enquires, "You require something more from me Wallace?" William enquires, "Did you campaign in Wales, and if so, did you ever save a young mans life called Bailey?" Sir Henry pauses for a moment, then a look of surprise lightens up his features, "Yes, actually I do remember him. And if I remember it rightly, his name was Wallace too, a kinsman of yours, am I correct?" William smiles, "Aye, Bailey Wallace, he was kin to me. He once told me that you were a tough, ruthless old bastard, who taught him much about having no mercy upon an enemy, but he also said you're a fair bastard too." Both Sir Henry and William laugh. William then continues "You will have my answer by the morn." Sir Henry replies, "Then go and find Marion. Though I know not where she is residing at the moment, I do know that she will be nowhere till you are by her side and you have her in your arms. Now... I shall bid you a good eve, or should I say what is left of it." Sir Henry walks away with Aylmer, who waves an innocent farewell to William and Blair.

"John Moor?" exclaims William. Blair says, "Aye, that's just close enough for those tiny wee English ears upon hearing the very name of Sean mòr." William says, "Then should I take up the offer of Sir Henry, that I may spend the rest of my days hunting down and never finding the warlord of the Loudoun hill massacre, John Moor." William's demeaner quickly changes, "Marion Blair, I must find her and the lassies, have you heard anything?" Blair looks at William, then he replies, "You look exhausted Wallace; you should take to rest some. Why not go up to the infirmary and lay there awhile. I will try and seek out Marion's whereabouts while you get some sleep. I think Ranald is up there at the moment with Sir Hugh." William, thoroughly exhausted, replies, "I cannot rest till I have her in my arms..."

There is a long pause as the two friends look at each other. William enquires, "Tell me Blair, has anyone seen her or Brìghde, do yie know of their whereabouts at all?" Blair replies, "Nobody has seen her since the abhorrent assault; though one of the Sisters up in Saint Kentigerns did say to me that she thought that Marion and Brìghde had fled the town with little Mharaidh, seeking shelter in the Wolf and wildcats, but she believes Marion will return to the infirmary in the morn to prepare Brannah's body for internment." William says, "And it's known that it was the son of Hazelrigg, Arthur, who is responsible for this assault placed on Marion and her family?"

"Aye," replies Blair, "There is little doubt about it, and from what I have gleaned, it was at the behest of his father, who was doing everything he could to find you." William enquires, "For what purpose?" Blair replies, "I don't know Wallace, but it's rumoured that Arthur Hazelrigg wants to have Marion as his wife." William is taken aback upon hearing the words from Blair. He exclaims, "No, no… this cannot be. Tell me this Blair, have I died and appeared in some hellish parallel dimension for some great misdeed that I have done, tell me this is not true…" Blair says, "If only it were so my friend, then I'd wake you with all that was within me to do so. But there are no other words to convey to you what has happened and what goes on in our lives."

"And Brannah…" enquires William, "is it true what I have heard of Brannah?" Blair replies, "It's all true Wallace, she's dead. It would seem that she was with child too, but after the rapine and abuse imposed upon her by Hazelriggs son Arthur and his men, she lost the child and bled out, there was nothing that anyone could do to save her." William drops his head once more; then he says mournfully, "She was so beautiful Blair, so full of life too. I don't know what Andrew Moray will do when he finds out what's happened to her." Blair says candidly, "Marion lost your unborn too Wallace." As William wipes the tears from his eyes, he replies, "I know. I'll tell yie Blair, I'll fuckin' slaughter those evil bastards. You be sure to be askin' your God to grant me the life of Arthur Hazelrigg and Marmaduke de Percy for what they have done to my family, for there are no Ceil Aicé nor any real Christians who do such evil things." Blair says, "We should go now Wallace." William enquires, "Aye, but where?" Blair replies. "Saint Kentigerns…" At that moment, a young priest arrives carrying a note for Blair. He quickly unfolds the note and reads the message. Blair looks at William while holding the note over a candle flame to ensure it is completely destroyed. William enquires, "What was in that message?" Blair replies, "We should go now Wallace, there are important people nearby urgently waiting to meet you."

"Who?" enquires William. Blair replies, "The message says that Lamberton is returned from Paris and must have urgent talks with you. He waits at Biggar in the company of Sir William Douglas and his son James. John de Graeme is there too; they wish to pursue the campaign you've started at the Loudoun hill, in the name of King John." William exclaims, "Sir William Douglas... the Hardy, James and young John too?" Blair replies, "The very same." William says, "Then we should go to them when I've found Marion and I've taken her to a place of safety." Blair says, "Come Wallace, we must make haste to Saint Kentigerns, there we shall find out more detail." William replies, "Tell me Blair, what have we done to deserve such pain and suffering?"

They immediately leave the Lanarch inn and walk up the hill towards Saint Kentigerns, talking intently and in great detail. Unbeknownst to them, Sherriff Hazelrigg, his son Arthur, Marmaduke and Thorpe are observing them both, while standing furtively in a darkened recess, their bile fermenting to such a degree of hatred...

"Let me kill them now father," says Arthur, "for I shall not tolerate such a fall of face and grace as was done to us in this town square, caused entirely by that murderous felon, he does not deserve to live." Hazelrigg says, "We must do this with planning, for de Percy appears to be enamoured by that Scotch bastard, what must be done should be in such a way, that no fault may ever be placed upon us by de Percy."

"I wish it were so..." says Marmaduke, "even though I be a bastard born m'lord Hazelrigg, that you were my father in his stead. For I have long sought this Wallace for several years now, and when I finally do have him within my grasp..." Hazelrigg says, "Have no fear Marmaduke. We shall have him dead this night and his blood will be running to earth like a stuck boar. No fool cur born of this realm shall live long enough to enjoy privileges for which he has no standing, nor any merit that could ever belong to one such as he. But it must be as I said before, his death must appear to be within the bounds of the law." Marmaduke enquires, "Then it must be done quickly my lord, for my father wishes it so that I leave this place for Glasgow before sunrise, we have very little time to do this, what can be done?" Arthur says, "Father, give me the opportunity to redeem our family honour, I think I may know of a ploy that will agitate Wallace to such a degree, he will have no other choice but to retaliate and make to assault me, and then my lord, with my men lying in wait nearby, we shall have him, then we will slay him most assuredly dead, and it would be caused only by his own aggravating circumstance and vile demeanor."

"That may be so," says Marmaduke. "My lord Hazelrigg, Arthur, I have an idea too, if I may be so bold. For us to trap Wallace, if he has any thoughts of being a man, he will undoubtedly be searching for that Braidfuite bitch, and it would appear to me that he is moving in the direction of Saint Kentigerns at the moment with that priest. If Arthur here were to follow him, then antagonise him within the sanctity and sanctuary of Holy ground to such a degree, he would have no option but to react, then I believe, there would be no inadvertent response of any worth nor merit from my father, what say you both?" Arthur says, "Let me do this father, I need only take a few men with me as my witness, also, a small number will not attract the attention of any misguided local fools who would follow us and perhaps interfere." Hazelrigg says, "Then we shall make it so this very night. You two, go now and make sure that Wallace is most assuredly going to Saint Kentigerns, I will retire to the castle to entertain the lord's Percy, Gray and Valence, but I will send a sergeant at arms and a small troop to meet up with you, just to make sure that nothing untoward should happen to you my son, and to you too Marmaduke. Though you be no son of mine de Percy, my sons and I will always welcome you into our home as a kindred spirit." Marmaduke replies, "Why, I thank you most profusely for your kind words m'lord Hazelrigg. One day I shall honour that offer." Hazelrigg replies, "I feel that is the least that you deserve Marmaduke. Now I must go, I will send some men to aid you very shortly while you both get prepared to act…" Hazelrigg wraps his cape close, then he leaves for the castle. "Thorpe, you shall come with us." says Marmaduke.

As William and Blair near the eastern cloisters of Saint Kentigerns, it is a long overdue and welcome sight. William remembers the last time he had been here was when he was with his beloved Marion, at a time when the world was very much a different place, and all he had to worry about then, was the forthcoming betrothal and wedding service celebrations in a Christian fashion, but now… Suddenly the noise of a door-guard sliding open distracts William. He looks and sees the eyes of a Sister appearing and scrutinising both him and Blair, then the door guard is slammed shut, followed by the noisy rattles of great bolts and hasps being released behind the door. The door creaks open and a Sister beckons them to enter. She says, "Come Wallace."

"They have entered the infirmary." Says Marmaduke. "Now we shall wait for him to come back out, and soon we shall have him very dead at our feet." Arthur enquires, "How long shall we wait out here for him?" Marmaduke replies. "Not long, for I have a plan to lure Wallace out of there very shortly." Arthur says, "We should only give him short time though, for it will not be too long before dawn starts to break, then sunrise." Marmaduke looks around, then he says, Thorpe, find out where the men are that sheriff Hazelrigg said would be in attendance with us." Thorpe replies, "Yes my lord, I shall go and find out right away." As Thorpe leaves, Arthur says, "By m'lady de Percy, I do believe your knees are all a tremble, what's to do?" Marmaduke replies, "I tell you Hazelrigg, Wallace is no wastrel when it comes to a fight. I know, I have seen him fight before, it will take a few more than just you and I to subdue him..."

As the doors of Saint Kentigerns close behind William, he is instantly struck by a heavy pungent odour, that, with the very claustrophobic and dimly lit passageway leading to the infirmary and the fumes from the tallow lamps on the walls, cause him to be nauseas and his head begins to spin. The Sister says, "Follow me." But William has to reach out to support himself against the walls to prevent himself from falling over. "Are you unwell?" enquires Blair. William replies, "I just need a little while to steady ma'self." Blair says, "You're in a real mess Wallace, what with you having fought a battle this day and having to travel here, then the beating you took at the gates earlier on, it's a wonder that you're standing at all. I told you, you should get some rest." William replies, "I'm fine, lets just get to where we're going, I'll get some rest there." Blair nods to the Sister then they proceed down the passageway.

Upon entering the main infirmary, the pungent odour is almost overpowering, the source apparently coming from the many different potions and liniments being applied to wounds on the survivors from the Loudoun hill. As they wander through the main infirmary, William notices that Stephen and Boyd are lying in cribs at the far end of the spittal. Both he and Blair walk over, only to see they are both sleeping like babies. "Would yie look at that," says William, "they look more like skinned piglets over-greased for a spit-roast." Blair smiles, then a Sister nearby says, "That's the potions and poultice-butter the strange old man applied to them, normally we would not approve of such things to be used in this Godly place, but they seem to be working for everyone." William enquires, "To what old man do you refer Sister?" Just then, the rear doors of the infirmary opens, for a moment no-one comes through, then the strange old man the Sister was talking about, walks from behind the door, grinding and stirring potions in a large clay vessel, William exclaims, "True Tam... what are you doin' here?"

True Tam looks up and an emotion of pure delight crosses his face. "Young Wallace, ah'v found yie at last. Where have yie been boy, we've missed yie so?" Unexpectedly, Kerlie and some of the Gallóglaigh follow on behind true Tam into the infirmary.

"You're here too Kerlie?" exclaims William, "How did you fella's get in here?" True Tam ignores William and proceeds to tend to Stephens many wounds, he says, "It's best Stephen here is well out cold as ah cauterize his wounds and sew him up, for ah wouldn't fancy to be doin' this to him when the boy's awake." Kerlie exclaims, "Fuck Wallace, but ahm sure glad to be seein' you here..." A loud clucking noise nearby causes them to look round, only to see a Sister frowning at them, she says "Would you please not be using that pagan language in the house of God... And if you do so wish to talk, then please go outside, for these patients in here need much rest and sleep, now begone, all of you."

William, Kerlie and Blair leave the infirmary and go out into the orchard; there they take in deep breaths of clean fresh air. "What a day this has been," says Kerlie. "We thought when the gates went down and the doors shut behind yiez that yiez were all done for, so tell us, what happened?" William replies, "Ah'll tell yie later Kerlie, for ah don't think that I even believe what's just happened." William hears a noise nearby; he turns to see the rest of the Gallóglaigh gathering in the orchard. "How did you fella's all get in here; the English have the place sealed off?" Handing William his Gallóglaigh battle armour and weapons, Kerlie replies with a grin, "Well eh, we climbed in here through the Sisters cludgie passages." William exclaims, "Yiez did what?" Kerlie replies, "You heard me." Blair says, "Even I haven't tried that one before, hmm, though I don't think I ever will, no matter how desperate I am for the company of a sympathetic Sister."

Everyone laughs; then they all take a long rest from the almost superhuman exertions they have expounded in the last few days. True Tam exits through the infirmary door and speaks to William. "It was a real bad business son, ahm so sorry for the lassies." William replies, "Have you seen Marion or Brìghde Tam, the only thing that I've heard is that she went to our camp in the Wolf and wildcats?" True Tam appears puzzled, "Have yie no' seen her yet Wallace? She did make sure that the young one was safe back at our camp, but both her and Brìghde returned to Lanark a right few hours ago?" Blair says, "I was down at their townhouse then the Bruin hoose, there was no answer, nor were there any lamps lit in any of the windows?"

"Where can she be?" enquires William. He hastily puts on his battle gear then straps on his weapons. His obvious concern is heart-felt by everyone as they all immediately assemble from their impromptu rest. "I've got to get out of here to find her," says William. "She must be somewhere close by." Kerlie says, "We will find her. When we get out there, we'll split up and scour the town. Ah'll wake up

Stephen, for he'll want to search for them too." True Tam says, "Ach Kerlie, Stephen won't be waking for many hours, for ah'v knocked him clean out cold with a potion, it was the only way to cauterize then sew up the many wounds the poor fella has." True Tam looks at William, "Ah see that you're need stitched up a' plenty there too Wallace." William replies, "Naw, not now Tam, I need to get goin' from here. Maybe later when this is all settled and I get back here safe enough with Marion and Brìghde."

"Wallace?" William turns and is surprised to see Alan O'Dale at the spittal door, he enquires "O'Dale, what are you doin' here?" O'Dale replies, "I came in with Kerlie, but I went to the les quartier des femmes in the east wing with Faolán Fiónlaidh and Eochaidh, Wallace they were badly wounded at the fight up at the Loudoun. Though the obviously hadn't said anythin' to you, they were in a real bad way, they've lost a lot of blood from slashes and deep cuts, they need some bolt n' arrow heads pulled too then all o' their wounds need seared." William says, "I must go and see them..." O'Dale says, "Naw, yie cannae, they're in the women's infirmary, but I need to tell you that I met with Faoláns outriders about halfway between here and the Wolf and wildcats camp, they said they were lookin' to see if Marion and Brìghde were there, but since I'd just came from the camp, I told them no, they weren't there. Wee Morríaghan is at the camp and bein' looked after fine and well enough by Daun and Dénnaigh, so we came back here as fast as we could to let yie know this."

"Where can they both be then?" exclaims William desperately, "We need to go, I need to find them..." William calls out, "Boyd, get everyone together, we're leavin.'"

While William and the Galloglaigh prepare to leave the infirmary orchard, a Sister comes through the door and speaks to William. "There was a young boy at the door a moment ago Wallace, he says that Marion told him to tell you that she's hiding with Brìghde down at the Bruin hoose. The messenger says that she wants you to go there and fetch her back here as quickly as is possible." William says, "Ah thank yie Sister." The Sister replies, "No need to be thanking me, but please, do try and keep silent as you pass through the infirmary and spittal, for those poor souls need as much peace as they do God in their wretched lives." William replies, "We'll be as quiet as church mice Sister." Blair says, "Wallace, maybe we shouldn't all go down there together, we sure don't want to be makin' any mistakes with the English, especially if you're bringing Marion and Brìghde back here." Kerlie says, "Blair's right, we'll all string out in a long line behind yie Wallace, we'll be making sure that yer path is covered all the way there and all the way back." William straps on his grandfather's dirk, then says, "Ah'll take ma sword with me, for even though there's a kind o' truce goin' on between me and that fella Lord Percy, ah don't fuckin' trust the fuckers all around him..." Hearing a now familiar clucking noise beside him, William looks around then down, there he notices a deep frown on the little sister's forehead. He says, "Eh, ahm so sorry about that cursin' there Sister, just a wee turn o' the phrase, that's all."

The Sister smirks, she says, "Then we will say no more about it Wallace, now, you follow me." The little Sister leads William and the Gallóglaigh quietly through the spittal and infirmary in single file, till they get to the outer doors leading onto the public walkways. William opens the door slightly ajar then turns to Kerlie, "Are yiez sure yiez are all ready to follow me down there?" Kerlie replies, "Ach Wallace, ah'll only be about ten paces behind yie for fucks sake. Ah... ahm sorry about that Sister." William leans his sword against the door-jam and walks outside a few paces.

Nearby, hiding discreetly, Arthur says, "It's worked, here he comes now." Marmaduke says, "Perhaps we should wait till Thorpe gets back here with more men." Arthur turns to Marmaduke and sneers, "Why de Percy, I do believe that you are shitting yourself now, by gad sir, who would ever have thought to have you by their side." Marmaduke replies, "I've warned you already, Wallace is more than just a peasant, I tell you, this Scotchman can fight better than any man I have ever seen." Arthur says, "Oh do shut up de Percy... Look, here he comes. If you are so scared shitless, then be so kind as to stay well behind me, now, I shall deal with this Scotch cad that appears to frighten you so."

Arthur suddenly turns and walks out from the recess, blocking the main exit path leading away from Saint Kentigerns. He calls out to William. "Halt there you Scotch felon, where do you think you're going?"

For a moment, William is unsure who it is that's blocking his path. He replies, "Who the fuck are you talkin' to Englishman?" Meanwhile, Marmaduke pulls his mantle hood over his head, in fear of William recognising him. He is also careful to stand far enough back, just in case he has to make a speedy exit. He whispers to Arthur, "Hazelrigg, perhaps this was not such a good idea, for that felon has now armed himself, and we've no armour." William hears the whisper and thinks he recognises the name. He calls out, "You, Englishman, your name, are you Arthur Hazelrigg?" Arthur moves closer, while slowly pulling his sword slightly ajar from the scabbard. "That's my name Scotchman. I have a question for you, have you yet kissed your sweetheart? For if you have done so, then surely you shall have tasted the seed of a real man that will still be lingering awhile upon your whore's lips, And I certainly don't mean any kind of seed that comes from a romantic and loving kiss."

"You…" exclaims William.

Suddenly Arthur lunges up the path towards William with his sword drawn, ready to strike him down. Kerlie shouts out from the main doors, "Wallace…" and throws William his sword, then, in one swift and devastating move, William reaches up, grips the handle of the sword, brings it down in a low arc while side stepping Hazelrigg, then he brings the blade straight back up between Hazelriggs legs with such a force, it cuts cleanly through the soft tissue of his genitals, splits the spinal tailbone and gets well embedded into Arthur's pelvis. In the same movement, William savagely head butts Hazelrigg, splintering the Englishman's nasal bones and fracturing the eye sockets. The momentum of both strikes, causes both of them to fall to the ground. As Hazelrigg shakes violently from the terrible wounds inflicted, William is struggling on top of Hazelrigg, who now begins to scream hysterically in absolute terror and agony. William pushes up and quickly paddles the sword blade from side to side, trying to pull it free, causing Hazelrigg extreme pain and agony. In a fury, William wrenches the sword free while still lying across the body of Hazelrigg, he turns the blade around then he rams the sword upwards with such a ferocity under Hazelriggs chin, the tip and blade travels up behind the bones of his face and exits through the top of his skull, spilling his brains and spraying blood asunder.

Marmaduke De Percy screams, "Wallace, you, you've murdered Arthur de Hazelrigg…" William, still feeling very weak and nauseous, looks up and peers into the darkness as Kerlie and the rest of the Gallóglaigh stream out of Saint Kentigerns. Suddenly William recognises de Percy, he calls out, "You…" At that moment, de Percy throws off his mantle and runs as fast as he can towards the Castle, all the while yelling and screaming, "Murder, murder, murder… William

Wallace has murdered Arthur de Hazelrigg, help me, someone please will you save me…" As William attempts to get up to give chase, he staggers just a few yards before he falls to his knees, he has no strength nor any energy left.

"Get him," cries William, "that's de Percy…"

Kerlie quickly arrives by William's side, "It's too fuckin' late Wallace, he's gone. We'd better get you out of here now, whatever arrangement yie ever had with de Percy, I reckon it's well and truly fucked now." Blair says, "Kerlie's right Wallace, we'd better get yie away from here before the English surround this place and catch us all." William is still kneeling on the ground, completely exhausted. Blair says, "Come on Wallace, let's go. It's likely best that we ride for Biggar, there we can meet up with the Douglas, Graeme and Lamberton, we can work out what to do from there." William looks up at Blair, "But what about Marion, I must go to her, I can't leave her here." Blair says, "Use your head Wallace, if you stay, you'll most certainly get caught by the English, for there sure will be hell to pay for the killing of the sheriff's son. And if that message truly was from Marion, I'll stay behind and go and fetch her and Brìghde back here, so you go, get going now before it's too late."

As dawn slowly breaks over Lanark, the entire precinct within the town walls is in a turmoil. Early springtime squalls and black thunderclumps lingering overhead, brings down torrential rain to flood the wyndes, vennel's and closes of the old town, while English soldiers doggedly comb through the empty streets, searching for the murderer William Wallace. Under a hastily enacted curfew, they kill without mercy, any Scot they find to be outside their own dwellings.

Hazelrigg meanwhile, is incandescent with rage and grief; all of his soldiers are searching for Wallace or guarding every port exit to the town, sealing Lanark off in its entirety.

Hazelrigg wails from the turret of Lanark castle to all who will listen... "Find this accursed felon Wallace, bring his head to me."

At the townhouse of lord Braidfuite, the outside wooden shutters are closed, leaving every room of the house in complete darkness. Marion, completely unaware of all the events that has taken place, lights a small candle and then tries to spoon feed her father, who no longer has the use of his arms after the barbaric torture he received at the hands of the Sherriff. Sir Hugh has not spoken a word since he was brought home from Saint Kentigerns infirmary, for his mind is gone, caused by the guilt felt in not revealing William's whereabouts to Hazelrigg. In his tortured mind, he alone has been the cause of the death of his only son, gentle Brian.

"Father, you must eat." says Marion. She carefully tips the spoon forward and pours a honey-based tinctured broth into his mouth, she says, "Brìghde, please help me, hold father's mouth open so that I may pour in his vittals." Marion looks over to Brìghde who is huddled in a corner, but she doesn't hear Marion calling out her name, for she is still in a terrified state of shock. Marion calls out to her once more.

"Brìghde, Brìghde, oh it's no use..."

Stubbornly she cups Sir Hugh's chin, opens his mouth and quickly pours the vittals inside, but as she withdraws the spoon, the contents simply dribble back out from his mouth. Now exhausted, frustrated, she throws the spoon on the table, folds her arms and rests her head for just a moment. She looks up at her father as Brìghde continues to weep inconsolably. Marion rises from her chair and quietly goes over to the wooden shutters on the window, she peers outside, in the vain hope William will come home and save her from this living hell. After a while, Marion eventually walks back over to the inglenook where a small peat fire glows. She sits down quietly and stirs some oatmeal to a swell in a soup pot, thinking of little Mharaidh, now safe in the Wolf and wildcat camp, far away from the reaches of the English and their barbaric ways, but It all becomes too much for her, she puts her hands to her eyes and begins to sob quietly, grieving bitterly for her brother and her sister, yet she suffers in silence great physical pains too, caused by the multiple rapines, and then her miscarriage…

"Oh my love, where are you…?"

Looking around the silent room, she then glares at her father, irrationally she knows, but he makes her angry and embittered, for he couldn't be moved, such are his injuries. When she did try to get him away to Lammington or to the safety of the Wolf and wildcat camp, he screamed and screamed like a madman, making it impossible for her to do anything other than to keep him in the townhouse and stay by his side. Suddenly, Marion hears an unusual noise outside, she rushes over to the shuttered windows, but sees no-one, nothing, then she hears a loud knocking at the front door. "William…." she cries. She runs over and quickly unlatches the door, suddenly it slams open with such a force of wind and rain, it knocks her violently to the floor where she strikes her head heavily on a ragged flagstone. As she attempts to sit up, her vision is extremely hazy, but she watches intensely, almost excited as a tall masculine-built character stoops under the low lintel of the doorframe, removes his great mantle and rushes over towards her. She exclaims, "William, close the door, quickly, if the English realise you are in here…" She raises her head and begins to find focus, suddenly, she cups her mouth with her hands, she whispers, "Hazelrigg…"

Warlord

To follow

Next in the
Wallace: Legend of Braveheart series

Book Eight: Guardian

www.ingramcontent.com/pod-product-compliance
Lightning Source LLC
Chambersburg PA
CBHW021141080526
44588CB00008B/165